YEARNING TO LABOR

YEARNING TO LABOR

Youth, Unemployment, and

Social Destiny in Urban France

John P. Murphy

UNIVERSITY OF NEBRASKA PRESS | LINCOLN AND LONDON

Unless otherwise indicated, all photographs in
this volume are courtesy of the author.

A portion of chapter 4 was originally published as "Baguettes, Berets, and
Burning Cars: The 2005 Riots and the Question of Race in Contemporary
France" in *French Cultural Studies* 22, no. 1 (2011): 33–49. Portions of chapters
4 and 5 were originally published as "Protest or Riot? Interpreting Collective
Action in Contemporary France" in *Anthropological Quarterly* 84, no. 4
(2011): 977–1009. Portions of chapters 5 and 6 were originally published as
"The Rise of the Precariat? Unemployment and Social Identity in a French
Outer City" in *Anthropologies of Unemployment: New Perspectives on Work
and Its Absence*, ed. Jong Bum Kown and Carrie M. Lane, © 2016 by Cornell
University. Used by permission of the publisher, Cornell University Press.

Library of Congress Cataloging-in-Publication Data
Names: Murphy, John P., 1977– author.
Title: Yearning to labor: youth, unemployment, and
social destiny in urban France / John P. Murphy.
Description: Lincoln: University of Nebraska Press, 2017.
| Includes bibliographical references and index.
Identifiers: LCCN 2016024929
ISBN 9780803294974 (cloth: alk. paper)
ISBN 9781496200266 (epub)
ISBN 9781496200273 (mobi)
ISBN 9781496200280 (pdf)
Subjects: LCSH: Youth—Employment—France—Limoges. |
Equality—France—Limoges. | Youth—Social conditions—
France—Limoges. | Riots—France—Limoges.
Classification: LCC HD6276.F72 M87 2017 | DDC 331.3/470944091732—dc23
LC record available at https://lccn.loc.gov/2016024929

Set in Sorts Mill Goudy by John Klopping.
Designed by N. Putens.

For Jillian

Contents

Illustrations

MAPS

TABLES

Acknowledgments

Since I began conceptualizing this project over twelve years ago, I have accumulated many debts. Now that this book is complete, it is with tremendous gratitude that I acknowledge them here. I begin by recognizing the young men and women in Limoges's outer city whose stories form the basis of the analysis in the pages that follow. France's *banlieues* have for many years now received a great deal of attention, most of it negative. For so patiently accepting yet another set of prying eyes and ears into their lives, I express to them my profound appreciation. I hope that they find here an honest reflection of their experience.

Conducting research for this project would have been far more difficult without the help of others in Limoges, especially the many social service providers who so kindly took time out of their busy schedules to explain their work to me and to introduce me to local youth. Although I have employed pseudonyms in this book to protect their privacy, I would like to note my appreciation to several individuals using their real names. I especially thank Jocelyne Mérand for taking me under her wing and introducing me to so many valuable contacts; Mélanie Bernadac and Isabelle Minot, who took a gamble when they agreed to let an American researcher volunteer in their association; Bernard Diverneresse for his insights on Limoges's urban development and his willingness to let me be part of the continuing education program he runs in one of the city's housing projects; Claude Monteil for his interest in my research and the many fine lunches we shared *chez Lise*; and Nicole Stephanus for coordinating initial meetings with many local youth and helping with a request after I left Limoges. I would also like to thank ARACT Limousin for generously providing me with office space during my fieldwork year. The insights into life in Limoges in general and the problems facing the region's workers in particular offered by its staff—Sylvie Cartoux, Catherine Gérard, Antoine Koubemba, and Benjamin Sahler—greatly enhanced this study, and their friendship made my stay far more enjoyable.

The research upon which this book is based would not have been possible without the generous support of several agencies and institutions. At New York University, I was the recipient of a GSAS MacCracken Fellowship, and for my primary period of fieldwork in France in 2005 and 2006, I was awarded a Bourse Chateaubriand from the French government and a Georges Lurcy Charitable and Educational Trust Fellowship. A Paul H. Rhoads Teaching and Professional Development Grant, awarded by Gettysburg College, permitted a month of follow-up research in Limoges in 2012. Additional funding from Gettysburg College helped with the final preparation of maps and the book's index.

This project began as a doctoral dissertation in the Department of Anthropology and the Institute of French Studies at New York University. I am deeply indebted to Susan Carol Rogers, who, during my time as a graduate student, deftly guided me through the rituals of initiation, always with warm wishes of "bonne continuation!" Her help defining this project at its earliest stages, her close readings of various versions of this text, the countless hours she spent discussing them with me, and her challenge to me always to think logically and write clearly have added immeasurably to the end result. I, of course, am solely responsible for any errors or shortcomings. Others at NYU also provided intellectual guidance and mentorship. In particular, I would like to thank Herrick Chapman, Stéphane Gerson, and Aisha Khan. Finally, I would like to express my gratitude to French anthropologist David Lepoutre, who served on my dissertation committee. His ethnographic field research in a Parisian outer city provided many interesting points of comparison.

During a semester of graduate study in Paris at the École normale supérieure and the École des hautes études en sciences sociales, I was fortunate to work closely with a number of scholars, who shaped in various ways this project. In particular, I would like to thank Nicolas Flamant, who first pointed me to Limoges; Serge Paugam and Christian Baudelot, whose seminars on work and inequality in France were both stimulating and extremely useful; and Stéphane Beaud and Florence Weber, who made time in their busy schedules to discuss field research strategies with me.

Throughout the research and writing stages of this project, many friends and colleagues provided consistent and generous encouragement, critical infusions of insight, and, at times, much-needed distraction. Lydia Boyd, Lindsay Kaplan, Kathryn Kleppinger, Amikole Maraesa, Arthur Plaza, Pilar Rau, and Ayako Takamori all enriched my time at NYU. During the two years I spent at Oberlin College as a visiting member of the faculty, I found in Grace An and Libby Murphy generous and insightful colleagues; I am especially grateful to them for their help navigating the difficult academic job market. At Gettysburg College, I have been fortunate to complete this book in the company of a dynamic community of scholars. In particular, I have benefitted from the support of my colleagues in the Department of French, especially Florence Ramond Jurney, whose steadfast mentorship helped me stay focused and finish this book on schedule, and Caroline Ferraris-Besso, whose *culture générale* is as impressive as her *brioches* are delicious.

I am tremendously fortunate to have found a home for this book at the University of Nebraska Press, whose team of professionals made the publication process as smooth as possible. In particular, I would like to thank Alicia Christensen, who first took an interest in this project and shepherded it through the review process; Sabrina Stellrecht for being so wonderfully patient and organized during the production stage; and copy editor Jonathan Lawrence, whose meticulous attention to detail much improved the final text. I am also grateful for the insightful comments and helpful suggestions offered by the two anonymous readers for the press.

Finally, I thank my family, whose support and encouragement have sustained me on this long journey. My parents, John and Patricia Murphy, are for me a constant source of inspiration. Their example of hard work, their respect for education, and their unflagging faith in me gave me the courage to take this "road less traveled." I also thank my sisters, Sarah, Kate, and Rachael, whose unique perspectives and good humor have helped ground me along the way.

I dedicate this book to Jillian Higgins, who has lived with this project from the very start. Throughout, she has provided unconditional love and support, even when an ocean separated us or chasing a tenure-track job meant moving and reinventing ourselves, not once but twice. Our sons—Liam, Declan, and Owen—were born during the course of this adventure. Children are both a reminder of the past and a link to the future. Becoming a parent helped me realize in ways I had not before the challenges facing my interlocutors in Limoges as they struggled to project themselves beyond the present. For this, I am thankful, but mostly I am grateful to my children for their tremendous patience as they shared me with this project. They are a welcome reminder that life should be about more than just work.

Abbreviations

BEP *brevet d'études professionnelles* (vocational training certificate)

BTS *brevet de technicien supérieur* (senior technician certificate)

CAP *certificat d'aptitude professionnelle*
(certificate of professional competence)

CDD *contrat à durée déterminée* (fixed-term contract)

CDI *contrat à durée indéterminée* (permanent contract)

CES Contrat emploi-solidarité (Solidarity employment contract)

CGT Confédération générale du travail
(General confederation of labor)

CNE Contrat nouvelles embauches (New jobs contract)

CPE Contrat première embauche (First job contract)

CTT *contrat de travail temporaire* (temporary work contract)

ENA École nationale d'administration (National school for civil service)

FJT *foyer de jeunes travailleurs* (home for young workers)

JOC Jeunesse ouvrière chrétienne (Young Christian workers)

PAIO *permanence d'accueil, d'information et d'orientation* (reception, information, and guidance center)

RMI Revenu minimum d'insertion (Minimum subsistence income)

RSA Revenu de solidarité active (Active solidarity income)

TUC Travaux d'utilité collective (Works of collective utility)

UNEF Union nationale des étudiants de France (National union of students of France)

ZEP Zone d'éducation prioritaire (Priority education area)

ZRU Zone de redynamisation urbaine (Urban revitalization area)

ZUS Zone urbaine sensible (Disadvantaged urban area)

Introduction

This book is about social inequality and how people make sense of it in everyday life. It is about the categories and distinctions they use to position themselves and others, the meanings and significance they give to these, the feelings of connectedness or difference involved, and the tensions, contradictions, and ambiguities that may arise along the way. This book is also about unemployment. Drawing on a case study I conducted in France amid widespread fears of rising job insecurity, I portray the daily struggle of a group of young people from the outer city of Limoges, one of France's poorer, multiethnic *banlieues*, as they confront more than triple the national unemployment rate. In the process, I aim to illuminate how changes in the global economy sometimes referred to as "neoliberalism" shape and are shaped by local frameworks of thinking and being.

To say that the timing of my research was fortuitous would be a tremendous understatement. During my fieldwork year, France found itself in the throes of what have come to be known as the fall 2005 riots, a conflict so unprecedented in scope—more than 270 cities, including Limoges, were simultaneously engulfed by violence for three full weeks—that it made front-page news across the globe. Just months later, also during my research period, trouble erupted again in France, this time in the form of massive opposition to a proposed government employment bill called the Contrat première embauche (CPE; First job contract). Both conflicts implicated young people, and both involved explicit claims about social inequality—specifically, the disproportionate number of youth affected by unemployment.

Since the early 1980s, contingent employment among working people under age thirty has nearly tripled in France. Today on average one out of every three workers in this age bracket is employed on a temporary basis. Meanwhile, unemployment is about as great for the under-thirty crowd as it was three decades ago, hovering at a much-higher-than-national-average of around 17 percent.[1] Such grim prospects undoubtedly rouse frustration, and this frustration, some commentators insisted, fueled the violence witnessed in late 2005 in France's troubled outer cities. Certainly, this was a view presented by France's leaders at the time, who, in response to the riots, proposed the CPE with the explicit goal of addressing unemployment among the country's youth.

More than a decade later, it remains the case that some young people in France do better than others in the precarious job market. In the disadvantaged outer cities, employment figures can be far worse than national averages: as many as two out of three young working people may hold only a temporary or part-time job, and unemployment levels can soar to a staggering 40, even 50 percent. A great deal of ink has already been spilled over this category of French youth. However voluminous, this literature tends to describe the question in terms of statistics or trends. Though often talked about, such young people, it would seem, are seldom listened to. A central question I attempt to answer in this book is how they *experience*, *understand*, and *manage* the unequal access to employment they face.

Put another way, this book is about young people's individual and collective perceptions of sameness and difference. It asks how youth struggling in the French job market position themselves both in relation to their peers, who may or may not experience similar difficulty finding or keeping work, and to previous generations, whose members came of age under different circumstances. Its title pays homage to a groundbreaking analysis of the social reproduction of inequality, *Learning to Labor*, published by British sociologist Paul Willis in 1977. Having conducted ethnographic field research among a group of twelve "lads" in a small, industrial English town in the early 1970s, Willis set out in that book to explain how distinctions of social position are sustained from one generation to the next at an individual level. He demonstrated that the youth at the center of his study actively participated in the reproduction of what he called "class identity" by consciously rejecting the "work hard, move forward" mentality of modern education, preferring instead to identify with their fathers, who worked on the shop floor.

A lot has changed since Willis wrote that book. Industrial restructuring and the implementation of neoliberal capitalist policies across much of the globe have had a profound effect on employment practices. Whereas long-term, stable employment had been the norm during the decades of economic boom following World War II, today unemployment is increasingly a chronic condition. The result, economist Guy Standing (2011) argues, is the emergence of a new "dangerous class" of people—a precarious proletariat, or "precariat." In the context of such claims, the question we need to raise, and one that anthropology, with its intense focus on people's everyday perspectives and practices, is particularly well positioned to explore, I argue, is not how today's youth "learn to labor," but rather what are their experiences *yearning to labor?* In other words, what are their desires and expectations about finding and keeping work, and what strategies of adaption, negotiation, or resistance do they develop in response to the bleak job prospects that await them once they leave school?

This question, in turn, raises another: In the absence of large-scale industrial manufacture, and stable employment more generally, does the label "working class," or even "class"—the lens Willis found so compelling in his analysis and which Standing adopted in his formulation of the precariat—still hold meaning for most or even many people today in places like France, as they attempt to make sense of their social world and the inequality they encounter in it? Certainly, "social class" was one category used by commentators in France and elsewhere to decipher the fall 2005 riots and the spring 2006 protests, but so too were a multitude of other distinctions, including, notably, race and ethnicity.

What interests me, and what this book tries to illuminate, is not whether one or another of these categories or distinctions better describes the riots, the protests, the difficult job market—or social life more generally and its unevenness in France or elsewhere, as if some fundamental truth were awaiting discovery. Rather, I seek to understand *how* such classifications get used. I ask who deploys them, when, in what context, and to what effect. It is my contention that such categories and distinctions are not in themselves meaningful or the root cause of social inequality in France or the world beyond. Far from the commonsense, immutable ideas they are often presented as encapsulating, they take on shifting meanings and significance over time and space. In this book I argue that social categories are used practically and strategically by people in the working out of everyday life (including during more exceptional moments, like the fall riots and the spring protests) to make specific claims and to achieve desired results. Depending on the intentions, understandings, and resources of those putting them into circulation, they can have vastly different consequences or outcomes.

To be sure, the transformations under way in the French labor market extend far beyond France's borders. Across much of the globe, greater flexibility in employment practices is widely viewed as vital for remaining competitive in increasingly interconnected, fast-paced, information-driven economies. Yet it is in the actions of individuals living in time and space that such extralocal forces are embodied, interpreted, managed, and negotiated. A primary objective of this study, then, is to explore how far-reaching social, political, and economic processes intersect with the everyday, situated practices of ordinary people. By tracing out the categories and distinctions people use to order their social world and the meanings they give to these, I aim to illuminate how large-scale change—specifically, shifts in the employment landscape sometimes described as "neoliberal"—may be shaped or molded in distinctly local ways.

For two reasons, France offers particularly fertile ground for exploring these issues. First is the glaring contradiction between the French Republican ideal of equality and the unevenness that pervades everyday life in France. By this I do not mean to suggest that inequality is any more of a problem in France than in other societies, or, even worse, that the

French are just a bunch of hypocrites—a view sometimes encountered in American popular discourse. Rather, because equality is, at least in theory, a foundational value of the French Republic (even if its definition has shifted in France over time), questions of equality, or more often inequality, frequently—and often passionately—enter into public debate. Inequality is very much a contemporary concern in France, a concern that the state is often formally called upon to address, much more so than in the United States. Second are the terms with which inequality gets understood and expressed in France, which, in my experience, can be similar to but also at times vastly different from those used in the American context. How might examining the ways people in France evaluate and classify themselves unsettle and illuminate some of our commonsense notions about the labels we use in social classification and stratification?

This question has particular resonance in the context of the shrill debates on race and ethnicity surrounding France's outer cities during the past several decades, debates that attracted widespread public attention in France and abroad at the time of the fall 2005 riots. The French Republic's universalist underpinnings, some critics contend, leave no room for difference, whether in skin color or in habits of mind and body, and this, these detractors insist, leads to frustration among oppressed racial or ethnic minorities. The violence witnessed in the outer cities, they argue, just offers more evidence in support of this claim. The question of how race and ethnicity are understood and used in France is very much central to this book. However, rather than taking these categories as my starting point and risk imposing ways of experiencing, thinking, and being that my interlocutors in Limoges might find erroneous, I take a step back to ask how they understand and express the inequalities they encounter in daily life. Race or ethnicity may—or may not—be important to some or all of them in this regard.

Instead of beginning with race or ethnicity (or class, for that matter), I adopt the less prescriptive—but locally more meaningful—concept of social destiny. People everywhere may have some sense of what their future holds. They will be doctors, plumbers, or teachers. They will live in their hometowns or move across the globe. They will marry or remain single. They will have children or not. They will be rich or poor, admired or scorned, content or unhappy. Regardless of what people think their future will be like, and whether or not these projections are actually realized, analyzing the terms in which they discuss their prospects, alongside observation of their everyday practices, has the potential to illuminate key understandings of social position. The period of transition between school and work life is particularly propitious for asking about social destiny, because it is often then that childhood aspirations are confronted with real-life challenges, especially in the context of a difficult job market.

This study, then, is both an ethnographic account of some members of the generation coming of age today in France, as they navigate an uncertain job market, and an attempt to bring into focus, through an examination of the categories and distinctions these young people use to order their social world, the mechanisms underlying the shifting inequalities of condition that are broadly part of the human experience at this beginning of the twenty-first century.

Neoliberalism in France

It is almost as if the nineteenth-century novelist Honoré de Balzac was anticipating current popular French sentiment when he linked "great fortunes" to "a forgotten crime."[2] According to an opinion poll conducted in 2006, only 36 percent of French people agreed that the free market was the best system available, compared to 71 percent of Americans and 66 percent of British.[3] Another survey, carried out in 2011, confirmed this result, placing France at the bottom of a list of ten advanced economies in terms of the popularity of capitalism; half of the French polled indicated that capitalism functions poorly, and another third said it should be abandoned altogether.[4] This perspective has been reflected in French economic policy, which, until recently at least, has exhibited a great deal of skepticism about the efficacy of market forces and has called for considerable state intervention in industry—a practice the French call *dirigisme*. Examining the structural and cultural factors driving this orientation should help us not only to better understand French reactions to the neoliberal turn but also to identify some important tensions in debates about France's thorny youth unemployment problem—and inequality, more generally—for consideration in later chapters.

"France's postwar regime," writes sociologist Monica Prasad, "might best be characterized as a strong state put at the service of capital, all in the service of nationalism" (2005, 360). In other words, the *dirigiste* model that emerged in France in the decades following World War II was not at all anticapitalist. On contrary, as the verb *diriger* suggests, it aimed at directing or managing industry, with the goal of helping France, which remained largely agrarian at the close of the war, catch up to its more industrialized European neighbors and the United States. The result was an unprecedented period of economic expansion and prosperity, which has come to be known in France as the *Trente glorieuses* (Thirty glorious years).[5] Building on liberation-era nationalizations, initial planning and financing efforts in the 1940s and 1950s centered on identifying and developing "priority" heavy industrial sectors, including coal, steel, and electricity (Massé 1965; Shonfield 1965; S. Cohen 1977; Bauchet 1986; P. Hall 1986; Rousso 1986). In the 1960s and 1970s, emphasis shifted to technological research and development. Thanks to the resources and support committed by the state, France became a world leader in such fields as nuclear power, transportation, and telecommunications, producing an array of dazzling innovations from the TGV (high-speed train) to the Concorde (supersonic jetliner) to the Minitel (pre–World Wide Web online service) (Bauer and Cohen 1985; E. Cohen 1992).

With its focus squarely on economic growth, *dirigiste* policy, especially that pursued through the 1960s, did not concern itself with issues of social equality. Whereas business reaped enormous benefits, including protection from foreign competition, exemption from price controls, and subsidized credit, labor saw few if any gains. Aggressive devaluations of the franc, the coordinated arrival of immigrant workers from former French colonies, and the relative impunity with which employers were able to violate workers' right to unionize all contributed to keeping wages low (P. Hall 1986). Moreover, during the early decades of *dirigisme* social spending was held in check so as not to drain resources away from industry; welfare expenditures increased by only 2 percent of GDP between 1950 and

1960 (Cameron 1991). Finally, the cost of *dirigisme* fell disproportionately on middle- and low-income earners. Most public revenue was generated on a regressive basis via sales tax and social security charges paid in large part by employees. By contrast, more progressive forms of taxation, including income, inheritance, and corporate taxes, were set at low levels and collected unevenly (Vail 2010). Ultimately, low wages, limited social spending, and regressive taxes contributed to the persistence of deep inequality in France. In fact, during the postwar period France had one of the most unequal distributions of wealth of any country belonging to the Organisation for Economic Co-operation and Development (OECD); by some accounts, French inequality in the 1960s and 1970s exceeded that of the United States (Sawyer and Wasserman 1976). It would be misleading, however, to claim that *dirigisme* caused inequality in France. As French economist Thomas Piketty (2003) has shown, although income inequality (including income from capital) rose slightly during the *Trente glorieuses*, it was far lower than prewar levels, and wage inequality remained fairly steady across the pre- and postwar periods.

If closing the income gap was not the main objective of *dirigisme*, economic development was, and in this domain progress was nothing short of spectacular. During the *Trente glorieuses* the French economy successfully transitioned from its agricultural and artisanal roots to a modern industrial and service base sustaining full employment. In the 1960s the economy grew on average by a remarkable 5.8 percent per year, twice the British rate (2.9 percent) and considerably more than the American rate (3.9 percent) (Girling 1998).[6] This expansion translated into an improved overall standard of living. By the mid-1970s, mean disposable income in France was roughly three times what it had been at the beginning of the 1950s (Dormois 2004). New consumer goods came to symbolize the country's growing prosperity. At the end of the 1950s, 26 percent of French families owned a television, 10 percent a washing machine, and 7.5 percent a refrigerator (Price 1993, 292). The car became a particularly visible emblem of France's leap into modernity: in 1939 there were an estimated 500,000 cars in the Paris region, in 1960 there were a million, and in 1965, two million (Ross 1999, 53). Sometimes referred to as the *années béton* (concrete years), the *Trente glorieuses* also witnessed rapid urbanization. Between 1946 and 1954 the total French population grew by 2.3 million, while cities expanded by 2.4 million (Voldman 1997, 322).

Such progress undoubtedly helped divert public attention away from persisting inequality, but ultimately *dirigisme* was predicated on an understanding that social hierarchy was necessary for economic development and ultimately social well-being. Steering the *dirigiste* wheel were a relatively small group of technocrats, who tended to share an educational pedigree—a diploma from one of France's premier *grandes écoles* (highly selective graduate schools), usually the École polytechnique (Polytechnic school) or the newly established École nationale d'administration (ENA; National school for civil service) (Birnbaum 1977; Suleiman 1979). In these prestigious institutions, students were groomed to become France's ruling elite. Describing ENA, writer, translator, and keen observer of the French Arthur Goldhammer remarks, "The training of *énarques* [graduates of ENA] instills hardheaded pragmatism, together with superb confidence in their subtle acuity at divining the persistent 'general interest' beyond the vagaries of the popular will" (2015, 36).[7] In other words, at ENA and other *grandes écoles* there has been from the beginning an implicit understanding that ordinary people (i.e., ones not holding a diploma from an elite school) do not or cannot know what is best for themselves; it is the responsibility of the ruling class to nudge the masses in the right direction. In his work, Pierre Bourdieu (1996) traced the ideological underpinnings of this stance to pre-revolutionary times, arguing that the *grandes écoles* produce a new nobility, what he called a "state nobility." Cloaked in the trappings of meritocracy, these elite institutions, he maintained, at once consecrate and concentrate in positions of command individuals from privileged backgrounds, who, like their pre-revolutionary predecessors, affirm the legitimacy of their superiority by invoking the collective good, most notably by claiming a commitment to "public service." This, Bourdieu reminds, is the meaning of the term *noblesse oblige*.[8]

This logic of social hierarchy and elite responsibility continues to inform discussions about social well-being in France today. Indeed, as I explore in this book, some of my interlocutors in Limoges expressed the belief that society was or should be ordered hierarchically. Along-side this understanding that social stratification is beneficial, however, runs a countercurrent equally embedded in French thought. Rooted in Enlightenment philosophy and collectivist revolutionary rhetoric, it is associated with such values as equality, universalism, and national unity—values that have frequently been invoked during French responses to the neoliberal turn.

Even before the global energy crisis of the 1970s, cracks began to appear in France's *dirigiste* model. After the near-revolution of May 1968, Charles de Gaulle, who had dominated French politics for more than a decade, was no longer the unquestioned leader of the country. His resignation a year later coincided with increased public awareness of and sympathy for workers, whose attempts at incorporation began at long last to rattle the labor-exclusionary framework of *dirigisme*. Heading into the new decade, France's center-right leaders progressively adopted a conflict-averse stance vis-à-vis labor demands, backing down at the first sign of street resistance, whether from farmers, workers, or shopkeepers. This was especially true after the establishment of a powerful Socialist-Communist alliance in the 1970s put them under electoral threat. Although in 1974 center-right presidential candidate Valéry Giscard d'Estaing beat Socialist rival François Mitterrand, the margin was an extremely slim 50.8 percent to 49.2 percent (Macridis 1987, 118). When the two squared off again in 1981, Mitterrand emerged the victor.

In 1973 an oil embargo imposed by members of the Organization of Petroleum Exporting Countries (OPEC) sharply increased production costs. As the stranglehold tightened on France's newly industrialized economy, leaders began to divert *dirigisme* away from its initial modern-izing mission to focus instead on rescuing faltering companies. Under the Giscard administration, the bankrupt steel industry was nationalized and a special agency, the Comité interministériel de l'aménagement des structures industrielles (Inter-ministerial committee for the develop-ment of economic structures), was created to bail out failing businesses. Alongside offering support for industry, the state sought to lessen the impact of the crisis on workers through tighter regulations on layoffs, rapid increases in the minimum wage, and more generous unemployment insurance. As a result, between 1974 and 1981, social spending increased from 19.4 percent of GDP to 25.3 percent (Palier 1999).

When Mitterrand entered office in 1981 he promised to take *dirigisme* to new heights in order to curb rising unemployment and, in the words of his campaign slogan, "reconquer domestic markets." However, it quickly became clear that his ambitious program, including a sweeping set of nationalizations, was untenable. "By 1983," writes political scientist Jonah Levy, "a number of firms were so heavily subsidized that it would have been far cheaper for the government to pay workers *not to produce*" (2008, 422). In what has come to be known as the "Great U-Turn," Mitterrand ultimately yielded to mounting international pressure, especially constraints imposed by the European Monetary System. After 1983, France's economic priorities shifted dramatically to focus on privatization, deregulation, and liberalization (Loriaux 1991; P. Hall 1990). These reforms were hallmarks of what some began calling in the 1980s neoliberalism.

The term *neoliberalism* is less common in the United States than in Europe or some other parts of the world and therefore may sound unfamiliar to American audiences, who are accustomed to having the phrase "free market" used to describe "American" capitalism. Because in the United States the notion of a free market is strongly associated with such positive values as individual liberty and opportunity, and is sometimes even described as a basis of national character, this economic system is difficult to question, much less challenge (Lane 2011). To complicate matters, American usage of the term *liberal* tends to refer to opposing values and ideas, including big government and redistributive policies (Bell and Stanely 2014).

Beginning around the turn of the twenty-first century, anthropologists began seriously engaging with the notion of neoliberalism. A review of the literature demonstrates just how polysemic the term can be (Ganti 2014). Indeed, as Aihwa Ong remarks, "Neoliberalism seems to mean many different things depending on one's vantage point" (2006, 1). Some research has narrowly defined the concept in relation to macroeconomic policy, notably the reforms pursued by Reagan and Thatcher in the 1980s or the structural adjustment programs imposed in the Global South beginning in the late 1970s. Deriving from a Marxist paradigm, this work has primarily been interested in questions of political economy, particularly how deregulation, liberalization, and privatization reinforce existing social hierarchies or work to create new ones. Other scholarship has treated neoliberalism more broadly. Drawing on a Foucauldian framework, this literature has examined how subjectivities are formed or refashioned in relation to values and ideas such as entrepreneurship, competition, personal responsibility, and self-improvement.[9] In his oft-cited assessment, David Harvey identifies what he views as a "cardinal" feature of neoliberalism: an "assumption that individual freedoms are guaranteed by freedom of the market and of trade" (2005, 7). For Harvey, neoliberalism is above all a class-based project that seeks to restore the power of global economic elites; he underscores its "pervasive effects on ways of thought to the point where it has become incorporated into the common-sense way many of us interpret, live in, and understand the world" (3). Harvey's appraisal of neoliberalism reflects a wider, critical stance within anthropology and the social sciences more broadly, where neoliberalism is often associated with deep inequality and escalating social and political strife (Boas and Gans-Morse 2009).

The recent focus on neoliberalism in anthropological scholarship has attracted a fair amount of criticism. Some observers have argued that accounts too frequently present neoliberalism as a monolithic, all-encompassing global force to the point where the idea becomes theoretically bankrupt. James Ferguson describes neoliberalism as a "sloppy synonym for capitalism" (2009, 171), and Tara Schwegler denounces it as "a handy way to bracket the global political economy without actively engaging it" (2009, 24). Others have maintained that as an analytical framework neoliberalism obscures ethnographic particularities and erases local categories of value and meaning (e.g., Gershon 2011; Kipnis 2008; Nonini 2008; Kingfisher and Maskovasky 2008; Richland 2009; Mains 2007). How, these critics implore us to consider, do neoliberal doctrine and policies interact with local dynamics?

In this book I take this question seriously, especially because in France there has been a fair amount of overt resistance to the sorts of neoliberal reforms observed in other national contexts. Indeed, in France neoliberalism is most often understood as a problem that needs to be managed or mitigated, if not an outright threat to be avoided. It is viewed as profoundly "un-French," imposed from without, most notably by the United States.[10] As such, it tends to be equated with "Americanization" (Kuisel 1993, 2012) and, more generally, globalization; in fact, the term *globalization* is frequently used in France as a gloss for neoliberalism. In an extended interview, Hubert Védrine, diplomatic adviser to President Mitterrand, presented what he saw as the French perspective: "The market economy, market society (unfortunately!), and ever-growing individualism go hand in hand. This has its merits, but it leads to the fragmentation of collective structures. The United States is very much at home in this sort of world. . . . I don't think France is ready to submit to this type of globalization without thoroughly examining it first" (Védrine and Moïsi 2001, 43–44). Bourdieu (1998) went even further, arguing that neoliberalism amounts to "the methodical destruction of collectivities," including first and foremost the nation, but also workers groups, unions, associations, cooperatives, and even the family. The result, he warned, is the emergence of a "Darwinian world," characterized by "the struggle of all against all." In the end, for both Védrine and Bourdieu neoliberalism is the opposite of collectivism; it is at once an ideology and a practice that gives priority to personal goals, desires, and motivations at the expense of social cohesion and well-being.

Despite his hesitation, Védrine did not expect France to withdraw from the world economy. On the contrary, he insisted that the French had an important role to play—that of "civilizing" the "savage" or "destructive" aspects of globalization (Védrine and Moïsi 2001, 134). In other words, for Védrine the free-market economy was a force of nature that the French, with their particular *savoir-faire*, could and should tame.[11] In practice this has translated in France into the implementation of what Levy (2008) calls the "social anaesthesia state," that is, a state committed to dulling the pain of economic liberalization. Thus, post-*dirigiste* France adopted a series of generous labor market and social policies designed to soften the blow to workers. These included the establishment of job-training centers, where workers could learn new trades; the creation of a guaranteed minimum income (RMI); the provision of subsidies to encourage early retirement; tax breaks and other incentives for employers who agree to hire hard-to-place workers, especially "at-risk" youth; and a multitude of training and internship programs. The number of workers enrolled in some kind of public labor market program leaped from 1.2 million in 1984 to nearly three million in 1999 (DARES 2000, 1996). The growth of social spending has been equally spectacular, rising from 21.3 percent of GDP in 1980 to 26.5 percent in 1990 and to 29.5 percent in 1998.[12]

Although the rapid expansion of social protection programs and policies in post-*dirigiste* France reflects at least partially a desire among French leaders to demobilize victims and quiet opponents of economic liberalization, the fact that these reforms have enjoyed support from members of both the political left and the right suggests a broad consensus in France concerning the need to shield workers and their families from the vagaries of the market. Whenever plans to reduce social protections have been announced in France, widespread public contestation has ensued. This was the case in 1995, when the Juppé administration proposed an extensive program of welfare cutbacks; it was also true in 2006 when Prime Minister Dominique de Villepin announced the CPE.

The sort of egalitarian collectivism espoused by Védrine and Bourdieu and evidenced in the French state's responses to the neoliberal turn appears to be at odds with the understanding of the importance of social hierarchy discussed above, particularly in terms of how much equality is viewed as desirable or even possible in society. Yet these social models converge on at least one point: *the pursuit of the common good*. Each stresses personal responsibility to ensure everyone's well-being. In short, the collective "us" is viewed as equally important, if not more so, than the individual "me," for the good of all. This, at its most basic level, is what the French call *solidarité*.

In this book I am interested in how French notions of solidarity articulate with neoliberal ideologies and practices, and how this articulation may produce new ways of imagining, experiencing, understanding, and living in the social world at the local level. Although the expansion of the French welfare state in the last decades of the twentieth century set France apart from many other Western economies, the redistributive policies pursued there have been applied unevenly. In France, young people in particular have often found themselves less protected than other groups. Until its discontinuation in 2009, the RMI, for instance, was only available to those twenty-five and older. Moreover, the French state has proven incapable of ensuring stable jobs for all French workers. Since the 1980s, France has witnessed a staggering rise in precarious work, especially among the youngest and the least qualified. This shift in the employment landscape has been said to upset vital categories of social distinction, especially class. At the same time, it has been blamed for summoning the divisive specter of racial politics. This linking of work, class, and race merits some attention.

Social Class, Race, and the Shifting Employment Landscape

Although, as Christian Topalov (1994) has demonstrated, policymakers and social reformers, eager to rationalize the functioning of the labor market, "invented" unemployment in the last decades of the nineteenth century, for much of the twentieth century, and especially during the postwar years, France experienced a chronic shortage of labor, not jobs. This, along with shifts in the social landscape, shaped workers' preferences and expectations pertaining to employment arrangements. Because seasonal work in nineteenth- and early-twentieth-century agrarian France required mobility, workers privileged jobs that afforded some measure of flexibility. For them, the idea of an unrestricted, open-ended contract too closely resembled older arrangements of vassalage or slavery. In fact, a popular 1922 electoral slogan called for "the abolition of the *salariat* [salaried as opposed to wage employment], the vestige of slavery" (Nicolet 1974, 54). Even as France began to industrialize, workers continued to prefer short-term contracts over open-ended ones. Being able to change jobs easily meant they could take advantage of the competitive wages resulting from the labor shortage that characterized the period (Fourcade 1992). However, during the *Trente glorieuses*, workers' attention gradually shifted from limiting managerial control over their mobility to ensuring that contractual obligations were respected.[13] Gérard Noiriel (1990) has linked this concern to a growing sense of hierarchy among workers, particularly between native-born ones and their immigrant counterparts.

France, even if not readily thought of as a country of immigrants, experienced at times during the twentieth century immigration rates comparable to those of the United States (Green 1991). Suffering a labor shortage linked to declining birthrates and native workers' unwillingness to be tied down to any single job, France became during the last decades of the nineteenth century and the first decades of the twentieth a destination of choice for many workers from Germany, Belgium, and Switzerland. The enormous loss of working-age Frenchmen during the two world wars, coupled with the dire need for labor for reconstruction efforts after and, later, native French resistance to low-paying, degrading work, encouraged the arrival of waves of Poles, Italians, and Portuguese, and then, increasingly, North Africans. Although the 1950s arguably witnessed a sort of working-class "consolidation," with all workers (immigrant and native) developing a shared sense of pride and an understanding of advancing toward a common goal of upward social mobility, as production shifted to new, increasingly mechanized factories turning out modern consumer goods, divisions in the labor force grew.[14] Whereas skilled workers used their seniority to avoid social and professional downgrading, unskilled workers, including many recent (North African) immigrants, found themselves relegated to the least desirable positions, with little hope of upward mobility (Noiriel 1990, 199–212). Following the 1970s global energy crisis, which spelled an end to the decades-long stretch of full employment in France, these divisions grew as the far right capitalized on native French fears of losing work to foreigners (Gaspard 1995).

Since the economic downturn of the 1970s, employment in France has been characterized by increasing flexibility in terms of work arrangements. Thus, nearly one million workers in the private sector held short-term contracts in 2001, compared to 320,000 in 1982—an increase of more than 200 percent over those two decades (Givord 2005). Most often this development has been discussed in terms of what the French call *précarité*.

Although generally translated as "precariousness," but also sometimes "precarity" (Paugam and Russell 2000), this concept, as sociologist Chantal Nicole-Drancourt (1992, 57) has noted, can and does mean many things in France, from a subcategory of nonstandard employment (short-term contracts, temporary work, internships, apprenticeships, etc.) to all forms of nonstandard employment to nonstandard employment and unemployment to the overall employment system.[15] It is this polysemy that makes the notion so difficult to translate (Barbier 2005). In the end, *précarité* for the French is not just about employment, underemployment, or unemployment; as the expression *précarisation de la société*—in widespread circulation among journalists, politicians, and other social commentators since the 1990s—suggests, it is perceived as a threat to society *in its entirety*.[16]

Why is increasing employment flexibility understood to carry this sort of danger in France, whereas in other national contexts it has sometimes, at least, been presented as an opportunity for personal or professional growth, even success?[17] A review of the rich sociological literature on the disintegration of the working class produced in France over the last two decades or so offers an answer: for a number of French scholars, transformations in the world of work have fundamentally destabilized various relationships of social obligation—relationships held necessary by many in France for good social order and function. According to Jean-Pierre Terrail (1990) and Olivier Schwartz (1990), France's working class has undergone a process of "individuation" (Terrail) or "privatization" (Schwartz), as individuals choose "me over us." The result, the authors contend, is not only a dismantling of the once powerful and widely respected French labor movement but also an unraveling of "primary" ties between coworkers, neighbors, and even family members. Stéphane Beaud and Michel Pialoux (1999) reach a similar conclusion in their investigation of French automobile workers. Despite the statistical significance of manual laborers in France today, they contend that the working class no longer exists as a class for itself, its members, and especially the generation coming of age, having to a large degree lost sight of collective goals and interests.[18] One particularly deleterious consequence of this development, Beaud and Pialoux suggest, is increasingly sharp intergenerational conflict. Nicolas Renahy (2005), in his research on young, rural blue-color workers, confirms Beaud and Pialoux's findings and argues that the sort of collective consciousness lacking across generations of today's workers is no more evident among young people themselves. According to Renahy, the fierce individualism he observed among his interlocutors generated feelings of depression, loneliness, and guilt and ultimately led to their withdrawal from society.

Critics of this literature have, however, questioned its terms of analysis (e.g., F. Weber 1991; Hidouci and Kundid 2001). In what ways, they ask, might it rely on an overly nostalgic and consequently homogenizing view of past workers' experiences?[19] More to the point, by taking social class—and the idea of a working class, in particular—as the most meaningful category of practice, how might this scholarship overlook or ignore other collective self-representations, which may hold more significance for people in their everyday lives? And how, as a result, might this work obfuscate some of the sources or consequences of inequality in today's job market? In other words, is asking about social class really the best place to start?

Carole, the director of a home for disadvantaged youth seeking employment in Limoges, did not think it was. "No one talks about class anymore," she insisted during an initial meeting with me, adding that the young people I would encounter would likely find the term "irrelevant."[20] She was right. During my fieldwork year, it became clear that class was not a particularly pertinent concept for any of the young people I came to know; some, for reasons I will explore in later chapters, even found the notion—and particularly the label "working class"—offensive. But what are the alternatives?

Following the 2005 riots, some commentators (e.g., Mdembe 2011; Lagrange 2010; D. Fassin and Fassin 2006; Castel 2007; Ndiaye 2008; Durpaire 2006) began to suggest that the social question was being replaced by a racial question—that is, that racial or ethnic identities were filling the void left by the disintegration of the working class.[21] This work, often through explicit comparison with the United States, particularly the civil rights movement of the 1950s and 1960s, presented this shift as a long-overdue awakening to repressed racial troubles in France. To be sure, a great number of my interlocutors in Limoges made references to race. Yet, asking if youth in France's outer cities, or people in France more generally, are positioning themselves less in terms of class or more in terms of race in everyday life does not seem to me to be the most useful or even interesting question. Beyond noting whether or not a social actor employs a particular category or distinction, I argue in this book that we need to draw out, to the extent possible, what that category or distinction means to that social actor at that moment and in that context, how he or she is using it, and why. Only by accessing what lies behind the classificatory terms people use will we begin to gain insight into local understandings of how the world works, and only then will we be in a position to elucidate the forms and dimensions social inequality takes on today in the labor market and beyond. In Limoges's outer city, I found critically interrogating my interlocutors' understandings and uses of the concept of social destiny helpful in getting at these meanings.

Social Destiny

The word *destiny* carries the idea of inevitability, and when discussed in terms of a person's social trajectory it may refer to his or her prospects for economic success, access to social goods or resources, or, more broadly, the likelihood of upward or downward social mobility. Some people may not consider themselves to have any particular social destiny; others, by contrast, may have more or less well-formulated ideas of what their future holds. In either case, analysis of the terms in which people discuss their prospects is likely to illuminate fundamental understandings of what goes into determining one's social position.

For my purposes, asking about social destiny proved particularly useful, not only because young people in Limoges's housing projects had a lot to say about it but also because it allowed me to take a step back in order to reflect critically on the categories of classification they used to understand and talk about the unevenness they encountered in daily life. Nearly a century ago, in his treatise on general sociology, Max Weber ([1922] 1978) evoked a similar idea—that of life chances (*Lebenschancen*)—to help explain social stratification. According to Weber, life chances are the opportunities each individual has to improve the quality of his or her life. These opportunities, Weber explained, are anchored in structural conditions, including income, property, norms, and rights, but they are also to a certain extent subjective. The ideas people have about their life chances ultimately affect their actions and as a result may alter, either positively or negatively, the positions they occupy in society.

Since its publication, Weber's work on life chances has been influential in debates among social scientists over the primacy of structure or agency in shaping human behavior. Bourdieu drew on Weber's writings in his formulation of habitus, arguing that one's present and future possibilities are neither entirely objective (the result of the resources, or to use Bourdieu's term, capital, to which one has access) nor subjective (a matter of free will, choice, or determination). Rather, according to Bourdieu, they are created by a kind of interplay between structure and agency over time. Thus, for Bourdieu, habitus is both a "structuring structure" and a "structured structure" (1984, 170). I am very much interested in this interplay between structure and agency in relation to inequality in the labor market. By considering my interlocutors' understandings and uses of the idea of social destiny, I explore more generally how the terms of classification people use in everyday life not only reflect but also work to produce, reproduce, oppose, or diminish social power differentials. I argue that the efficacy of any given category depends not only on the resources, whether social, economic, or cultural, of the social actor putting that category into play, but also—and equally importantly—on the cultural context in which the use of that category takes place. The work that categories of classification are able to accomplish in the social world, I contend, is fundamentally shaped by local systems of meaning and value.

I am not the first observer of France's disadvantaged outer cities to discuss the concept of social destiny. In a contribution on urban youth and violence, sociologist Laurent Mucchielli (1999) highlighted the use of this concept by some young people as a means of understanding and explaining the obstacles to upward social mobility and the risks of downward social mobility they faced. For Mucchielli, social destiny in this instance functioned as a "stand-in" (he used the term *représentation*) for "class." Still, the youth at the center of his study, like my interlocutors in Limoges, did not use that term. Why?

The answer, I argue in this book, has everything to do with the rise and persistence of unemployment and underemployment, especially among certain segments of today's youth. Linked to global transformations, notably the precipitous expansion of neoliberal ideologies and policies, the underlying causes of this inequality have become increasingly diffuse. This has in turn generated a problem of naming. Whereas the word *class* may have seemed both evident and compelling to many people in the context of past labor struggles, in the absence of work today it is arguably neither. On a practical level, naming is, however, of vital importance, for it is the first step to mobilization, to collective resistance. By focusing on my interlocutors' understandings and uses of social destiny, I attempt in this book to trace out how they grapple with this problem of naming. It is my hope that this case study will help us think comparatively about similar struggles as they play out across the globe today.

Methods and Organization

Writing in 2006, Angela Jancius bemoaned anthropologists' tendency to treat unemployment as a mere "sub-theme," despite its being an "extremely relevant topic" (141). As if in response to this reproach, anthropologists have since produced a number of fascinating monographs focusing on unemployment in locales ranging from Dallas (Lane 2011) to Ethiopia (Mains 2011), from Kentucky (Kingslover 2011) to Japan (Allison 2013). By and large, these authors have been concerned with how the global forces behind shifts in the employment landscape are perceived and negotiated at a local level. Joining this small but growing body of literature, I tackle this same problem, with special attention to the question of social classification and categorization laid out above. The location of my study: the medium-size, centrally located French city of Limoges (see map 1).

Limoges may seem better suited to a study exploring agriculture, the elderly, or even luxury goods than urban youth and unemployment. The Limousin, of which Limoges is the regional capital, is one of the most rural

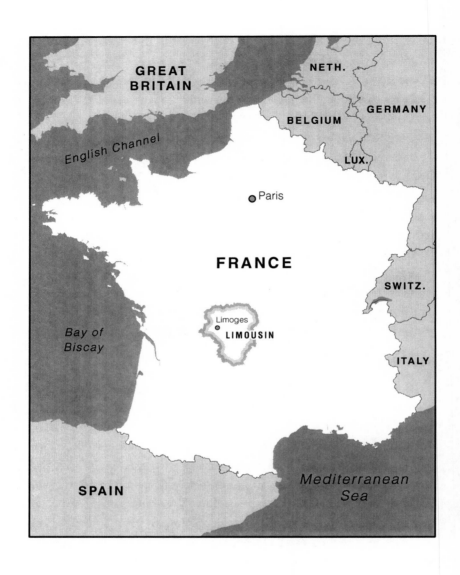

MAP 1. Limoges and the Limousin region. Cartography by Erin Greb.

FIG. 1. Herds of chestnut beef cattle, known as *la Limousine*, dot the region's upland pastures. Breeders from Texas regularly visit Limoges to select the best specimens.

areas of France. It is also one of the least populated, with a disproportionate number of seniors. In 2008 the Limousin had the highest percentage of inhabitants aged sixty or over of any French region (Desplanques 2008, 12–13). Famed for some of the best beef farming in the country—herds of chestnut red Limousin cattle are a common sight—it also boasts extensive oak and pine forests, making timber an important industry (fig. 1). Heavy industrial manufacturing such as that which developed in the north or east of France has never been associated with the Limousin; neither has the kind of large-scale immigration other regions have experienced. As for Limoges, this medium-size city, unlike larger urban centers, such as Paris, Lyon, or Marseille, is not especially known for its troubled public housing. Rather, its name tends to evoke images of the fine china that has been manufactured there since the eighteenth century, and perhaps to a lesser extent, its long history of producing enameled, leather, and paper goods.

FIG. 2. As is the case in many French cities, *grands ensembles* dominate the periphery of Limoges. These large-scale, mixed-income housing projects were built during the decades of economic prosperity following World War II to meet the demand of the city's growing population.

Limoges was, however, a strategic choice. Despite its lack of heavy industry, the city has a significant and well-documented working-class history, grounded in a deeply rooted left-wing tradition dating back at least to the Revolution, and resulting in a precocious labor movement (Corbin 1975; Merriman 1985). In fact, Limoges is the birthplace of the Confédération générale du travail, one of France's most important labor unions, long affiliated with the once-powerful French Communist Party. This leftist tradition spurred the construction of a multitude of worker housing developments beginning as early as the first decades of the twentieth century (Wright 1991). Today, a number of large-scale housing projects (some with more than two thousand units and one boasting almost four thousand) circle the city (fig. 2). And because Limoges was never the site of heavy industrial manufacturing, the effects of deindustrialization have been less significant there; a sizable working population remains, with little out-migration of young people from what might be called "blue collar" backgrounds (Lavaud and Simonneau 2010).[22] Finally, with a population of roughly 140,000, Limoges provided an urban environment but was still conducive to the kind of ethnographic research my project demanded. The city's modest size afforded frequent chance encounters with interlocutors; word quickly spread about my presence, so that on more than one occasion I was identified as the "American researcher" before introducing myself; and I was fairly easily able to access local people in a position to facilitate my work, including, most notably, the city's many social service providers.

Another reason why I chose Limoges for my study has to do with the lack of scholarly work to date on provincial outer cities, especially those of smaller agglomerations. In effect, most examinations of France's fractious *banlieues* concentrate on the Parisian periphery, particularly housing projects in the ill-famed department of Seine-Saint-Denis. What might a study focused on a smaller city reveal? Are locals' experiences similar to or different from those recorded and analyzed by researchers elsewhere? How and in what contexts do Limougeauds (the name used to refer to inhabitants of Limoges) position themselves in relation to people living in larger urban centers? By seeking answers to these questions, this study aims to help us rethink familiar assumptions about the French *banlieues*.

Some clarification about my use of the term *outer city* is in order. Without context, *banlieue* simply translates as "suburb." Although there certainly are affluent suburbs in France (Paris's western periphery is a well-known example), *banlieue* more readily calls to mind the large-scale, architecturally monotonous, and often-rundown housing projects that ring many French cities, as well as the problems—academic failure, juvenile delinquency, unemployment, and drug abuse, to name just a few—linked to them.[23] This negative understanding of the word *banlieue*, it seems to me, has far more in common with the American notion of inner city than that of suburb, which in the United States tends, on the contrary, to evoke visions of middle-class stability. As Loïc Wacquant (2008) insists, there are, however, important differences. Whereas American inner cities tend to be ghettos in the true sense of the word, concentrating one ethnic group within close spatial proximity, French outer cities are far more ethnically diverse, including a "mix" of Franco-French and other ethnicities.[24] Furthermore, statistics show far fewer homicides in French outer cities than in American inner cities. Although violence is a frequent complaint of residents living in French outer cities, reported cases mostly concern the degradation of property. Finally, unlike what tends to be the case in the United States, public housing in France has historically accommodated workers and lower-level salaried staff, as well as the very poor. In 2005 in Limoges, a three-member family (two adults and one child) with a combined annual income of 34,000 euros qualified for public housing. For purposes of comparison, in 2005, 34,000 euros was the equivalent of 41,000 American dollars, roughly 2.5 times the poverty threshold for a household of three ($15,720), as defined by the U.S. Census Bureau.[25]

The data on which this book is based were collected over an eight-year period. In the spring of 2004, while still completing graduate coursework in Paris, I made two preliminary trips to Limoges, during which I visited Limoges's outer city and met with municipal officials and a few social service providers to discuss the feasibility of my project. Then, beginning in the summer of 2005, I conducted twelve months of intensive, uninterrupted fieldwork. Six years later, in the summer of 2012, I returned to Limoges for a month of follow-up research. Between stays, I remained in touch with several primary interlocutors through sporadic email and Facebook exchanges. I have also kept up with the happenings in Limoges through daily reading of the online editions of the two main local newspapers (*Le Populaire du Centre* and *L'Écho de la Haute Vienne*).

Before arriving in Limoges in 2005, I had planned to rent an apartment in one of the outer-city housing projects as a way to meet local youth, but this strategy proved impossible. According to the agent who greeted me at the municipality's public housing office, the city suffers from a shortage of low-income housing, with waiting lists for units typically averaging six months to a year.[26] Because I ended up renting a small apartment toward the city's northern periphery, near one of the housing projects but not in it, I had to find another means to meet youth. Ultimately, I turned to the city's social service sector for assistance. As a result, although my project focused on young people aged sixteen to twenty-four in the process of transitioning between school and the working world,[27] my first interlocutors in Limoges were social workers and case managers, outreach workers and employment counselors, association leaders and program coordinators. With the help of these social service providers, I identified entry points into three of the largest housing projects. These included a municipally funded *bar sans alcool* ("dry" bar) that also serves as a youth employment information center, a *maison des jeunes* (youth house) that aids in the coordination of leisure activities, and an *atelier d'aide aux devoirs* (after-school homework-help program), in which I volunteered several days a week. I also attended a weekly support group for unemployed youth sponsored by the local chapter of Jeunesse ouvrière chrétienne, an international faith-based organization for "blue-collar" youth. Through these associations, organizations, and programs, I was able to meet many local youth and, thanks to their social networks, I eventually expanded my base of interlocutors to include young people who might not necessarily frequent any of them.

France's urban peripheries tend to be ethnically diverse, including both immigrants and their descendants and "Franco-French" people, and Limoges is no exception in this regard. Although it was never an important destination for immigrants, immigration patterns to Limoges have followed national trends. Drawn by the promise of economic opportunity (mostly in logging, mining, and, later, construction), successive waves of migrants came first from neighboring European countries and then from North Africa (Marsac and Brousse 2005; Desbordes 2004). Beginning in the mid-1970s, with the implementation on the national level of stricter immigration policy, the number of immigrants settling in the city steadily decreased. However, since 1990 new immigration has been on the rise. Because of the availability of public housing in Limoges, administrators of the often-overwhelmed public housing systems in some of France's larger urban centers encouraged many political asylum seekers (mostly from Sub-Saharan Africa and Asia) to settle in Limoges. According to 1999 census data, 5.3 percent of Limoges's population was foreign-born compared to 7.4 percent on the national level (Boëldieu and Borrel 2000). Within Limoges itself, most immigrants live in the outer city, where the majority of the municipality's low-income housing is found. In 1999, 16.9 percent of the outer city's residents were foreign-born compared to 3 percent in the city center (Duplouy 2003, 15). In France it is illegal to collect data on race or ethnicity. The presence in Limoges's housing projects of individuals of immigrant background (but born in France) is therefore not accounted for in these statistics. My interlocutors in Limoges's outer city included roughly as many young people with deep roots in France as children or grandchildren of immigrants.

I collected data through participant observation. I hung out at bars and cafés, made trips to the unemployment office, sat in on meetings with employment counselors, and attended neighborhood festivals and concerts. I also participated in other, less quotidian activities, such as a croissant drive and a rummage sale to raise money for a local association and the production of a homemade police thriller, filmed "just for fun" over the course of several months using one industrious youth's video camera, purchased with earnings from a summer of odd jobs. Throughout, I always took notes (usually after returning to the quiet of my own apartment) and sometimes snapped photographs, some of which are included in this book.

In addition to ethnographic observation and informal discussion, I tape-recorded "life-history" narratives. These more-formal interviews, carried out in two or three one-hour sessions over the course of several months, allowed me to probe the backgrounds and trajectories of thirty-three young people. Topics covered included family life and childhood, school, employment experiences, and plans for the future. The timing of these interviews was strategic. I undertook them during my last few months in Limoges, by which time all of the respondents knew me well and were more comfortable discussing personal information with me. Furthermore, I was able to ask them to reflect critically on the fall 2005 riots and spring 2006 protests. What they had to say greatly enriched data collected during the heat of those two galvanizing events.

Finally, I amassed a great deal of printed material, including pamphlets outlining the goals and activities of the different associations and organizations I frequented, handouts distributed at individual meetings, official state and municipal literature concerning youth unemployment, public housing, or urban renewal, and leaflets dispersed by labor unions and other organizations during the CPE demonstrations. I also combed through the national and local press for pertinent articles, especially during the fall riots and the spring protests. Many times, this material formed the basis of exchanges with interlocutors.

Although the material upon which this study rests thus comes from a variety of sources, the most significant of these is unquestionably the young men and women who so trustingly shared their lives with me. Although many of them asked to be cited by name in future publications, not all of them did. In an effort then "to return to them at least a small part of the power to decide whether or not to reveal themselves" (Rogers 1991, xiii), I have chosen to employ pseudonyms throughout this book and have altered any particularly personal (and potentially damaging) information they shared with me.[28] They will, however, undoubtedly recognize themselves in the pages that follow.

By contrast, I have retained place-names, including the actual name of the city and the names of the individual neighborhoods where I carried out my fieldwork. This seems important for at least two reasons. First, to understand where these young people are coming from, referencing Limoges's working-class past is crucial. This would have been very difficult (if not impossible) without citing the historical work on the city, particularly John Merriman's (1985) well-known study. Second, the focus on France's outer cities for nearly forty years now in public debate has proved to have a reductionist effect. Indeed, many of the young people I came to know complained to me that outsiders forget that these are distinct places where real people make real lives. It is my hope that by calling them by name, I will help to return to Limoges's outer-city neighborhoods at least a small portion of their individuality.

"Ethnographic fieldwork, like most research," writes Daphne Berdahl, "is often a matter of structured serendipity" (1999b, 14). My work in Limoges certainly supports this claim. That the fall 2005 riots and the spring

2006 protests, conflicts that thrust the question of youth unemployment into public debate, took place during my fieldwork year offered me a remarkable opportunity to explore how my interlocutors understood and positioned themselves in relation to this issue, particularly as it was presented in the national and local media at the time. I devote a chapter to each of these events. But first, I examine the context that gave them their meaning.

Chapter 1 introduces readers to Limoges and its outer city. Discussion centers on popular fears associated with these outlying neighborhoods and municipal and state measures implemented to address those fears. Noting that the emergence of structural unemployment coincided with an alarming shift away from social reform and the redistribution of resources toward an emphasis on personal accountability, restitution, and retribution, I chronicle the birth of a new dangerous class—"outer-city youth"—in the popular imagination. This discussion sets the stage for chapter 2, which considers how youth in Limoges's outer-city housing projects pushed against this negative narrative through comparison of their condition with what they imagined their parents' prospects to be like when they were their age. I argue that these young men and women's nostalgia for a bygone era of full employment served to eschew guilt and shame over their inability to find work today. Furthermore, the collective nature of this nostalgia suggests an awareness of a shared social destiny darkened by the cloud of economic decline.

Chapter 3 shifts focus to the more than eighty measures implemented by the French government over the last several decades to favor job growth, many aimed directly at reducing youth unemployment. I examine discourses surrounding these measures, from those produced by their architects at the national level to what employment counselors and social workers in Limoges had to say to the perceptions of young people themselves. In addition to creating more jobs, the idea of *solidarité*, I note, was frequently presented by stakeholders as a highly desirable outcome. In other words, these measures were often described as a way of drawing the unemployed—and young people in particular—into responsible social life. I argue that this definition of *solidarité*, founded on an opposition between included and excluded, has deleterious consequences. It reinforces neoliberal discourses of personal responsibility and masks underlying structural inequalities, effectively recasting "at-risk youth" as "risky youth."

In many respects, chapters 4 and 5 form the core of the book. Starting with the rioting that ripped through France in the fall of 2005, chapter 4 focuses on race as a potentially meaningful category of distinction. Long denounced in France as a dangerous basis for social classification because of its perceived potential to cleave society into ethnic enclaves, the notion of race nonetheless took center stage in media, political, and academic commentary on the riots. Rather than applaud or condemn this development, as so many others have already done, I take a step back to ask what meanings race may hold for people in France today. Noting that my interlocutors in Limoges's *banlieue* linked racism to a decline in *solidarité*, I argue that their uses of the concept had a lot more to do with making sense of the complex problems they faced in the new economy than with any claims to the right to difference. Chapter 5, in turn, considers other categories of social classification that were put into play during the CPE protests in early 2006, notably that of the precariat. The CPE, which promised to create more jobs for young people by slackening France's rigid labor code, provoked a great deal of anger among many people in France. Precarity, they insisted, would only worsen if the proposal became law. Curiously, few young people from Limoges's outer city participated in the protests. Why was this the case, and how might answering this question raise others about the rise of the so-called precariat?

If chapters 4 and 5 focus on more exceptional events, chapter 6 explores everyday life in Limoges's outer city. In an attempt to move beyond popular depictions of the *banlieues* as either epicenters of advanced anomie or seething crucibles of radicalism and dissent, I portray the creative and adaptive strategies my ethnographic subjects in Limoges implemented as they improvised new forms of sociality and personhood in response to persistent, long-standing unemployment. Although *galère*, the term they used to describe the challenges they faced, may be seen as contributing to a common group identity, many factors, I argue, not the least of which was a shift toward more flexible employment arrangements, precluded the development of any organized collective movement.

Finally, in the epilogue I check in with some of my research subjects seven years after my initial fieldwork. No longer the youth they were, and some with children of their own, I ask them to reflect on their personal and work history and encourage them to discuss how their experiences have compared to the social destiny they imagined for themselves when we first met in 2005 and 2006. The word *luck*, whether qualified as "good" or "bad," I discovered, was often on the tip of their tongue. How, I ask, does this idea match up with that of social destiny, and what can interrogating it tell us about perceptions of social position over time in the face of long-term unemployment?

1 On Edge

(Un)Employment and the Bad Reputation of Limoges's Outer City

"What," the bank employee asked me, "could an American possibly be doing in an as out-of-the-way place as Limoges?" I had arrived in the city the previous evening and was eager to get down to business, but I had a number of practical concerns to attend to first, including opening a bank account. When I explained to the woman who sat down to help me that I would be conducting research in the city's outlying housing projects, her expression turned grave. "Don't go into those neighborhoods," she whispered. "They're full of Muslims, and they don't like Americans." According to her, four years earlier, on the afternoon of September 11, 2001, when word of the terrorist attacks in the United States had reached Limoges, residents of the housing projects descended into the streets of their neighborhoods. Car horns rang out in celebration, and cries of joy filled the air. This "appalling clamor," the bank employee told me, was heard all the way in the city center.

A few days later I had lunch with Christophe in the pleasant court-yard behind the medieval timbered building where he lives, just steps from the Cathedral of St. Étienne, a landmark of Limoges's city center. A teacher at a vocational high school, Christophe is well versed in the problems facing youth as they transition between school and work life. As we discussed ways of making contact with potential research subjects, I mentioned my recent visit to the public housing office, where I had been told that long waiting lists would prevent me from renting an apartment in the outer city.[1] "It's probably for the best," Christophe said with a shrug. "No one would have talked to you anyway. People in the housing projects keep to themselves. There's no sense of community. Besides," he continued, "there's a lot of gang violence. It's better you steer clear of *those* neighborhoods."

Soon after my discussion with Christophe, I met with Louise in her city-center office. A municipal official who directs various community service and outreach initiatives, she was interested in my project for the practical insights she thought it might provide the city. She was careful, though, not to sugarcoat what she expected my experience in the housing projects to be like. "You're in for a difficult year, I'm afraid," she told me. "The housing projects are not a pleasant place. So many of the buildings are run down, there's trash everywhere, and no one seems to care. To be sure, budgets have been cut in recent years, but the city can only do so much. Now more than ever, we need residents to take on their share of communal responsibility. They need to be active participants in turning their situation around."

Commentary like this is not surprising in France. Since the early 1980s, when riots erupted on the outskirts of Lyon, the *banlieue*, or outer city, has been the focus of intense, if intermittent, media attention. It has also figured prominently, mostly in a negative light, in a number of popular feature films, including the 1995 blockbuster *La Haine*. One result is that today the word *banlieue* evokes for many French people all sorts of fears and anxieties about an unraveling of the social fabric, from a breakdown of cultural consensus, to uncontrollable drug and alcohol abuse, to rampant youth violence, to an overall lack of sociability and collective responsibility.

In this chapter I trace the development of Limoges's outer city, focusing not only on the physical construction of these neighborhoods but also the ideas associated with them—ideas that have led many in Limoges to be "on edge." The long-standing bad reputation of these areas, I argue, belies an important shift: whereas in the past outer-city residents were viewed as potentially dangerous because of their collective, working-class consciousness and proclivity for group militancy, today's outer-city inhabitants—especially young people—are feared for their perceived individualism and cultural isolationism. This discontinuity, I maintain, maps onto transformations in the employment landscape, especially the end of full employment and the spectacular rise in short-term work contracts, particularly among the youngest and the least qualified. Feared by many, today's unemployed outer-city youth are viewed as particularly visible representatives of what some are calling "new dangerous classes."

Workers Rising

By some accounts an urban center and by others a provincial backwoods, Limoges is known for many things, not least of which the fine china that bears the city's name. But what is perhaps one of Limoges's most defining characteristics is its deep-rooted leftist tradition, evident even to casual observers of the city by its many street names paying homage to heroes of the French left.[2] Although a relatively understudied region of France, a number of scholars—notably, American historian John Merriman and French historian Alain Corbin—have produced works examining the city and surrounding countryside.[3] What, they have asked, accounts for the precocious development of leftist politics in this remote part of France? Why did Limoges become "the Red City," France's "First Socialist City"? The answer, these authors suggest, lies in part in patterns of industrialization and urbanization that were specific to Limoges.

Understanding Limoges requires situating the city's economic development in relation to more general trends in France. Most historians agree that a working-class consciousness emerged in France around the middle of the nineteenth century, when artisans, exposed to the developing logics of capitalism, began to understand themselves as exploited. In pre-revolutionary times, artisans were a driving force of the French economy, producing everything from clothing and furniture to farm tools and weaponry. Each craft had its own guild, and each guild had its own internal hierarchy, with highly codified rules pertaining to recruitment, retention, and promotion. Revolutionary legislators initiated important economic change in this regard. Viewing guilds as a vestige of ancien régime privilege, they abolished them, a move resulting in a flood of newcomers into the trades. No longer protected by guilds, artisans were forced to accept piecework at rates the new market could support, which were often below those they had been able to command before the Revolution. Historical research suggests that artisans thus began to identify their situation with that of less skilled workers, whom they mobilized in part through the creation of mutual-aid societies (Sewell 1986). These voluntary clubs provided social and economic assistance to their members, especially during times of unemployment. At first tied to particular crafts, these mutual-aid societies eventually paved the way for organizations that stretched across trades. The resulting "confraternity of proletarians," William Sewell (1980, 211) has suggested, climaxed in the 1848 Revolution in Paris, when workers demanded not only the right to assistance but also "the right to work."

Given this record, historians tend to contrast the French context with that of England. Whereas England's economy was mostly industrial by 1850, France remained a predominantly agricultural and rural society well into the twentieth century.[4] In France, organizational change, far more than technological innovation and development, appears to have been responsible for the emergence of a working-class consciousness.[5]

As Merriman has shown, Limoges did not entirely follow this pattern. First, the group responsible for organizing workers was not strictly speaking made up of artisans, although its members, the *artistes en porcelaine* (decorators who hand-painted intricate patterns on the china) shared "the same pride of craft and sense of dignity" (1985, 105). Second, in nineteenth-century Limoges, technological innovation and concentration played an important role. Indeed, "large-scale industry in Limoges," writes Merriman, "manifested some of the features of the English model of large-scale industrialization" (105).

Production of porcelain in Limoges began toward the end of the eighteenth century, after kaolin, the fine white clay that constitutes its principal ingredient, was discovered near the town of Saint-Yrieix, some thirty kilometers southwest of the city.[6] By 1819, four porcelain factories had been established in Limoges (Merriman 1985, 28). This figure rose to seven in 1828, then to twenty-seven in 1861 (84). Although by century's end only an additional seven factories had been built, the number of workers employed in the porcelain industry had increased dramatically. Whereas in 1892 there were just over five thousand porcelain workers in Limoges, by 1905 this number had jumped to nearly thirteen thousand. Some 40 percent of the city's overall workforce was directly engaged in porcelain production at the beginning of the twentieth century. The four largest companies, including the one bearing the name of its American industrialist founder, Haviland, turned out half of all production in Limoges (167).

Technological advances, Merriman contends, drove this rapid development and concentration. The arrival of the railroad in the city in 1856 brought with it coal, which largely replaced timber as a source of fuel for the porcelain kilns. At the same time, factory owners were devising ways to streamline production and reduce dependency on labor. These included larger kilns (made possible in part by the increased heat generated from coal), new heating methods, the introduction of presses to mass-produce flat pieces, and the mechanical production of molds for sculpted pieces (Merriman 1985, 168–69). All of these innovations resulted in reduced labor costs. Consider, for example, a machine to crush kaolin, which was introduced around 1875. Not only did this invention generate a more uniform paste that was less likely to break during firing; it also replaced the workers who had previously performed the same task, albeit less efficiently, using their wooden shoes (169).

Of all the changes to the porcelain industry, those in the area of decoration, Merriman contends, had the most far-reaching effects. Porcelain production involved a number of steps, from the extraction of kaolin in nearby quarries to the preparation of this substance for shaping on pottery wheels or in molds to baking, enameling, and then finally, for some pieces, decoration. At each stage, the skill of the workers increased. Thus, the *artistes en porcelaine* occupied something of a privileged position. "Dignified, literate, prosperous, and relatively independent, they were as close to an 'aristocracy of labor' as existed in Limoges" (Merriman 1985, 29). Unlike most porcelain workers, *artistes en porcelaine* often labored at home or in separate workshops, and their efforts were (relatively speaking) well rewarded. As tastes shifted during the nineteenth century away from plain white porcelain toward more ornate pieces, Limoges's industrialists sought ways to cut the high costs associated with decoration. David Haviland proposed, as a first step, combining the operations of production and decoration under one roof (81). However, the most significant innovation involved the development and perfection of decoration plates by impression and chromolithography, which, by the end of the 1880s, had largely replaced hand painting. Although at century's end a much smaller number of *artistes en porcelaine* continued to find work painting the edges of plates with gold, touching up pieces, or embellishing special orders, female workers called *décalqueuses* accomplished the lion's share of decorating by applying mass-produced decals to the porcelain. Even though they turned out finished pieces at a much higher rate than previously possible when the painting was done by hand, they were paid far less, earning at best one-fourth of what an *artiste en porcelaine* had been able to command (168).

Alongside these technological innovations, employers increasingly sought ways to control or discipline workers. In this regard, Merriman notes that for most observers one of the most striking features of the new Haviland factory, which by the mid-1860s had become the largest single producer of porcelain in all of France, was the imposing clock over the main entrance. Although admired by visitors to the city, this "handsome Wagner," as one guidebook described the device, served more than an aesthetic role; it "regulated the arrivals and departures of the Haviland workers" (Merriman 1985, 81). Limoges's other porcelain manufacturers, Merriman explains, soon followed Haviland's lead, imposing similar measures of control.

In the factories, working conditions were atrocious, both from the stifling heat generated by the enormous kilns and the noxious fumes that permeated the air in the decoration sections. Workers experienced much higher than normal rates of illness, such as chronic bronchitis and tuberculosis, which could be directly linked to these conditions.[7] Indirectly, alcoholism was rampant (Merriman 1985, 170).

Against this backdrop of declining working conditions, "the foreman,"

FIG. 3. Once avoided by outsiders because of its putrid smell, the historic butchers' quarter, with its narrow, cobbled streets and crooked, timbered buildings, is now a landmark of the historic city center.

writes Merriman, "became a symbol of capitalism" (1985, 170). Responsible for enforcing the rules set in place by the Union des fabricants, the trade organization established by porcelain manufacturers, foremen were often depicted by workers as cruel, denying them permission to leave the factory to get fresh air or to attend to personal matters, such as caring for sick children. Such was their understanding of being held captive during their long shifts that some workers described themselves as "convicts," the foremen as "guards," and the factories as "prisons" (171). This understanding, Merriman argues, generated resentment, which in turn provided fertile ground for revolt. When in 1864 the French government legalized strikes, porcelain workers immediately struck, followed by workers of Limoges's other major manufacturers, including the shoe industry. This coopera-tion across trades—a first that drew national attention—led Limoges's prefect to describe the disturbance as "a war between capital and labor"

(Merriman 1985, 112). According to Merriman, spatial organization in the expanding city, particularly what he describes as "class segregation," favored such cooperative militancy.

During the nineteenth century, Limoges did not benefit from any clear urban planning. Writing about the city, Corbin contrasts the newly developed "open" and "anonymous" industrial suburbs with the densely populated "traditional" city center (1975, 83) (fig. 3, page 39). He explains that as industry developed—especially the porcelain and shoe trades— peasants from the surrounding countryside migrated to the city in search of work. For the most part, these newcomers settled in modest dwellings in the industrial *faubourgs* on the city's edge.[8] These neighborhoods, Corbin notes, expanded in a haphazard fashion, often following the main arteries of circulation. He likens the result to a star, with the old city at its center, its radiating points representing the *faubourgs*, and vast empty spaces in between. Communal worker gardens, small farms, or swamps occupied these vacant areas (83).

Although the laboring populations of Limoges's peripheral neighborhoods may have enjoyed easier access to open space than residents of the overcrowded city center, their living conditions were far from ideal. Merriman explains that life in the new industrial suburbs was nasty, brutish, and, for many, short. Quoting one local observer, he offers the following description of the workers' quarters: "wooden houses, generally inordinately high and without proportion to their width and to the width of the streets. The alleys are somber and fetid, the narrow stairways give way underfoot; the landings are encumbered with garbage, the rooms poorly ventilated, the walls are bare or covered with old wallpaper that serves as a refuge for a variety of insects. To these powerful causes of insalubrity one must add the piling of too many people in rooms that are too small (1985, 171). Improvement was slow to reach the *faubourgs*. Merriman reports that for much of the second half of the nineteenth century, when other urban centers, most notably Paris under Baron Haussmann, began to modernize, Limoges's elected city government did not seriously carry out a policy of urban renewal or give much attention to either city planning or public health. Only near century's end were the sewer and water systems expanded into the *faubourgs*, which helped to alleviate some of the workers' discomfort (206).

These poor living conditions reinforced ideas among city-center dwellers, particularly the growing industrial bourgeois elite, about irreconcilable cultural and social difference. "For many bourgeois," Merriman writes, "the faubourgs seemed menacing and forbidding; perhaps they associated them with the traditional uncertainties of the immediate countryside, particularly the wood, where robbers, brigands, and prostitutes were said to lurk" (1985, 87).[9] Corbin quotes a nineteenth-century guidebook, which indicates that newcomers on the periphery were sometimes perceived as backward or coarse: this "newly implanted working population," the travel guide reads, "is much preoccupied with re-creating on the city's edge the conditions of rustic life" (1975, 83). In these liminal spaces, where some "houses still lacked identifying numbers [and] day laborers and weavers mingled with gardeners, sharecroppers, truck farmers, and tenant farmers," urban was muddled with rural (Merriman 1985, 87).

Bourgeois fear of the *faubourgs*, however, eventually centered on the proletarian character these quarters assumed. As production became increasingly standardized, so too did workers' experience, even that of women, who by the turn of the twentieth century had largely been integrated into factory life. Whereas workers' conversations and movements were tightly controlled in the factories, the peripheral neighborhoods provided spaces for greater freedom of thought and expression, and mingling among workers from different trades occurred. According to Merriman, bars and cafés, which by 1864 numbered over six hundred in Limoges, played an important role in shaping a working-class community. These drinking establishments "served as the 'just judiciary,' or parliament, of the people," where, he suggests, workers learned the fundamentals of socialism (1985, 106).

During the second half of the nineteenth century, efforts by activists to channel workers' solidarity into political action grew. Reformers founded trade unions, including in 1895 the Confédération générale du travail, which quickly became in the early decades of the twentieth century France's most powerful labor organization; they organized festivals, such as May Day and Bastille Day, to promote workers' rights; and they preached anticlericalism to break the hold of conservative churchmen. At the same time, influential speakers, including Jean Jaurès and Jules Guesde, visited the city. The open meetings they held "helped draw average citizens into political life" (Merriman 1985, 188). In this climate, workers came to understand their interests as at odds with those of their industrialist employers. The situation grew ripe for collective action.

The strikes of 1864 were followed by others, culminating in massive protests in 1905, which Merriman describes as "revolutionary in scale" (1985, 239) and "the most violent that Limoges had ever seen" (221). Demonstrations outside the homes of company owners and foremen became especially confrontational. In a move uncannily similar to more recent bouts of outer-city violence, angry workers set ablaze the car of Theodore Haviland, the son and successor (along with his brother Charles) of David Haviland's porcelain enterprise (229). Merriman contends that actions such as these, which involved the participation of workers from across the trades, "seemed to highlight the solidarity of workers on the periphery" (248). Associated with workers, the *faubourgs* came to be seen as a hatchery for insurrection, the nesting place for a social alternative subversive of the property-respecting, bourgeois order.

By the turn of the twentieth century, then, Limoges's periphery had already earned a bad reputation among many city-center dwellers, a reputation tied to employment or, more specifically, the collective militancy of the periphery's proletarian inhabitants. The urban periphery I discovered a century after the tumultuous events of 1905 still suffered from a negative reputation, but these neighborhoods resembled little the descriptions offered by Merriman or Corbin. Long gone were the raucous crowds of porcelain and shoe workers and their squalid dwellings and boisterous bars and cafés. Modern high-rise apartments arranged in tidy clusters and shiny big-box shopping centers were now the main features of the periphery. As I explore in the following section, concern over controlling workers, but also integrating them into mainstream society, helps to explain this radical transformation.

Promoting Social Order through Housing

Less historical work has examined Limoges in the twentieth century. Perhaps this is because revolution is an alluring topic, and worker insurgency aimed at transforming the social order dropped off markedly in Limoges following the 1905 strikes. Merriman attributes this decline to workers' "general acceptance of the rules of the game" (1985, 250). In other words, workers' increasing integration into the political process seems, to him, to have forestalled any inclination on their part to overturn it. This is doubtless an accurate assessment, but the role of housing in promoting social order in twentieth-century Limoges must also be taken into account.

A defining feature of Limoges's urban landscape throughout the nineteenth century and up until the middle of the twentieth century was a persistent lack of housing, especially for workers and their families. This shortage was at least partially due to the inability of construction to keep up with demand. Indeed, the growth rate of Limoges during this period rivaled that of Paris. Between 1846 and 1896 Limoges's population more than doubled, rising from roughly thirty-eight thousand to nearly eighty thousand (Desforges 2002, 112). This expansion continued unabated into the twentieth century, nearing the one hundred thousand mark only a decade later (130).

Industrialization was principally responsible for this increase. As new factories opened and old ones expanded, peasants flooded into the city looking for higher wages and a better life. According to one estimation, by 1921 nearly two-thirds of the city's total population was made up of workers and their dependents (Perrier 1924, 362). Losses suffered during World War I and then the economic crisis of the 1930s, which dealt a severe blow to both Limoges's porcelain and shoe industries (Perry 2007), slowed further growth. However, during World War II the city's population increased dramatically, as refugees fled Nazi persecution in the occupied north (Fogg 2009).[10] Although in the decade following the war Limoges's population declined, a municipal report published in 1949 recognized that an additional ten thousand apartments were still needed (Diverneresse 1986, 40). As in any context where demand outweighs supply, beggars cannot be choosers, and those who possess a coveted good occupy a position of power. When this good is essential to life, as housing is, this power is particularly great. In Limoges, employers were able to turn this situation to their favor.

Despite growing housing demand and increasing misery in the *faubourgs*, Limoges's municipal government was slow to take action. In fact, it was not until 1919 that the city, in a delayed response to a 1914 national law freezing rents, established the Office public d'habitations à bon marché (OPHBM; Public affordable housing office). In the meantime, workers had organized a small number of collective residences. The vast majority of housing was, however, under the control of factory owners.

To be sure, worker housing represented a practical concern for Limoges's industrialists. Efficient production depended on a readily available workforce, which in turn required nearby worker housing. Practicality, however, may have been a disguise for a more insidious agenda. By renting housing to workers, Limoges's industrialists were able to create a symbolic universe where they were no longer necessarily the oppressors of workers but their natural intermediary in dealings with capital. Housing, in this view, was not only essential for maintaining the labor force but also for preserving a social order where industrialists occupied a privileged position. Thus, even after the creation of the OPHBM, factory owners continued to invest in worker housing, founding in 1948 an interprofessional housing committee, whose mission was to collect subsidies from area entrepreneurs and work with municipal authorities to increase Limoges's housing stock (Diverneresse 1986, 36–38).

This coexistence of private and public interest in worker housing may help to explain why, up until the late 1950s, Limoges's outer city expanded in a haphazard fashion, much as it did during the nineteenth century. The only real consideration appears to have been the availability and accessibility of land. In general, the modus operandi was to build as quickly and as cheaply as possible. The result, as one local observer bemoaned midcentury, was often unsightly: "A multitude of developments . . . gives a sad and disorderly appearance to the peripheral neighborhoods. The accumulation of housing causes vehicles to amass inharmoniously at the base of the apartment buildings" (qtd. in Diverneresse 1986, 40).

Another jump in Limoges's population during the *Trente glorieuses*, that three-decade period of economic development following World War II, changed all of this. Although the porcelain and shoe industries had long since receded under the pressures of foreign competition, opportunity in construction, new industry, and the burgeoning service sector lured job seekers from the surrounding countryside.[11] This time, the resulting demand for housing coincided with efforts on the national level to bring order to the incoherent development that had characterized the *banlieue* (Fourcaut 2004). The scientific rationalization of space, founded on social hygiene principles developed a century earlier, would leave an indelible mark on Limoges's periphery.

In France, the social or public hygiene movement emerged in the second half of the nineteenth century. Building on new medical discoveries, particularly the work of Pasteur concerning the transmission of pathogens, hygienists posited that the manner in which people live—that is, the buildings they inhabit, the work they perform, and the people with whom they associate—plays a central role in the spread of contagions. More than just a question of disease, however, social hygiene came to encompass a broader range of concerns. "Hygiene," writes Janet Horne, "evolved into a commanding social metaphor that fostered new representations of urban life, industrial society, and even democracy itself" (2002, 225). For hygienists, the sort of social unrest witnessed in Limoges at the turn of the twentieth century constituted a social malady, born of undesirable conditions, including poor working conditions, but also inadequate or unhealthy housing. These conditions, hygienists argued, could be reformed or eliminated to promote better social order and, ultimately, avoid further political turbulence.[12]

Early efforts in France aimed at the rehabilitation of housing included Haussmann's sweeping transformation of Paris.[13] During roughly the same period, reformers undertook similar, albeit less ambitious, renovations in Limoges, including the razing of the poverty-stricken, crime-infested Viraclaud and Verdurier neighborhoods (Merriman 1985, 206–7). These efforts, however, largely consisted in chasing unwanted elements from the city. Haussmann's critics argued that he added to the problem of social strife in Paris by encouraging the development of working-class slums on the city's outskirts.[14]

As the social hygiene movement gained momentum in the twentieth century, concern shifted to include the well-being of all of the city's inhabitants, from the most prosperous industrialist to the least fortunate factory worker.[15] Worker housing became, according to one well known reformer, "the first of all social questions" (qtd. in Horne 2002, 230). In other words, housing was seen as a tool to avoid class conflict and promote better social order.

By the 1920s, young planners and architects trained in the new discipline of urban planning began to set their sights on France's *banlieues*. Borrowing from the British model pioneered by Ebenezer Howard, they proposed the creation of garden cities to "relieve congestion, improve urban hygiene, and order growth" (Wakeman 2004, 124). In line with these ideals, Limoges witnessed in 1924 the construction of a planned community of more than two hundred apartments contained in two-story buildings, each with an individual garden and communal lavatories (Desforges 2002, 136). Economic crisis and war slowed further development of this type. However, in the postwar boom years efforts to bring order to Limoges's periphery were renewed, this time on a much grander scale. In a matter of just a few decades, huge blocks of high-rise housing—the *grands ensembles* that today typify the landscape of the French *banlieue*— mushroomed on the city's edge.

Often held up today as an example of everything wrong with postwar, state-sponsored public housing, from their visual monotony to their "inhuman scale," France's *grands ensembles* were nonetheless the source of a great deal of optimism when they initially were designed and built. The first *grands ensembles* were erected on the outskirts of Paris in 1954, on the heels of public outcry when labor unions and the Christian group Emmaüs, led by Abbé Pierre, brought to light the substandard living conditions endured by workers and others in the crowded, decaying slums on the capital's edge. The *grands ensembles*, by contrast, would offer modern, hygienic apartments, complete with running water, flush toilets, heat, and electricity (Rudolph 2015). The goals of the *grands ensembles*, though, were far loftier than the provision of modern comforts. According to one planning commission's report, they would do no less than "regenerate the worn urban fabric of the *banlieue* [and] restore order to the Paris metropolitan region" (qtd. in Fourcaut 2004, 212).

To this end, the *grands ensembles* were meant to house a balance of the poor and the middle classes, workers and families. Such *mixité sociale*, planners argued, would soothe class conflict as neighbors from different social strata mingled and, ideally, members of the lower classes adopted middle-class norms and values. It would also, they insisted, promote the assimilation of foreigners into French society—a major concern as France received increasing numbers of workers from abroad, especially North Africa. "Far from being pushed out and marginalized, immigrant groups," Beth Epstein writes, "were to be dispersed and gradually inserted into French life, on the assumption that if they were a relatively small presence, their needs could be attended to and they would better adapt to French social life and practices" (2011, 39).

Designed to wipe clean difference, whether difference in social class or difference in ethnicity, the *grands ensembles* tended to encourage individual rather than collective practices. The architecture itself of these imposing structures limited social interaction. Although home to thousands of people, in general very little common interior space was made available to residents save cramped entryways, stairwells, and elevators. Furthermore, most *grands ensembles* were built around anonymous big-box stores, where shopping became less about consuming a product and more about consuming an aspiration. Deprived of the regulating effect of the "collective eye" of their former social networks, some rehoused workers succumbed to the pressures of consumer society, burying themselves in debt. Other residents, especially those who were the best off, used the *grands ensembles* as a stepping-stone to more prestigious forms of accommodation. Chasing the dream of private home ownership, they demonstrated little interest in socializing with neighbors, whom they viewed as temporary and perhaps inferior (Noiriel 1990, 208–9).

FIG. 4. The last of Limoges's *grands ensembles* to be constructed, Beaubreuil was supposed to be a self-sufficient "city of tomorrow," complete with mixed-income housing, industry, services, and entertainment. Never finished because funding dried up after the economic downturn of the 1970s, today Beaubreuil has the reputation of being a particularly rough neighborhood.

The first *grand ensemble* in Limoges rose in 1958 and was quickly followed by others. Today the city counts a half-dozen such housing developments, some with close to two thousand apartments and one boasting nearly four thousand apartments. To be sure, these huge housing blocks were a response to population growth, since by 1975 there were nearly 144,000 people living in the city (Desforges 2002, 144). However, some research has suggested that municipal officials, in giving the green light to these housing projects, were equally concerned with the city's reputation (e.g., Diverneresse 1986; Lazzarotti 1970).[16] Dissatisfied with Limoges's long-standing status as an insignificant and undesirable place—the verb *limoger* is the French equivalent of "to send to Siberia"—they wanted to emulate housing initiatives in Paris or Lyon to bring their city grandeur and renown. This preoccupation may have clouded their judgment, at least with regard to Beaubreuil, the last *grand ensemble* to be erected in Limoges (fig. 4).

Built on the heels of another large housing project that had been declared a success by city officials, Beaubreuil was supposed to be even better. Inspired by the recent construction of the *villes nouvelles* (new towns) in the Paris region, plans called for private and public housing, a variety of municipal and recreational services, and businesses.[17] Beaubreuil, its developers insisted, would be an attractive, self-contained community where a range of people would want to live. Yet many of these aspirations were never realized. Construction, begun in the early 1970s, was halted less than a decade later when funding dried up (Diverneresse 1986, 76–91). Today, Beaubreuil has a particularly rough reputation, and for those who grow up there the walls seem to be closing in. The young people who during the day congregate around its dreary, concrete-slab buildings face an unemployment rate in excess of 50 percent (Duplouy 2003, 21).

From Inclusion to Exclusion

Since the 1980s, French commentary on the management of the *banlieues* has dramatically shifted. Whereas in the past housing development on the city's edge had been promoted as a tool for addressing the structural inequalities of capitalist production, whether to quell rebellious workers, improve the condition of the less fortunate, or both, more recent urban renewal policy has tended to focus less on the redistribution of resources and more on personal responsibility and individual accountability. As Zygmunt Bauman (2001) has established, in today's "individualized society" emphasis on personal accountability is widespread, with the unfortunate result of hiding from sight the deeper, sociological causes of the problems we face. In the context of the French *banlieues*, the effect is especially perverse. Not only do residents of these disadvantaged neighborhoods struggle to explain to themselves and others why they experience the difficulties they do, but they also almost certainly incur the stigma that being from the *banlieues* entails. That is, rather than being viewed as unable to turn their situation around, many are perceived as willfully refusing to uphold their end of the social contract and therefore contributing to the misery they face.

Sylvie Tissot (2007) has traced this shift to personal responsibility in discourse on the *banlieues* to the ten-year period spanning 1985 and 1995, when the negatively charged category *quartier sensible* (disadvantaged neighborhood) appeared. Far from a mere reflection, even a distorted one, of social life, this category, Tissot insists, represented above all a new and paradoxical approach to looking at urban poverty and vulnerability in France. Its emergence, she explains, owed much to interactions among urban policymakers and administrators, the media, and scholarly representations of the "problem" of the *banlieues*.

Beginning in the 1960s the *grands ensembles* faced growing criticism. Vigorously denounced for everything from their gigantism and lack of adequate public transportation to their homogeneity and flimsy construction, these "rabbit hutches" were said to be responsible for a particular kind of neurosis—*la sarcellite*, named after the city of Sarcelles, where the first *grand ensemble* in the Paris region was constructed. Critics of the *grands ensembles* also condemned the top-down, authoritative approach of government officials and planners, which, they argued, left little room for alternative solutions to the housing crisis France faced in the postwar years. Such dissent only grew louder as the country sank into economic recession following the oil crises of the mid-1970s. In response, the state established the Politique de la ville (Urban Development Program), aimed at tackling the problems facing the *grands ensembles*. The approach was twofold, involving both the renovation of the aging housing stock and, above all, *accompagnement social* (social support) for its residents. Confronted by budgetary restrictions and an overly complex bureaucratic structure, administrators chose the battles they felt they could win, or at least where defeat seemed less likely. "We cannot solve the big issues, such as unemployment," suggested one elected official in the Paris region, "but we can help with the development and promotion of social relations. We must mend the bonds among residents" (qtd. in Tissot 2004, 533). In other words, the residents themselves, rather than the structural problems they faced, became the focus of post-1970s urban renewal efforts in the *banlieues*.

This focus was asserted and reasserted by planners and administrators of the Politique de la ville through liberal use of a number of keywords. Residents of the outer cities, Tissot explains, were called to demonstrate good "citizenship" through active "participation" and "dialogue." The goal was to strengthen "social bonds." To this end, notions such as "proximity" and "local" were frequently invoked (2007, 9). Practically, reformers encouraged residents to demonstrate these "virtues" through engagement in town hall and neighborhood council meetings, local associations, and community picnics and festivals. These venues, they insisted, would enable residents not only to voice their needs but also to participate in fulfilling those needs. A guiding principle explained in the abundant literature produced for the new social service professionals, whose presence in the housing projects was established under the Politique de la ville, consisted in the belief that "it is better to teach a man to fish than to give a man a fish" (qtd. in Tissot 2007, 245).[18]

Both humanist and progressive, such rhetoric, Tissot notes, was hard to challenge, particularly in a political climate charged by questions of immigration and insecurity. The 1980s in France were marked by the rise of the anti-immigrant, extreme-right National Front party, whose platform consisted largely in blaming immigrant workers for the decline of the French economy and skyrocketing unemployment (Gaspard 1995). At the same time, the figure of the *beur* (French-born child of North African immigrants) emerged on the national stage, calling for equal opportunity and an end to racism during a highly publicized, two-month-long march across France. Any hopes entertained by the French that worker immigrants and their families would return to their homelands were at that moment effectively dashed. Finally, the media began to focus on disorder in the *banlieues*, describing these disadvantaged neighborhoods as "ethnic ghettos," especially in the late 1980s, when concern over homegrown Islamic fundamentalism intensified in the context of a number of troubling events abroad (Boyer and Lochard 1998; Wacquant 2008; Champagne 1993; Sedel 2009).[19] The ethnic difference of some residents was cast as a problem—even a danger—for the rest of society, drowning out any concern over the racism directed toward them (Amselle 2011).

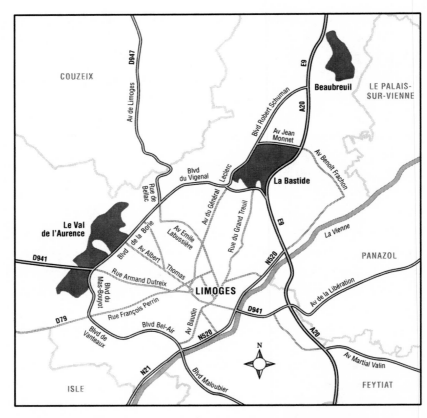

MAP 2. Limoges's *zones urbaines sensibles*: Beaubreuil, La Bastide, and
Le Val de l'Aurence. Cartography by Erin Greb.

Intellectuals, Tissot explains, also had a hand in shifting discourse on
the *banlieues*. As trade-union activism plummeted and unemployment
soared, researchers, drawing principally on the work of Alain Touraine,
began to map the notion of exclusion onto France's urban landscape. The
banlieues, they maintained, had been a site of structure and integration
for workers and their families. The collapse of the working class had left
a void, leading to a breakdown of social relations and the emergence of
new, corrosive forms of individualism. In this analysis, the excluded,
shiftless outer-city delinquent became the inverted figure of the integrated,

hardworking factory laborer. At the same time, the *banlieues* became sites of "segregation" or "exile" rather than of economic exploitation and domination (Tissot 2007, 74–82).[20]

In 1995 the state officially delimited 744 *zones urbaines sensibles* (ZUSs; disadvantaged urban areas; see map 2), including three in Limoges. It was in these neighborhoods that I conducted the majority of my fieldwork.[21] In line with previous urban policy, the goal driving the ZUS initiative was to help residents help themselves, primarily through neighborhood associations that would receive state subsidies to hire local youngsters in paid internships. The ZUS plan also aimed at combating crime, particularly the intensification of youth involvement in the parallel economy. The idea was that employment, even temporary and often part-time employment, would lure young people from the streets with the promise of a salary as well as professional experience that could be highlighted during future job searches. Finally, the ZUS initiative sought to attract commercial venture to the outer cities by providing various tax incentives. Alongside neighborhood associations, multinational corporations, the plan's architects hoped, would function as agents of change in the *banlieues*.

In the years following the implementation of the ZUS plan, measures favoring security progressively overshadowed social reform efforts. This was due in part to fiscal belt-tightening necessitated by France's preparation for entry into the European Monetary Union. Politicians' desire to divert public attention away from economic concerns, especially as unemployment soared to record heights in the late 1990s, also doubtless played a role. Indeed, it was easier to highlight and then crack down on crime than it was to address the social and economic problems driving criminal behavior. The ZUS initiative already called for an additional two hundred plainclothes officers to patrol France's troubled *banlieues*. In 1999, Prime Minister Lionel Jospin mobilized another thirteen thousand riot police and seventeen thousand military gendarmes. During his tenure as minister of the interior, Nicolas Sarkozy further increased the police presence in the outer cities while simultaneously criminalizing various everyday activities, including the assembly of residents in entryways and basements. This "militarization" (Silverstein and Tetreault 2006) of the *banlieues* was accompanied by the rise of a punitive model of juvenile justice, replacing previous efforts at rehabilitation and prevention (Coutant 2005; D. Fassin 2011; Karpiak 2013; Terrio 2009). It was against this backdrop that Sarkozy offered a particularly harsh assessment of outer-city youth around the time of the 2005 riots. After branding them as *racaille* (scum) and vowing to clean up the *banlieues* with a pressure washer, he declared: "The leading cause of unemployment, of despair, of violence in the outer cities, is not discrimination or the failure of schools . . . it is drug trafficking, gang law, the dictatorship of fear, and the resignation of the Republic" (Ridet 2005). Long gone were the days when urban policy focused on strengthening social bonds among neighbors. Recast in neoliberal terms with an emphasis on individual accountability, the problem of the *banlieues* was ascribed to residents themselves, not the social and economic dilemmas they faced.

Returning to where I began this chapter, the cautionary words offered to me by the bank employee, Christophe, and Louise when I arrived in Limoges to begin fieldwork find their place in this overarching discursive frame. It is not this frame, however, that is the focus of this book. Rather, in the chapters that follow I examine how the young people I came to know in Limoges's outer city tugged at and pushed back against it as they attempted to understand why their future seemed so dark.

2 Longing for Yesterday

The Social Uses of Nostalgia in a Climate of Job Insecurity

"There's my mom and there's my dad. Look at that moustache! And those are my sisters . . . and there I am, *la petite*! I couldn't have been more than four or five at the time." Bright eyes and happy grins jumped out from the small frame Hanan held before me. Now faded, the photograph, she explained, had been taken in the mid-1980s during one of her family's summer trips to her parents' native Morocco. "They'd load us up in the car and we'd drive for hours," she recounted. "The car wasn't big, mind you. With all our luggage and gifts for family in Morocco, we were packed in like sardines. But it was so much fun! I cherish those memories. It was simpler then." *Simpler, easier, carefree*—these were words that rolled off the tongue of many of my interlocutors in Limoges's outer city when discussing the past, whether their childhood or a more distant past, one they had not experienced themselves but had heard their parents and other members of the previous generation talk about. Those times, they told me, were, in a word, *better*.

"Nostalgia," writes Fred Davis, "despite its private, sometimes intensely felt personal character, is a deeply social emotion" (1979, vii). It is this aspect of nostalgia—its social dimension—that interests anthropologists and other social scientists. Nostalgia is a particular kind of memory, one where pleasant experiences are given priority and painful ones are screened out. It therefore feeds on the past, but it is never about just the past. Rather, as Kathleen Stewart suggests, "its forms, meanings, and effects shift with the context—it depends on where the speaker stands in the landscape of the present" (1988, 227). In other words, nostalgia is a reaction to present-day social stimuli, often ones that provoke fear or anxiety. The way it is expressed and the work it is able to accomplish in the social world are culturally dependent. It can, for example, play a central role in the maintenance of self during periods of transition in the life cycle. It can also help to reaffirm or establish a sense of solidarity or common purpose in the face of political, social, or economic upheaval.[1]

In this chapter I explore my interlocutors' reflections on the past with the aim of better understanding how they framed the challenges they faced as they transitioned between school and work in an uncertain job market. The nostalgic discourse they produced, I argue, served an important purpose: it was an adaptive response to the individualizing effects of neoliberal policy. These young Limougeauds, I contend, used nostalgia to blunt the rhetoric of personal responsibility that has characterized the French state's reform efforts in the fractious *banlieues* since the 1980s, a rhetoric responsible in large part for the creation and circulation of the negatively charged category *jeune de quartier* (outer-city youth). At the same time, their idealization of a past that predated their own experience—the "golden age" of full employment that the previous generation knew—served, I suggest, to challenge the myth of meritocracy promoted by the education system. By pointing to generational shifts in employment opportunity, my interlocutors eschewed guilt and shame over their own failure to advance socially. In the end, their narratives of the past, whether of their childhood or the experience of their parents, point to an understanding of a shared social destiny darkened by the ever-lengthening shadow of economic insecurity.

Although it was a powerful weapon in the face of neoliberal challenges, the sword of nostalgia these youth wielded proved to be double-edged. Part of what made the past so appealing to them, I suggest, was not only greater employment opportunity but also an understanding that such prosperity generated explicit, collective class identities. Their parents, they told me, were members of something greater than themselves; they were born into a support community composed of family, neighbors, friends, and colleagues. This class system, they maintained, has crumbled, and chaos and confusion now reign over the rubble. In some sense, then, their longing for yesterday can be likened to what Rebecca Bryant (2015) has called a "longing for essentialism"—that is, a search for stable identities in the shifting sands of the contemporary social landscape. This backward-looking, essentializing gaze, I conclude, leaves little room for new models of competent adult identity.

Before examining these issues in more depth, I spend some time considering the economic transformations Limoges underwent in the twentieth century. Highlighting this context is important for at least two reasons. Not only will it provide a backdrop for the stories my interlocutors told me about themselves and previous generations, some of which I relate here. Against the state's hegemonic discourse of personal responsibility and the rhetoric of meritocracy encountered in the school system, it will also help bring into focus some of the structural causes of the difficulties they faced.

Economic Change in Twentieth-Century Limoges

Never the site of heavy industrial manufacturing, Limoges did not witness the same devastation as some other French cities following the economic downturn of the 1970s. This is not to say that Limoges has been immune to unemployment or its consequences. The story of Limoges in the nineteenth century was one of conflict and agitation, but also great progress. As we saw in the previous chapter, this "Red City," with its deeply rooted socialist tradition, was at the forefront of the nascent workers movement. Twentieth-century Limoges, by contrast, has been scarred by decline, particularly the retreat of the porcelain and shoe industries.

Already at dawn of the twentieth century, the china industry in Limoges was heading toward trouble. Although business was good, fierce competition was emerging abroad, especially in Germany and Czechoslovakia. Mostly family-owned and -operated, Limoges's porcelain firms lacked the capital and injection of fresh ideas needed to remain viable in this context (Lazzarotti 1970, 60). Whereas during the last decade of the nineteenth century between thirty and thirty-five porcelain factories

FIG. 5. Located along the banks of the Vienne River, Royal Limoges is one of the city's few remaining porcelain factories. Visitors can peer inside the historic Casseaux kiln (no longer operational) and tour the production and finishing workshops before perusing the fine china on display in the onsite outlet store.

operated in Limoges and employed upwards of ten thousand workers, by 1914 an increasingly tight market had shuttered ten of these businesses, resulting in nearly four thousand layoffs (Perrier 1924, 359). World War I added to the problem of foreign competition by seriously reducing the demand for luxury goods, including fine china. By the early 1920s, porcelain production in Limoges was two-thirds what it had been before the outbreak of the conflict (Perrier 1924, 359). The global economic crisis of the 1930s added the final nail to the coffin: by 1938, porcelain production in Limoges had dropped by an additional 75 percent (Desforges 2002, 132–33). By the time I conducted my fieldwork, only a handful of porcelain firms remained (fig. 5).

Whereas World War I dealt a serious blow to Limoges's porcelain firms, it was a boon to the city's shoe manufacturers, who saw themselves inundated with orders from the military when the usual providers, located too close to the front, were unable to meet demand. On the eve of the war, seventeen factories were turning out shoes in Limoges. By 1920 this number had increased to forty-six. That Limoges had a readily available labor force, thanks to the recent contraction of the porcelain industry, helped fuel this growth. The success of the shoe industry was, however, short-lived. As production picked up elsewhere following the war, Limoges's shoe manufacturers had to face growing foreign and domestic competition (Perrier 1924, 360–61). This and the global financial crisis were more than many firms could handle. Between 1931 and 1936, sixteen shoe factories folded; in 1938 alone, another eleven closed their doors permanently (Desforges 2002, 133–34).

The collapse of the porcelain and shoe industries left a gaping hole in Limoges's economic fabric that would be felt for decades to come. In fact, whereas many other French cities began to recover, even prosper, soon after the end of World War II, relief did not come to Limoges until well into the 1960s. Historical research has attributed this delay to a number of factors, including the relative poverty of the surrounding countryside, high rates of out-migration, a lack of adequate transportation linking Limoges to other cities, the municipal government's reticence to improve the city's infrastructure, Limoges's reputation in France as a "red" or anti-capitalist city, and locals' supposed attachment to "irrational tradition" (Lazzarotti 1970, 61–66, 71).

Beginning in the late 1950s, a shakeup in city hall, including the election of a new mayor and the injection of young blood into the municipal council, brought much-needed dynamism and determination to Limoges. Industry, new city officials recognized, was too dispersed, too artisanal. They proposed and implemented the creation of a number of "industrial areas" to the north and south of the city and sought to lure big business with various tax incentives (Lazzarotti 1970, 66–69). At the same time, they launched a massive construction campaign, erecting the *grands ensembles* described in the previous chapter but also building roads, extending water and sewer lines, and creating public parks and squares. Between 1968 and 1972, ground was broken on three important projects: an international airport, the University of Limoges, and the University Hospital (Desforges 2002, 147–48).

Alongside well-established occupations, new jobs thus appeared. Although some Limougeauds still labored in the porcelain or shoe trades or other long-present albeit dwindling industries, including textile, enamel, and print production, workers were increasingly employed in metalworking, construction, and public works. Two corporate giants dominated the new industrial scene in Limoges: the porcelain-turned-electrical-components manufacturer Legrand and Saviem, a Renault subsidiary specializing in the construction of commercial trucks and buses (Larivière 1968). At the same time, the service sector was expanding, and new jobs could be found in retail, banking, food services, and tourism, among other areas. The construction of three large shopping complexes accompanied this shift. Two were built on the periphery, in proximity to the *grands ensembles*, and a third rose near the city center, on the former site of the Haviland porcelain factory (Desforges 2002, 148). Civil service jobs were also on the rise, particularly with the opening of the public University Hospital in 1975. By 1999, service sector work, including civil service jobs, accounted for nearly 73 percent of all employment in Limoges (INSEE 2014, 15).

Limoges, like many other places, suffered following the energy crises of the 1970s. Take, for example, Saviem. Whereas this manufacturer of commercial vehicles employed roughly three thousand workers in 1974, in 2011 the company, now called Renault Trucks Défense, only counted 662 employees on its payroll, and 80 of these were in temporary positions (Fougeras 2011). In general, though, the lack of heavy industry in Limoges helped soften the recession's blow, as evidenced by the city's rate of unemployment since the 1980s, which has consistently been below the national average and far below rates registered in France's former bastions of industry (INSEE 2008).

During the last two decades of the twentieth century, the city has attempted to rebuild and rebrand itself as a cutting-edge technological and scientific center. In spite of significant investment, including the construction of a major research and development facility to the north

FIG. 6. Perched atop a hill overlooking the city, ESTER Technopole is Limoges's futuristic-looking scientific research and development center. Work at ESTER is concentrated in five areas: engineering, biotechnology, industrial ceramics, water treatment, and optics.

of the city (fig. 6), Limoges suffers a brain drain to larger urban centers. Those young people who choose to remain in the city (or who lack the means to leave) are not as likely to hold university degrees and generally earn less (Lavaud and Simonneau 2010).

Unemployment in the Limousin region has tended to follow national trends, with peaks ranging from just over 7 percent to just under 9 percent in the late 1980s, late 1990s, and the middle of the first decade of the twenty-first century (fig. 7) (INSEE 2013). Figures relating to youth unemployment are higher and in Limoges vary widely between the city's central neighborhoods and the periphery. In 1999, 18.1 percent of youth aged sixteen to twenty-five living in the city center declared they were looking for work, compared to more than double that number (39.2 percent) in the outer city (Duplouy 2003, 20).

Unemployment statistics alone do not offer a full picture of youth

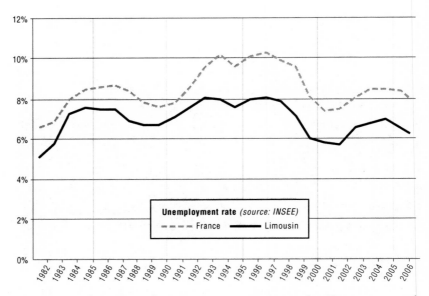

FIG. 7. Unemployment in the Limousin region compared to France in general, 1982–2006. (Courtesy of www.insee.fr.)

joblessness at the turn of the twenty-first century, however. It is also necessary to consider the work arrangements of those young people who are employed. These include the permanent *contrat à durée indéterminée* (CDI), the fixed-term *contrat à durée déterminée* (CDD), and the temporary *contrat de travail temporaire* (CTT), also called *intérim*. The CDD usually covers a nine-month period, although there is no minimum. In most cases a CDD may be renewed, but generally only once, for a total employment period of eighteenth months, after which employment ceases, or the contract must be converted into a CDI.[2] The CTT offers employers even greater flexibility. Unlike a CDD, which is established between an employer and an employee, the CTT involves three parties: an employer, an employee, and a temporary employment agency. Workers remain the employees of the agency that places them. They complete *missions* (short-term assignments) and are paid on an assignment-by-assignment basis. They may be removed from an assignment without explanation, and in most cases

FIG. 8. The first temporary employment agency in France opened in 1954 in Paris. Since then, temp agencies have mushroomed in cities and towns across the country. In 2004, sixteen such outfits operated in Limoges alone, according to the local phone book.

agencies operate without any obligation to provide a minimum number of assignments.

All forms of temporary work are on the rise in France. In March 2001 nearly one million workers held a CDD compared to just over 300,000 in March 1982. During the same period, the number of CTTs increased from about 100,000 to more than 600,000 (Givord 2005, 130). Temporary work is less likely to lead to a permanent position than in the past (Cancé and Fréchou 2003), and young people are hired on a temporary basis more often than older workers. On average, one in three workers aged twenty-five or under holds some sort of short-term contract (Givord 2005, 129).

In Limoges, the number of young people who are employed in temporary positions has grown steadily and exceeds the national average. Whereas in 1990 nearly 39 percent of workers aged twenty-five or under were employed on a non-permanent basis, by 1999 this figure had jumped to 50 percent for youth overall and to nearly 53 percent for young people residing in the outer city (Duplouy 2003, 21). The slogan in figure 8—"Temporary work is a career. You'll love working with us"—suggests that temporary forms of employment may well be considered a new employment paradigm rather than merely a stepping-stone to more permanent work arrangements.

Recession, rampant unemployment and underemployment, and declining opportunity: these were the conditions into which the young people I came to know in Limoges had been born. To be sure, these problems affect all of French society to some extent. However, my interlocutors also faced the stigma of being from the outer city, a stigma based on the widely circulated idea that they were at least partially responsible for the difficulties they encountered. How did they perceive and experience the label *jeunes de quartier* (outer-city youth)? As we will see, they looked back on yesterday not only to escape the negative assumptions associated with this term but also—and especially—in an attempt to redefine who they are in the present.

Coming of Age in Outer-City Limoges

"It was great! Tom Sawyer, that's who we were," exclaimed Noureddine. "We built forts, we jumped across ravines, we stole plums and pears from people's yards. We were Tom Sawyer, I'm telling you, that's who we were!" In this exchange, Noureddine, a twenty-two-year-old unemployed mechanic, echoes comments I recorded during other conversations with young people in the outer city. As children, they told me, they never remained idle in the housing projects. Literally at their doorsteps, the surrounding countryside, they said, offered endless possibilities for amusement (fig. 11, page 72). This idealized recollection of childhood stands in stark contrast to popular commentary on outer-city youth, commentary whose consequences my interlocutors were forced to confront as they began to leave their neighborhoods to look for work or continue their studies.

Anyone who has had at least a little high school or college French probably remembers that the word *quartier* means "neighborhood." In Limoges I quickly discovered that, when used in the plural, *les quartiers*, the term refers specifically to the outer city. This practice is not uncommon in France. As Sylvie Tissot (2007) has shown, the word *quartiers*, sometimes preceded by the adjective *sensible* (disadvantaged), began to be employed by politicians, reformers, journalists, and others in the mid-1980s to designate France's fractious *banlieues*. Tissot argues that this change corresponded to a fundamental shift in how disadvantage was understood and dealt with in France. Whereas prior to the 1980s poverty was most often linked to structural factors, and state aid was directed toward programs and projects aimed at reducing social inequality, since 1980 disadvantage has increasingly been explained in terms of personal responsibility.[3]

The shadowy figure of the *jeune de quartier* embodies this shift. Rather than being recognized as the victim of disadvantage, discrimination, or both, he is routinely depicted as a lazy, thieving, lying, raping drug addict whose religion (Islam) is at odds with French republican secularism (Bowen 2010; Terrio 2009; Mucchielli 2005; Coutant 2005).[4] Although the term *jeune de quartier* is usually marked as male, a female version also exists. Even if she may be seen as more "assiduous" or "discreet" by teachers (Beaud 2002; Lepoutre 1997), in popular discourse she is most often equated with the veiled Muslim girl, who has largely been presented as either too submissive in the face of male (Islamic) domination or too aggressive in her demands for the recognition of cultural difference (Bowen 2007). In short, the outer-city youth, either male or female, is viewed as a threat to the very fabric of French civil society.

Some adolescents in the peripheral neighborhoods told me that they played off of these fears. Karim, a quick-witted, sharp-tongued eleven-year-old whom I tutored after school, related how he and his friends routinely hung out in the atrium of their neighborhood's shopping center. There, he said, they passed their time playing the role of the "perfect juvenile delinquent."[5] Both the Val de l'Aurence and Beaubreuil housing developments include a large shopping complex. Built at the same time as the housing blocks, these retail malls, with their Wal-Mart-like anchor stores, were meant to serve both the residents of these neighborhoods and people from the city center, whom developers hoped to lure with

FIG. 9. The shopping complex in Beaubreuil contains two anchor stores (a Walmart-like super center and a major home furnishings chain) and a number of smaller retailers, offering everything from clothing and shoes to cell phones, jewelry, cosmetics, and perfume. There are also several restaurants, including a McDonald's, as well as a pharmacy, a post office, bank branch offices, and a branch of the municipal library. Shoppers from the city center have access to a large parking lot at the front of the shopping complex (pictured here). Residents of Beaubreuil enter in the rear, where a small pedestrian bridge spans a gully separating the shopping complex from the housing projects.

the convenience of one-stop shopping.[6] To this end, the shopping centers were constructed on the edge of the housing projects, close to main arteries of circulation for easy access to the city center, and each provides ample parking (fig. 9).

I was familiar with the phenomenon described by Karim, having witnessed it several times myself. During an afternoon of observations in one of the shopping complexes, I noted a group of mostly hooded adolescents loitering just inside the main entrance. At first they kept to themselves, but then they began to harass passersby, either by jumping into their conversations or by making offhand remarks about their appearance. When security personnel finally approached the group and ushered them to the door, they began spouting all sorts of profanities. Just before exiting, one youngster shouted at the top of his lungs the name of the housing project in which the shopping center was located.

Although Karim was not among the group, I later asked him to interpret the meaning of this final outburst. "The people who come here," he replied, "they're just a bunch of fools [bouffons]. We gotta represent!" In the end, it seems that exchanges such as this were used by outer-city adolescents as a way to reappropriate and revalue the negative label *jeune de quartier*. Those who "represented" the "bad" or "dangerous" outer city the best were rewarded with the esteem of their peers.[7]

Youth in their late teens or early twenties, by contrast, did not take part in such behavior. As they transitioned from school to work life, the shopping complexes became the arenas of a different sort of struggle. No longer did these young adults express concern about impressing their peers. Nor did they suggest that playing the role of the perfect delinquent was a way to achieve respect. Instead, they sought to shed the yoke of the term *jeune de quartier*. For them, the shopping complexes were a shiny sliver of the mainstream, consumption-oriented, consumption-driven society that lay beyond the confines of their neighborhood. In the current climate of job insecurity, their chances of achieving access to this world seemed slim at best.

Although these retail malls may have been conceived with the needs of residents and non-residents alike in mind, these older youth told me they no longer serve this purpose. According to them, inhabitants of the outer city in general, and young people from the peripheral neighborhoods in particular, are not considered desirable customers. The Beaubreuil shopping center, interlocutors explained to me, has two main entrances: one large entrance in the front that opens onto an expansive parking lot, with direct access to the A20 highway leading back to city-center Limoges, and one smaller entrance in the back, which fronts a pedestrian bridge spanning the gully between the shopping center and the housing blocks. This second entrance is "practically hidden," they insist, because management wants to draw attention away from the housing projects—and, by extension, their "undesirable" tenants—so as not to "frighten" and thus deter potential shoppers from other areas of the city. "You see," complained nineteen-year-old Yasmina, "we're made to feel unwelcome in our own neighborhood, whereas people who are not even from here are encouraged to come!" Twenty-one-year-old Malik expressed a similar understanding: "Have you seen all the security guards in the shopping center? Yesterday, one of them followed me all the way to the back aisle of the grocery store. I just wanted to buy some laundry detergent, but I'm sure he thought I was going to steal something."

If these young people experienced the shopping centers in their neighborhoods as sites of exclusion where they were defined as different and potentially dangerous, for them the city center could be even worse. They told me that as children they avoided Limoges's central districts out of fear or distrust. Now older, many of them had to go there for school or for work, but they did their best to blend in.

Limoges's peripheral housing projects, particularly Beaubreuil, were designed as self-sufficient communities.[8] In addition to their expansive housing blocks and the large shopping complexes found in most of them, each neighborhood contains a range of state and municipal services, including schools through the junior high level, post offices, police stations, libraries, playgrounds, and other recreational facilities. There is even a *mairie-bus*, a van dispatched by city hall to field residents' questions and offer assistance completing official paperwork.[9] The close proximity of these services means that many adult residents of the housing projects only leave the outer city for work. As for local youngsters, they rarely leave their neighborhoods, if at all.[10] Many of my interlocutors reported that their first prolonged encounter with the city center did not occur until they entered high school or began their job search.[11]

"It's like a wall," Noureddine told me. "When you're from the other side of it, everyone knows. They treat you differently." He was referring to the *boulevard périphérique*. Constructed in the 1950s and 1960s to alleviate traffic in the city center and facilitate access to the quickly expanding suburbs, this boulevard runs along the northern and western edge of

FIG. 10. In Limoges, the outer city is generally thought to begin beyond the six-lane *boulevard périphérique* that travels along the northern and western edge of the city. To facilitate outer-city residents' access to the city center, a number of pedestrian bridges and tunnels have been built. Pictured here is a bridge spanning the peripheral boulevard near the Val de l'Aurence housing project.

Limoges. The municipality's three largest housing projects are all located outside of it: two just beyond it (La Bastide and Le Val de l'Aurence) and the other (Beaubreuil) about four kilometers to its north. Even though this six-lane thoroughfare is heavily trafficked during rush hours, its speed limit, which is frequently controlled by radar, is only fifty kilometers (about thirty miles) per hour, and there are numerous crosswalks along it, each outfitted with traffic lights, as well as several pedestrian bridges and tunnels (fig. 10). Nonetheless, many of my interlocutors echoed Noureddine's description. For them, the *boulevard périphérique* was a boundary beyond which their "difference" became palpable.

What, according to these young people, gave them away as being from the outer city when they crossed the boulevard? Answers to this question varied, and although sometimes interlocutors cited race or ethnicity as a factor, "white" (Franco-French) youth just as frequently claimed they were the victims of discrimination in the city center. Consider, for example, what twenty-four-year-old Jonathan had to say: "People have an idea about us, residents of the *quartiers*. It's happened to me at work.[12] 'Where do you live? Le Val de l'Aurence?' You see, they're gonna distrust you. They're gonna say, 'Oh yeah, a *jeune de quartier*. You'd better watch your back!" To avoid this negative outcome, Jonathan told me, he always dodged questions about where he lived when in the city center and, if pressed, would give a vague answer—"near the shopping complex, near the sports stadium"— since that could be understood in various ways. In the end, though, this strategy usually failed. "You see, the thing is," Jonathan explained, "we more or less have an accent compared to them, and we don't speak as well. People judge you. They say, 'He's a *jeune de quartier*, he's a *racaille* [street scum].'"

In chapter 4, I explicitly take up the question of how race was understood and used by young people in Limoges's housing projects as they struggled to comprehend why their chances for success seemed so uncertain compared to other French youth who had not grown up in a troubled *banlieue*. For now, it is important to note that according to Jonathan, at least, the category *jeune de quartier* was above all based on two traits that had nothing to do with physically observable difference: residency in the disadvantaged outer city and, following Bourdieu (1986), a lack of "legitimate"—that is, bourgeois—linguistic capital. As we saw in chapter 1, in Limoges these markers have historically been associated with lower positions in a social class hierarchy. But how in 2005 and 2006 did Jonathan and other young men and women from the housing projects experience the label *jeune de quartier*? To be sure, some interlocutors told me that their fears of the city center were largely unfounded. This was particularly true for those young men and women who left the peripheral neighborhoods to attend Limoges's centrally located *lycée général* (general-track high school) or the University of Limoges. Some reported that they made good friends among their mostly city-center classmates. However, for the majority of my interlocutors, especially those seeking employment, a term that frequently fell off of their lips when describing their experience was that of *citoyen de seconde classe* (second-class citizen). "We may have the same rights as everyone else on paper," remarked Timothée, a nineteen-year-old unemployed, aspiring baker, "but in most employers' eyes, we're first and foremost outer-city youth and all the negative things associated with that term: irresponsible, unpredictable, aggressive. Why take a gamble on us? In the end, employers hold all the cards, and we're just *citoyens de seconde classe*."

This understanding of being a *citoyen de seconde classe* carries with it an understanding of structural inequality that is at odds with the neoliberal rhetoric of personal responsibility that has dominated public action directed toward France's *banlieues* since the 1980s, a rhetoric whose primary outcome, as we have seen, has been the classification of outer-city youth as social parasites at best and dangerous deviants at worst. Is the plight of outer-city youth mostly their own fault, or are larger forces to blame? It is in the context of the struggle over this question that we must understand Noureddine's comparison of himself to Tom Sawyer, with which I opened this section of the chapter. Noureddine's description is unexpected, because it is the polar opposite of received ideas about outer-city youth. With it, he attempts to redefine who he and his peers are. Far from the image of the urban thug that so many in France associate with the troubled *banlieues*, Noureddine presents himself and the young people he grew up with as mischievous, perhaps, but also fun-loving and ultimately harmless. That he situates their play in the forest is important (fig. 11). Removed from the stigma with which the outer city is stained and concealed from the gaze of the city center, the forest in his account can easily be interpreted as a symbol of freedom. By this I do not mean individual freedom or independence, which, as we have seen, is one trait for which outer-city youth are routinely rebuked. On the contrary, Noureddine emphasized the collective nature of his bucolic adventures. The freedom he longed for was the chance to live without the shackles of the negative assumptions associated with the label *jeune de quartier*. In short, he wanted the freedom "to go unnoticed," a freedom he assumed that "normal" French youth— that is, youth not from the outer city—took for granted.[13]

FIG. 11. Unlike the old industrial *faubourgs* of the nineteenth century that were swallowed up by urban expansion, the *grands ensembles* of Limoges were completed in the 1970s, when the city's population began to decline. Today, they stand on the city's edge; beyond them are pastures and forests.

Struggling to Grow Up

More than a natural yearning for lost childhood, the nostalgia expressed by Noureddine and other young men and women in the housing projects conveyed a deeper longing for stability in the life course as economic insecurity loomed large, threatening to derail their transition to adulthood. Anthropologists and other social scientists have long shown how the notion of adulthood is culturally and socially derived. In France, at least, it has been linked to employment. During the decades of economic prosperity following World War II, the term *troisième âge* (third age) appeared as a euphemism for older people who, having left the workforce, were at last able to reap the benefits of their labor. The understanding was that the *premier âge* (first age) designated childhood (the time of learning and preparation for work) and the *deuxième âge* (second age) designated adults, those who work or should work (Trincaz, Puijalon, and Humbert 2011; Lenoir 1979).[14] The end of full employment in the 1970s and the increasing role of temporary work since have meant that people coming of age today face vastly different circumstances from those the previous generation experienced. My interlocutors' reflections on the past sometimes included comments about this shift. Although they did not experience themselves this bygone *âge d'or* (golden age), they mourned its passing just the same.

"It's like we've gone back in time . . . back to the time of our grandparents. They had to work really hard, they struggled for very little pay, just to make ends meet. At the same time, there were really rich people. They didn't lift a finger." This remark, made by Hélène, a twenty-four-year-old part-time cashier at a grocery store, fairly well sums up a perspective shared by many of the young people I came to know in Limoges's housing projects: for them, society today is characterized by a sharp divide between "haves" and "have-nots," between those who are *inclus* (included) and those who are *exclus* (excluded). Far from being novel in any way, this condition of extreme inequality signaled for them a return to past ways, some sort of undoing of social progress. Some even compared the conditions they faced with pre-revolutionary France and its system of feudal privileges. For example, Gaëtan, an eighteen-year-old apprentice carpenter, said: "The aristocrats are back! We may have cut off the king's head, but the *privilèges* have returned."[15]

Such commentary only makes sense if these young people understood that things had been better at some point in the past. Youth in Limoges's housing projects tended to situate this improvement around the time their parents entered the workforce. "Our parents," Hélène went on to say, "had it a lot better than us." She continued:

They found work much more easily. They left one job and had no trouble finding another. Now the tables are turned. Employers will fire you if they don't like the way your hair looks—I'm not kidding, it's happened to me! They can have someone prettier or skinnier or funnier by the end of the day. What do they care that I'm twenty-four and can't afford a driver's license, much less my own apartment!

Although Hélène's comments suggest that appearance and disposition were deciding factors when it came to finding and keeping work, she could have just as easily said something about the kind of music she liked to listen to, as did another interlocutor when attempting to explain why he had recently been let go from a job. The point is that for Hélène and others, one's willingness to work seemed to matter very little, and employers could fire anyone on a whim. This, they insisted, was a fundamental difference between their experience and that of their parents. As we will see below, they described this difference as barring their access to adulthood.

I hesitate to label these young people's idealization of the pervious generation's experience "nostalgia," since, according to some researchers (e.g., Davis 1979), that term should be reserved for memories of a lived past, not events that predate one's own personal history.[16] Nevertheless, I cannot ignore the similarities between the two kinds of longing, at least as they were expressed and used by my interlocutors. Not only did a majority of these young Limougeauds describe the previous generation's experience as eminently personal, but they also used it—or rather a reconstruction of it— to push against a discourse of meritocracy that they encountered at school. Their longing for a bygone era ignored, however, the fact that the previous generation faced very real difficulties that prompted many parents, at least in the words of their children, to push for the next generation's social advancement. As the following two accounts suggest, these expectations were in large part entrusted to the school system, particularly education beyond the high school level. Presented as egalitarian and merit-driven, the school system was supposed to be a "social elevator" by which each student, through hard work and perseverance, could ascend society's ranks.

Hanan

I met Hanan at the Val de l'Aurence homework-help center, where she worked and I volunteered several days a week. Tall and slender with striking green eyes, Hanan was soft spoken and reflective. Pursuing a degree in education at the University of Limoges, she had recently taken a course in sociology and was thus particularly interested in my research. We often chatted about the progress of my work in between helping the junior high and high school students who visited the center; toward the end of my fieldwork period Hanan agreed to sit down with me for a taped life-history interview.

Hanan's parents emigrated from Morocco, where they were married in 1969. In 1971 her father left his new bride behind to take advantage of the employment opportunities available in France. He first settled in northeastern France, where he worked in the construction industry. This work was unstable, however, and during periods of inactivity he returned to Morocco, where Hanan's oldest sister was born. Dissatisfied with his situation, Hanan's father moved to a town just south of Limoges where a relative owned a butcher's shop. In 1975, following France's closing of its borders to new immigrants, his wife and daughter joined him, thanks to a law permitting the reunification of families. They settled in Limoges, where Hanan's father, along with many other immigrant men, found work in construction. Another daughter soon followed the first, and then in 1982, Hanan was born.

Hanan talked fondly about her childhood in her family's apartment, surrounded by "attentive" parents and "protective" sisters. But she also recognized that she grew up in a sort of "cocoon." This revelation came to her when, at age fourteen, she took the public bus for the very first time to attend high school in the city center. Kids from her neighborhood, she told me, usually did not go to that school; there was another high school far closer to the housing project, but it had a bad reputation, at least according to her father. "He did everything in his power to make sure I went to the right high school," she explained. "For him, it was my ticket to university, and continuing my studies was extremely important. In his view, it was how I could get ahead, get a good job." Although a serious student, Hanan avowed not wanting to attend the high school in the city center, and described how out of place she felt, from the clothes she wore to the inflection of her voice, which at first at least invariably gave her away as being from *les quartiers*. She told me, not without a touch of pride, that she had made a conscious effort to "lose that accent." Hanan ultimately earned her *baccalauréat* (high school finishing exam) and headed off to the University of Limoges, but without a clear idea of what she wanted to study. She decided somewhat haphazardly on a two-year degree in Spanish, explaining that it brought her back "toward the south, to her roots." After a rocky first year, she ended up having to repeat the second year, ultimately unsuccessfully. Discouraged, she left school to work part-time as an *animatrice* (counselor) in a youth association located in her childhood neighborhood, where she still lived with her parents.[17] Realizing this was a dead-end job, and encouraged by her father, she re-enrolled in the university, this time with the objective of becoming a teacher. In hindsight, Hanan wishes she had never pursued university study. "My parents didn't know anything about the school system. They pushed me to go as far as I could, but I would have been better off with a BTS [*brevet de technician supérieur*]." This advanced vocational degree, she said, would at least have given her some work experience through an internship. Confronted by several more years of school and then the all-important and in her words "very difficult" CAPES exam (the state-administered certifying exam, required of all secondary school teachers), she was uncertain of her future.

When reflecting on her parents' generation, Hanan was ambivalent. On the one hand, she recognized the difficulties her mother and father had to overcome. "Can you imagine the shock they must have felt, arriving in a place like this from where they came? The climate alone must have been terribly difficult to get used to." According to her, the younger generation, born in France, has it easier, if only in terms of acculturation. "I'm French to the core," she insisted, adding that "assimilation is not a problem I face." But at the same time, she bemoaned her lack of direction in life and her limited job prospects, which at this point seemed to hinge on her all too uncertain success at the university. Although twenty-four years old, she told me she was still "waiting to become an adult."

Jonathan

Jonathan also worked at the homework-help center, and it was in this context that I got to know him. "Full of energy" and "upbeat" are the best ways to describe his personality, which always seemed to me to be strangely at odds with his small, unassuming frame and ever-pale countenance. Jonathan, like Hanan, grew up in the Val de l'Aurence housing project. They had known each other as children but had not become friends until working together at the homework-help center.

Jonathan is Franco-French, although his parents are not from Limoges. They were born and raised in the surrounding Limousin hinterlands, where their parents (Jonathan's grandparents) worked in the agricultural sector. This lifestyle, Jonathan explained to me, was hard, not only because of the backbreaking nature of the work but also due to its unreliability. The family's income depended a great deal on weather conditions: an overly dry or wet season could spell disaster for an already tight budget. After marrying in the early 1970s, Jonathan's parents moved to Limoges in search of more stable, better-paying work. The first years were tough, Jonathan explained. Although in the countryside rumors of plentiful employment in "the City" circulated widely, by the time his parents arrived in Limoges the well of job opportunities seemed to be drying up. Jonathan's father ended up working odd jobs in construction, mostly in the housing projects (where he and his wife settled). Meanwhile, Jonathan's mother worked as a housekeeper, mainly in the city center in the homes of what Jonathan called "bourgeois" families. In the mid-1970s, Jonathan's father got a break: after working on the construction of Limoges's University Hospital he was hired full-time in the new facility's maintenance department, thanks to the recommendation of a colleague. Several years later, Jonathan's mother found full-time employment at city hall, also in janitorial services. Both of Jonathan's parents still occupied these positions in 2005 and 2006. After a number of failed pregnancies, Jonathan was born in 1981; he is their only child.

Jonathan suspects that his status as an only child resulted in his parents' focusing all of their hopes on him. And fulfilling these hopes, they made it known to him, meant pursuing his studies as long as possible. "My parents have great respect for education. They wouldn't dare contradict a teacher," he recounted. Jonathan, by contrast, did not have the same depth of faith in the school system, as evidenced, for example, by his playful distortion of the French term for school guidance counselor (*conseiller d'orientation*): "They're all *disorientation* counselors, if you ask me!" Jonathan explained that after completing a vocational high school degree in electronics he was ready to try his luck in the job market, but his mother was opposed to that idea. "She pushed really hard for me to continue. She even found a BTS program in Brive [a town about sixty miles south of Limoges] for me. She filled out all the paperwork and everything." To please his mother, Jonathan headed off to Brive, where he completed the two-year program and passed (on his second try) the final qualifying exam. Because the program included hands-on experience, Jonathan had in the meantime earned enough hours to qualify for unemployment insurance. With this extra income, he returned to his parents' apartment, where, prodded yet again by his mother, he enrolled at the University of Limoges for a technical bachelor's degree in fiber optics. "I really wasn't interested in continuing school, but I had all this extra income. It was more than double what I'd get with a student stipend alone, so I figured why not."

Looking back at his parents' situation, Jonathan was just as ambivalent as Hanan. He recognized that staying in school had for the most part spared him the kind of hard labor his parents had undertaken when they were his age. But at the same time, he felt that he had put his future on hold. Twenty-four when I met him in 2005, he still lived with his parents, whereas they, he recognized, had already married and moved to Limoges by that age. Furthermore, he was not certain his advanced degrees would do him any good. Though armed with a BTS and a bachelor's degree, he had in his estimation applied to over one hundred positions in the previous year but had yet to secure a stable job. His parents, he told me, struggled to comprehend why this was the case.

Shifting Destinies

In a recent book, Jennifer Silva (2013) tackles the question of what it means to grow up in the post-industrial, neoliberal age. Focusing on the narratives of young "working-class" men and women living in the eastern United States, she found that her research subjects tended to look inward, often by embracing therapeutic models of selfhood, to understand the difficulties they faced, rather than link those problems to larger, public issues. This search for individualized solutions, Silva contends, has spilled over into conceptions of adulthood, especially as traditional markers of what it means to be an adult—including steady employment—increasingly become beyond many people's reach. The result, she suggests, is a withdrawal from various forms of social engagement. "In an era of short-term flexibility, constant flux, and hollow institutions," Silva writes, "the transition to adulthood has been inverted; coming of age does not entail *entry into social groups* and institutions but rather the explicit *rejection of them*" (2013, 84; emphasis added).

Rather than looking inward, like Silva's research subjects, young people in Limoges's *quartiers* preferred to look backward to make sense of the roadblocks to adulthood they encountered. For them, their nostalgia was more than just a simple retreat into an idealized past. It was an arm they wielded to blunt the neoliberal rhetoric of personal responsibility, individual accountability, and retribution that has surrounded France's troubled *banlieues* since the 1980s. Their yearning for the conditions under which their parents entered the workforce demonstrated a capacity to see beyond themselves, to sense, if not entirely grasp, a systemic shift that had left them with far fewer chances than the previous generation.

How might we explain this observation compared to Silva's research subjects, who appear incapable of making such a conceptual leap? The following remark offered by Fariba, a twenty-two-year-old outer-city resident who held a state-subsidized temporary job at the municipal library, provides clues:

Basically, a worker's son [*fils d'ouvrier*] has the same chances as everyone. If he works really hard, he can get ahead. But, you know, you don't get the same education when you're from the outer city. And once you're done [with school], you can't afford the prep courses or fees for the entrance exams to get the really good jobs in the public sector. We're at a real disadvantage in the job market. The only way I'd be rich is if I won EuroMillions [the lottery]. Right now, I'd settle for a decent job and an apartment in Beaubreuil near my family. You can't have everything in life!

Although Fariba is seduced by the idea of a meritocracy, she acknowledges the validity of markers associated with status in a hierarchy (social, cultural, and economic capital) and ultimately accepts her lot in life. Her comments, which reflect broader French attitudes and beliefs (e.g., Bourdieu 1984), contrast sharply with dominant American assumptions and expectations about success, centered on the promise of a better life to all those willing to put in the time and effort (Kingston 2000; Mantsios 1995; Weakliem and Heath 1999). The figure of the "self-made man," that rugged and hardworking individual who trades his rags for riches, plays a central role in this utopian narrative (Wyllie 1954). Tellingly, the idea has no equivalent in the French cultural repertoire. Defying easy translation, *le self-made man*, as the French say, is viewed as a fundamentally American concept. By contrast, the French are responsible for the expression *noblesse oblige*. Equally untranslatable, this idea holds that the rich and powerful have a social obligation to the poor and weak, because social position is mostly a result of fate, not merit. In other words, the material, social, and cultural conditions into which an individual is born are likely to have a greater impact on his or her social position in life than that person's achievements or failures.[18] Whereas the idea of the self-made man rests on a logic of personal responsibility and individual accountability more or less in harmony with today's neoliberal rhetoric about work and autonomy, the concept of *noblesse oblige* is predicated on a commitment to social responsibility and solidarity that is largely at odds with such discourse. This may help to explain my interlocutors' appeals to the past. By looking backward, they were recalling a time when not only a social class system seemed far more evident, but also a unified working class in particular was perceived as forming a fundamental base for the rest of French society.

In the end, were the young people in my research sample any better off than their American counterparts studied by Silva? As the commentary offered by Hanan and Jonathan in the previous section suggests, they were hardly any closer to developing new models of competent adulthood. Yearning to labor, they were also longing to grow up. Furthermore, although their backward posturing may have allowed them to see beyond themselves when attempting to explain their misfortune, it is unlikely that it prepared them to understand, much less act upon, the problems they encountered. Indeed, if for them nostalgia was a sword against neoliberal calls for personal responsibility, it risked being a double-edged one because of nostalgia's own structural limitations. Nostalgia, by its nature, raises questions of continuity and discontinuity. A positive appraisal of the past in response to a negative evaluation of the present, it posits a break or a rupture. As sociologist Stuart Tannock has noted, this bipartite structure "contains the implicit assumption that decline to the present is caused by forces *external to* a previously stable and utopian system; the nostalgic subject or author returns to the past to find sources of identity and community, not sources of alienation or oppression" (1995, 460; emphasis added). This is dangerous, Tannock concludes, because it denies the possibility that present-day problems or worries are in any way the result of pressures or processes internal to the system itself. In other words, nostalgic subjects risk misidentifying—or ignoring altogether—the real origins or causes of the troubles they face. As I explore in later chapters, among my interlocutors this issue amounted to a problem of naming. Although youth in the outer city of Limoges were clearly conscious that a systemic shift had left them worse off than the previous generation, they struggled to explain to themselves and others why this was the case. There was far less opportunity for good stable employment, they easily remarked, but why had this happened and what could be done to change it? In France this problem of naming has been complicated by the establishment of a long string of legislation aimed at treating the symptoms of youth joblessness without addressing the root causes. These measures and the discourses surrounding them are the focus of the next chapter.

3 Jobs for At-Risk Youth

State Intervention, *Solidarité*, and
the Fight against *Exclusion*

In the early spring of 2006, I attended a roundtable on youth employment at city hall. Organized by the faith-based collective for blue-collar youth Jeunesse ouvrière chrétienne (JOC; Young Christian workers), it was meant to provide an opportunity for local youth (both members and non-members of JOC) and municipal officials to come together to discuss the results of a recent national survey on youth employment and employment practices. During the Q and A that followed the formal presentation, young people in attendance openly criticized the city's social service system. They complained that no general reduced bus fare was available to them, whereas elderly Limougeauds rode public transportation for free.[1] They also pointed out that when looking for work they had to make multiple trips to numerous agencies and organizations. The bureaucracy they encountered at each step, they protested, made them feel "alone" or like "simple numbers." During her concluding remarks, the president of the local JOC chapter thanked participants for the lively discussion, which she hoped would "better enable young people to create a France in which they could become the autonomous actors of their destiny."

The contradiction in terms was striking. On the one hand, young people in the audience insisted that the social service support they received was neither sufficient nor personalized enough. On the other, the local JOC president—a young person herself—expressed the desire that members of her generation become self-reliant. It is this tension between assistance and autonomy that is the focus of this chapter, particularly how it plays out in relation to a term—*solidarité* (solidarity)—that frequently came up in the conversations about social services I had with various stakeholders in Limoges. Looking at diverse and sometimes divergent perspectives, from official state policy to remarks made by social service providers to what young people themselves had to say, I attempt to unravel what exactly *solidarité* means today in France. Rather than an opposite of individualism, *solidarité*, I found, was more frequently contrasted with the notion of *exclusion* (exclusion), itself a word that defies easy translation. Although my interlocutors unanimously viewed *solidarité* as a highly desirable outcome, this understanding of it, I argue, risks masking deep social inequalities that would otherwise help to explain why some people in France faced far more limited access to employment than others.

State Interventions

Although the economic downturn of the 1970s affected all of French society, its impact on young people has been particularly great. In 1975, 3.5 percent of the total workforce was unemployed, but more than double that number (7.1 percent) of young people aged fifteen to twenty-four were out of work. By the mid-1980s the picture was even grimmer: as youth unemployment soared, surpassing 20 percent, nearly half of all French job seekers were under the age of twenty-five (Aeberhardt, Crusson, and Pommier 2011, 154–55). Faced with this alarming spiral, the French government scrambled into action. Resulting legislation aimed at helping youth secure jobs, both indirectly through education and directly through employment policy.

Education, some state officials insisted, was the key to getting France's youth back to work. In 1985, Minister of Education Jean-Pierre Chevènement announced an ambitious program: the government would work toward the goal of having 80 percent of every graduating class earn the *baccalauréat* or its equivalent. At the time only about one in three young people in France achieved this level, and diploma holders hailed disproportionately from the middle and upper classes. In the years following Chevènement's call to action, a number of concrete steps were taken to "democratize" education, including reducing the number of students per classroom, establishing personalized tutoring for those in need of extra help, and increasing funding for schools in disadvantaged neighborhoods, labeled by the state as *zones d'éducation prioritaire* (ZEPs; proriority education areas). Furthermore, a new vocational *baccalauréat* was introduced. This diploma, along with the creation of the Mission générale d'insertion, whose function was to strengthen outreach to vocational students and their families, aimed at improving the overall reputation of vocational education in France (Gendron 2009).

The success of these efforts has been debatable. To be sure, more and more young people are staying in school.[2] But what, some researchers have asked, are the costs? The price paid by young people from disadvantaged backgrounds, their work suggests, seems particularly high. Many report an overwhelming sense of personal failure and shame at not succeeding beyond the high school level and express dismay upon discovering that their academic credentials, especially the *baccalauréat*, do not carry as much weight in the job market as they thought they would (Beaud 2002; Beaud and Amrani 2005). For young people lacking even the lowest credentials, such as the *certificat d'aptitude professionnelle* (CAP; certificate of professional competence) or the *brevet d'études professionnelles* (BEP; vocational training certificate), whose numbers have stubbornly held steady in recent years, the situation is particularly dire.[3] They often find that the doors to stable employment, even unskilled positions, are locked.

Alongside efforts to raise young people's education level, the French government has since the 1970s put into place a staggering number of measures—more than eighty in all—to favor job growth. Many, although not all, of these policies have targeted young people. In 2005, whereas 4.7 percent of the general workforce held a position benefiting from some sort of state intervention, 26 percent of young people aged twenty-five or younger did (Aeberhardt, Crusson, and Pommier 2011, 154). This difference is partly the result of persistently disproportionately high rates of youth unemployment in France. It is also, however, the consequence of a consistent choice made by legislators to focus on developing employment opportunities among young people rather than redistributing wealth to them in the form of welfare or other social programs (Lima 2005). Although the Revenu minimum d'insertion (RMI; Minimum subsistence income) was established in France in the late 1980s to assist the growing masses of long-term unemployed, access to it was reserved for those twenty-five and older.[4]

As officials looked to employment policy as a way out of the economic crisis, they faced two fundamental questions: What form should the policy take, and who should be its beneficiaries? The measures adopted since the 1970s, many lasting for only a short period of time, present a great deal of heterogeneity (see table 1). Some called for permanent positions (CDIs); others anticipated short-term contracts (CDDs).[5] Some required full-time employment; others permitted part-time work. Some were directed toward what the French call the *secteur marchand* (market sector); others concerned only the *secteur non marchand* (non-market sector). Some schemes were made available to anyone *éloigné de l'emploi* (estranged from employment); others were restricted to young people under twenty-five and therefore ineligible for the RMI. Still others targeted specific categories of young people. In this last instance, references to educational attainment and work experience were frequently used to define eligibility. The terms *sans qualification* (without qualification), *peu ou pas qualifié* (with little or no qualification), and *peu ou pas diplômé* (with little or no academic credentials), found in these measures' guidelines, reflect France's highly differentiated education system.[6] At the same time, a broader category—*jeunes en difficulté* (literally, "youth in difficulty," but a more natural translation might be "at-risk youth")—appeared. Although this label was also linked to educational underachievement, it came to describe the victims of any number of personal and social disadvantages, including, especially, residence in one of France's *quartiers sensibles* (Bartkowiak 2005).[7]

In the literature accompanying these policies, the word *insertion* (insertion) repeatedly turns up. *Insertion professionnelle* (access to employment) is, according to the policies' authors, an essential first step to *insertion sociale* (integration into society). The idea of insertion implies a preexisting state of separation, marginalization, or isolation, and indeed many measures were touted as important weapons in a *lutte contre l'exclusion* (fight against exclusion).[8] Exclusion generated by joblessness, policymakers argued, risked undermining the very foundations of society itself. Maintaining the social fabric was, in this view, inextricably linked to employment.

Even if most policies have focused on creating jobs in the non-market sector, legislators have been more successful at putting young people to work in the market sector. The designations "market" and "non-market" can be loosely thought of in terms of private and public organizations, respectively. There is, however, a difference. "Market" in this context refers to the creation of goods and services intended to be sold at a price covering at least the cost of their production. In France, firms in the private sector are responsible for the majority of market production, but some market production takes place in public or semi-public companies, such as the utilities provider EDF or the rail operator SNCF. "Non-market" corresponds to the creation of services provided at little or no cost by France's public administrations or by various private nonprofit groups, including unions, political parties, associations, and charities.

Most employment policies pursued in the market sector have aimed at reducing the cost of employment to employers to compensate for the lack of experience and therefore what would likely be the lower output of young new hires, especially those with low education levels (Gautié 1999). The short life of many of these measures reflects both a process of trial and error, by which legislators aimed at finding the right balance of incentives to lure potential employers, and shifting priorities in a divided political climate.[9] Thus, the Plan d'urgence en faveur de l'embauche des jeunes (Emergency plan for hiring youth), passed in 1986 and abandoned a year later, granted payroll tax abatements of up to 50 percent to employers hiring new employees under the age of twenty-six. In 1994, Aide au premier emploi des jeunes (Allowance for young new workers), another program lasting for little more than a year, subsidized the salaries of new employees without any previous work experience during their first nine months of employment. The Contrat initiative-emploi (Employment initiative contract), introduced a year later, combined these incentives. Not only could employers collect a two-year subsidy toward the salaries of new hires, but they were also eligible for a reduction in the payroll tax. Although this plan was open to the long-term unemployed in general, irrespective of age, its guidelines cited particular groups, including *jeunes non diplômés* (young people without diplomas), as the intended beneficiaries.[10]

Such state-aided contracts, some critics have argued, have failed to meet the mark. Rather than combat exclusion, these measures, they insist, have created more of it. Even if increasing numbers of young people were hired, overwhelmingly these policies have resulted in part-time temporary work. Moreover, many have not included training or professionalization, and for those that have, such as a few internship programs, employers have tended to skirt around this requirement.[11] To add insult to injury, in this case the young worker's status as an intern means that he or she can be paid less than the minimum wage and is ineligible for various social protections. Interns "appointed" (the term "employed" was not used) under the Stage d'initiation à la vie professionnelle (Initiation to the world of work internship) beginning in the mid-1980s, for instance, only earned 17 to 27 percent of the minimum wage, could not count the hours they worked toward the lifetime retirement requirement, and could not collect unemployment insurance at the end of their appointment. According to critics, the only arrangements where training has in reality been a priority include the apprenticeship model, which has existed in France since the 1920s, and what the French call *alternance*, where formal coursework, usually dispensed in a training center, is combined with work experience (Aeberhardt, Crusson, and Pommier 2011, 160–61).

TABLE 1. Overview of youth employment policy in France, 1977–2010

Data compiled from the following websites: cnle.gouv.fr, jeunes.gouv.fr, travail-emploi.gouv.fr, www.assemblee-nationale.fr, and www.senat.fr.

State-Subsidized Jobs in the Market Sector

Pactes nationaux pour l'emploi (1977–82)

ELIGIBILITY: young people under twenty-five; reduction of employer's social security contributions (100 percent under the first Pacte, 50 percent under the second and third).

Contrat de qualification, CQ (1984–2004)

ELIGIBILITY: young people aged sixteen to twenty-five; training both inside (mentoring) and outside firms (training centers); the employer received a partial exemption from social security contributions, a training subsidy of FRF 60 (EUR 9) per hour, and, beginning in 1993, a lump sum at recruitment; young people were paid below the national minimum wage (SMIC), according to their age and tenure; maximum duration: two years.

Contrat d'adaptation, CA (1984–2004)

ELIGIBILITY: young people aged fifteen to twenty-five; in-firm training; the employer received a partial exemption from social security contributions, a training subsidy, and beginning in 1993, a lump sum at recruitment; young people were paid the minimum wage or 80 percent of the contractual wage corresponding to their qualifications; maximum duration: one year.

Stage d'initiation à la vie professionnelle, SIVP (1985–91)

ELIGIBILITY: young people aged sixteen to twenty-five, without job experience; very low pay (under the minimum wage) in exchange for "on-the-job" training; duration: between three and six months.

Plan d'urgence en faveur de l'embauche des jeunes (1986–87)

ELIGIBILITY: young people under twenty-five; reduction of employer's social security contributions (50 percent for a young person exiting another employment scheme, 25 percent for others).

Exo-jeunes (1991–94)

ELIGIBILITY: unskilled youth under twenty-five; reduction of employer's social security contributions (100 percent for one year, 50 percent for the next six months, up to 120 percent of the minimum wage).

Aide au premier emploi des jeunes, APEJ (1994–96)

ELIGIBILITY: young people who never held a job entitling them to unemployment benefits, whatever their level of skill or education; the employer was paid FRF 1,000 (EUR 152) per month for the first nine months of employment.

Contrat initiative-emploi, CIE (1995–2005)

ELIGIBILITY: variously defined groups, including, "young people without diplomas"; in addition to receiving a monthly subsidy of FRF 2,000 (EUR 305), the employer was exempted from paying social security contributions for the first twenty-four months of the job.

Contrat jeune en entreprise, CJE (2002–7)

ELIGIBILITY: young people between the ages of sixteen and twenty-two not holding the *baccalauréat*; the employer was paid a monthly subsidy between EUR 225 and EUR 292, depending on the youth's salary, for a maximum duration of three years; contracts could be for either full-time or part-time work but had to be permanent (CDI).

State-Subsidized Jobs in the Non-Market Sector

Travaux d'utilité collective, TUC (1984–90)

ELIGIBILITY: youth aged sixteen to twenty-one, or up to twenty-six if they were unemployed for over a year; "intern" (*stagiaire*) status: less social protection, low pay, 30 percent of salary paid by the state; maximum duration: one year, except in special cases.

Contrat emploi-solidarité, CES (1990–2005)

REPLACED TUCs; extended to other at-risk groups (in particular the long-term unemployed); half-time work contract, paid at an hourly rate based on the minimum wage; 60 to 100 percent of salary paid by the state; maximum duration: one year, except in special cases.

Contrat emploi ville, CEV (1996–98)

ELIGIBILITY: young people between eighteen and twenty-six living in a neighborhood designated by the state as "disadvantaged" (ZUS); thirty-hour-per-week work contract, compensated based on the hourly minimum wage; 35 to 75 percent of salary paid by the state; duration: one year, with the possibility of renewal up to four times, for a maximum total of five years.

Emplois-jeunes (1997–2002)

ELIGIBILITY: young people up to the age of twenty-six (or thirty for those not entitled to unemployment benefits); wages according to industry-wide collective bargaining agreements; duration of no more than five years; these jobs had to correspond to "new services" not existing in the "regular" market.

Contrat d'accompagnement dans l'emploi, CAE (2005–9)

ELIGIBILITY: persons encountering difficulty finding work; the proportion of the cost of employment underwritten by the state varied according to shifting priorities: in 2005, the state subsidized 90 percent of the minimum wage for young people under age twenty-six, compared to 83 percent on average for other age groups.

Accompanying Support Measures

Trajet d'accès à l'emploi, TRACE (1998–2003)

ELIGIBILITY: young people under twenty-six "faced with failure and risking social exclusion"; provided youth with "individualized support," including one-on-one sessions with employment counselors (*mission locale*, PAIO) and access to training programs; duration: six months, with the possibility of extending up to eighteen months.

Contrat d'insertion dans la vie sociale, CIVIS (2005–)

> ELIGIBILITY: young people between sixteen and twenty-five with little or no academic credentials or those out-of-work for at least twelve months; provides the same support as the TRACE program, plus a stipend of up to EUR 450 per month (but no more than EUR 1800 in a single year); duration: one year, with the possibility of renewing on a yearly basis until *insertion* is achieved.

Contrat d'autonomie (2009–)

> ELIGIBILITY: young people under twenty-six living in a neighborhood designated by the state as "disadvantaged" (ZUS); support provided is similar to that of the CIVIS program, but the monthly stipend is EUR 300 (with no lesser yearly maximum); duration: open until successful *insertion* (defined as finding a job, opening a new business, or enrolling in a training program), after which there is a six-month follow-up phase.

Conscious of their limited ability to control employers' hiring decisions in the market sector, lawmakers have simultaneously tried another tack: the direct creation of jobs in the non-market sector. The state, they have argued, can put the unemployed to work, especially *jeunes en difficulté*, to help meet unfulfilled community needs (Lefresne 2010, 195). The result would be a sort of symbiotic relationship where the unemployed are "reinserted" into society for their own good and for the good of all. This focus on collective engagement was made explicit in the titles of two of the most widely used policies of this type during the 1980s and 1990s: the Travaux d'utilité collective (TUC; Works of collective utility) and the Contrat emploi-solidarité (CES; Solidarity employment contract). Paying at or below the minimum wage, the TUC and CES programs generated temporary (three to twelve months) part-time (twenty hours per week) work in public or nonprofit organizations.[12] Beneficiaries performed a wide range of tasks based on their experience and skill sets and the needs of the community, from sweeping the floors of local associations to maintaining signposts along area hiking trails to organizing activities for neighborhood children to painting the walls of municipal buildings (Villalard 1985).

These schemes have however elicited the same objections as the market sector policies discussed above. They, say detractors, primarily produce part-time, short-term, low-paying work that includes little or no opportunity for professionalization. Perhaps even more problematic, according to some critics, they carry a stigma not always seen in the market sector programs. In this respect, the Emplois-jeunes (Youth employment) initiative offers an instructive case study. Launched in 1997, Emplois-jeunes was, according to its originator, Minister of Employment and Solidarity Martine Aubry, a radically new approach to the tenacious problem of youth unemployment in France. The program, she insisted, would create the "jobs of tomorrow," including, notably, positions aimed at protecting the environment. The program's scale was ambitious: 350,000 jobs were to be created in the non-market sector. These would be temporary or permanent positions (CDDs or CDIs) paid at the minimum wage and subsidized by the state at a whopping 80 percent for five full years. Ultimately, Aubry hoped to develop new services that would eventually spill over into the market sector, as private businesses recognized the profits to be gained by responding to the unmet needs the program revealed. Recognizing the criticism leveled against previous initiatives, Aubry declared from the start that Emplois-jeunes would not focus on training or professionalization. Rather, the program was to be for young people who were "immediately employable," meaning those holding at least a vocational certificate (CAP or BEP) or, preferably, the baccalauréat. The fact that, during the initiative's first three years, 40 percent of participants had completed high school and two years of postsecondary education (bac+2) suggests that the state was fulfilling its mission to keep French youth in school longer; however, rising levels of educational attainment did not necessarily translate into secure employment after graduation (Aeberhardt, Crusson, and Pommier 2011, 159).

Aubry's preemptive justification for the exclusion of vocational training from the Emplois-jeunes initiative did not stop critics from denouncing its absence. The program, detractors argued, did not adequately prepare young people for employment beyond the initial five-year subsidized period. A lack of training, they maintained, was part of the problem, but so too was the type of work participants ended up doing. By and large, they were given the nebulous job title of *médiateur social* (social mediator). Stationed for the most part in the *quartiers sensibles* where they had grown up, their work included everything from telling people the time to helping elderly residents off the bus to breaking up fights among local youngsters. "It's not a real job" was a refrain recorded by Sophie Divay (2002) in her study of social mediators. Some of Divay's interlocutors were so ashamed of the title that they admitted to excessively laundering the state-issued jackets they had to wear at work in an attempt to make the words *médiateur social* fade, or else tried to scratch them off (2002, 138). According to Divay, employers in France tended to share this negative perception of the Emplois-jeunes program and consequently hesitated to hire anyone listing it on his or her résumé (136). Beginning in 2002, Emplois-jeunes was phased out.

Over the years, as different state schemes aimed at favoring job growth in the market and non-market sectors have come and gone, one constant has been an emphasis on *accompagnement*. In 1981 the Mauroy administration commissioned a study on the state of youth unemployment in France. The resulting report, made available later that same year, issued a number of recommendations, including the establishment of an official agency whose sole purpose would be to facilitate young people's "professional and social insertion."[13] The state responded in 1982 by creating a national network of *missions locales* (youth unemployment offices) and *permanences d'accueil, d'information et d'orientation* (PAIOs; reception, information, and guidance centers). Staffed by counselors trained in career-readiness preparation, these agencies' charge was to *accompagner* (accompany) young people aged sixteen to twenty-five in their job search by helping them overcome the "barriers to employment" they may face, including, among other issues, mobility problems, health care, and housing (Aeberhardt, Crusson, and Pommier 2011, 162). To this end, counselors, in partnership with local associations, would propose a variety of interventions. These were to include the provision of information regarding area services and resources, help navigating the long and ever-changing list of state-sponsored youth employment opportunities, individual and group advising sessions, and hands-on work experience. The ultimate goal was to assist young people in developing a *projet professionnel* (career plan). Since 1982, the presence of *missions locales* and PAIOs has increased dramatically across the country. Already in 1994, roughly 900,000 young people had visited one of these agencies at least once. By 2005 this figure had risen to 1,146,000, or about one in every eight sixteen- to twenty-five-year-olds living in France (Bonnevialle 2011, 2).

The notion of *accompagnement* in this context is not easily translated into English. Is it advising? Is it counseling? Is it a more general kind of support? Writing on the use of this term in the school system in French-speaking Canada, Arcand and Leblanc (2011) proposed the English word *companioning* as an approximation. To be sure, this term captures the idea of a journey or a voyage that the frequent use of the words *parcours* (path), *itinéraire* (itinerary), and *trajet* (trip) in *mission locale* and PAIO documentation imparts. The job seeker, program descriptions and titles suggest, is on a journey toward employment and ultimately *insertion sociale*.[14] However, the word *companioning*, it seems to me, fails to convey the inequality understood with *accompagnement*. Generally speaking, a companion is an equal or someone who presents complementarity. He or she is a friend or a partner, depending on the context. The notion of *accompagnement*, by contrast, carries an imbalance. Initiative comes from one party in the relationship, while the other follows along. This is especially evident in the way the verb *accompagner* is used to express the action "to take someone somewhere." In French, I "accompany" my friend to the doctor's or to the airport, not because I have a need or a desire to go to these places myself but because I want to help my friend, who has already made the necessary arrangements (she scheduled an appointment, he bought an airline ticket). *Accompagnement* as an answer to youth unemployment implies something similar. Staff counselors are present at the *missions locales* and the PAIOs to help job seekers and guide their efforts, but ultimately the job seekers alone are responsible for their own successes or failures. In other words, at least part of the solution to unemployment, according to the logic of *accompagnement*, resides in the unemployed themselves.

At-Risk Youth or Risky Youth?

Toward the start of my fieldwork period, I contacted Isabelle. An *animatrice* (activity leader) at the *maison des jeunes* (youth house) in Beaubreuil, she had been recommended to me by a contact at city hall as someone who might be able to put me in touch with potential research subjects. After we spoke briefly on the phone, Isabelle agreed to talk with me in person at the *maison*. When I arrived for our appointment, however, I wondered if I had written down the wrong address. The nondescript cement building looked more like a storefront than a house, and its mechanized metallic shutters were rolled nearly completely to the ground. As I bent down to look underneath, a voice called out from behind me: "You must be the American researcher!" It was Isabelle. After introductions, she explained that earlier that day her colleague's cell phone had gone missing. When it failed to turn up after a search, they assumed it had been stolen. In protest, the *maison* was closed down for the remainder of the day, and Isabelle's colleague went to report the theft to the local authorities. Shrugging off the incident, Isabelle ushered me into her small office where she described the purpose and function of the *maison*. I learned it was established as a *point information jeunesse* (youth information site). Through partnerships with various local agencies, including the *mission locale*, it provided a "first stop" for young people, one where they could familiarize themselves with the resources available to them in areas ranging from employment to housing to education. "A lot of the young people we see come from disadvantaged backgrounds [*milieux défavorisés*], a lot of them are at-risk [*en difficulté*]," Isabelle explained. She continued: "They face exclusion, so we're here to help draw them back into society, we accompany them on the road to *réinsertion*. Practically, this means informing them of the services out there for them, services they can take advantage of to become active participants in their own development. By linking them up to these services, we accompany them in their projects, both personal and professional." As we continued our conversation, Isabelle gave me a tour of the facility, which contained an old television set, a couple of computers, and a foosball table, as well as a rack displaying the glossy brochures of the state's latest youth employment initiatives. "I wish I could tell you that we have a lot of success stories, a lot of kids who do well," Isabelle went on to say, "but in the end, much of our work consists of keeping them occupied so they don't get into trouble. Let's face facts: this is a difficult neighborhood [*quartier difficile*], and these are difficult kids [*jeunes difficiles*]." Before we took leave of each other, Isabelle gestured to the messenger bag I had slung over my shoulder. "Don't ever let that out of your sight at the *maison*," she warned. "Otherwise, you may just find yourself at the police station filling out a theft report too."

I highlight Isabelle's comments here not only because of the remarkable similarity between how she defines her work and the official language used by the state to describe its programs for young people (it is almost as if she is reading from a script), but also because of the way she slips between *jeunes en difficulté* and *jeunes difficiles* when describing the young people who visit the *maison*. This reflects a tension I noted when speaking to other social service providers in Limoges, whether in neighborhood associations, at the *mission locale*, or at the public housing office. At-risk youth, many of them suggested, were also more often than not risky youth. As a result, any efforts "to accompany" them, they told me, frequently had to take a backseat to a more pressing demand—that of making young people aware of their responsibilities, an idea they usually rendered succinctly in French with the verb *responsabiliser*. "Before any personal development can be achieved, before any progress toward social or professional insertion can be made, we must first make young people responsible," a caseworker at the *mission locale* maintained. "They have to understand the stakes. They have to learn what it means to live responsibly in society with other people." This tension crystallized around the juxtaposition of two recurrent themes: fragility and unpredictability.

Close relationships can develop between social service professionals and the young people they serve.[15] A number of the providers I interviewed spoke of their clients as if they were their own children: "My kids behave for the most part," an *éducateur de rue* (neighborhood educator) told me one day as we toured the housing project where he worked.[16] Sometimes, young people used nicknames evoking familial ties to address providers, especially older ones. A retired worker-priest in one housing project was affectionately known as Pépé (Grandpa) Vincent, even among non-Christian families, and a longtime youth activities coordinator in another was referred to as Tantine (Aunty) Marie.

It follows that some social service professionals were fiercely protective of the young people they worked with, so much so that I encountered a fair amount of resistance at the beginning of my fieldwork period when I requested their help as intermediaries to connect with local youth. Many of the messages I left with recommended contacts went unreturned, and those providers who did agree to meet with me often expressed concern. For example, Bernadette, the director of a *foyer de jeunes travailleurs* (FJT; home for young workers), told me during our first meeting that my project made her "uneasy."[17] "You have to understand," she went on to say, "these kids face an accumulation of hardships . . . they are extremely fragile. We have to weigh the costs and the benefits of the sort of research you are proposing. I am worried your study will only stigmatize them further."

"Fragile," "vulnerable": these were adjectives social service professionals used frequently to describe the young people they worked with. Although the use of these descriptions could be interpreted as their understanding that the youth they served were somehow personally defective, that they were simply not robust enough to withstand the pressures of today's world, this was not the case. Rather, social service providers insisted, sometimes passionately, that the economic system itself played a large part. Often highly educated (at least one program coordinator held a doctorate in sociology, and many other social service professionals had earned master's degrees in various social science fields), they tended to be familiar with recent sociological scholarship on the question, which they did not hesitate to cite when talking with me. *Précarité*, they maintained, was the real culprit. By this they meant job insecurity, to be sure, which they linked to a fundamental shift in the dominant employment paradigm over the last several decades. But they did not stop there. For them, *précarité* was something greater, something even more ominous. It was the gathering storm cloud of a frightening new social condition characterized by ever-increasing numbers of *exclus* (socially excluded people). In their view, this swelling underclass, unlike the *classe ouvrière* (working class) it replaced, could not provide the stable base society needed to function properly. *Solidarité*, according to them, was at stake, as society's members increasingly looked inward for answers to the problems they faced. Something, they insisted, had to be done before it was too late.

Part of the solution, providers agreed, was for society's haves to reach out to its have-nots. In this respect, many criticized recent budget cuts to social programs in the *banlieues*, arguing that they no longer had the resources necessary to carry out their work effectively. However, they also insisted that those facing exclusion had to want to be helped. This meant at-risk populations making a concerted effort at reintegration into the workforce and ultimately society, not only for their own good, but also for the good of all. Providers thus urged young people to move beyond themselves, to see the larger picture. In sum, they exhorted them to be socially "responsible." Yet, according to professionals, it was precisely this quality that many of the young people they worked with lacked.

"Aujourd'hui, les jeunes, c'est du zapping," the director of Limoges's *mission locale* sighed as I concluded an interview with her early during my fieldwork. The noun *zapping* comes from the colloquial verb *zapper*, which describes the action of channel surfing (*zappette* is in French an informal word for remote control). *Zapper* can also be used to express the idea of going abruptly from one thing to another, or ending something without warning. It is, for example, roughly the equivalent of "to dump" when discussing a romantic breakup. The director of the *mission locale* used the term to describe what she viewed as the unacceptable tendency among the young people who pass through her agency never to follow through on the projects they start. This judgment, I would discover, was shared by many social service professionals in Limoges. For example, a school guidance counselor complained to me about the "countless" students she sees who, despite her advice not to do so, drop out of school. "Come next fall, when they see all their friends back in class while they're unemployed or have some low-paying, menial job, they think twice. They come back to me saying they've made a big mistake." Likewise, a volunteer at a local association recounted how he had spent hours helping a young woman craft a résumé and cover letter tailored to the "job of her dreams," only to discover by word of mouth several months later that she had never submitted the application materials. A social worker at the public housing office described the young people she works with as "extremely volatile," explaining that they frequently turn down the apartments she helps them secure. Their change of heart, she asserted, more often than not was the result of ephemeral romantic relationships: "They're together when we fill out the paperwork," she commented, "but have already broken up by the end of the month." Even Bernadette, mentioned above, seemed to hold a similar opinion of the young people she worked with. After finally agreeing to give me access to the FJT she oversaw, she told me not to waste any time setting up appointments. "These kids change plans very frequently," she warned. "Many of them vanish into thin air."

In an influential book, Pierre Rosanvallon (2000) argues that an increasingly widespread belief that some people lack self-control and a sense of personal responsibility is a leading cause of declining solidarity in today's welfare states. Current welfare schemes, founded on the Rawlsian assumption of a homogeneous population facing similar risks, must be rethought, he contends. According to Rosanvallon, a new form of solidarity, deriving from a framework of inclusion built on the expectation of mutual obligation, is the answer. He explains that in practice this would amount to using public funds "to pay workers rather than indemnify the unemployed" (2000, 57). Looking to France, Rosanvallon cites the RMI as a model leaning in this direction. In return for this minimum subsistence allowance, beneficiaries signed a *contrat d'insertion* (integration contract), according to which the state, as a community of citizens, committed itself to protecting its members against deprivation, while each recipient pledged to make a concerted effort to participate in the social and economic life of the nation. Yet as we have seen, young people under twenty-five were excluded from the program. Why was this the case?

This question has received some scrutiny in French public debate. Most often, familial solidarity has been offered up as a response. Relatives, and especially parents, it has been suggested, can and should come to the aid of those young adults who are as yet unable to support themselves. Critics of this line of reasoning have argued, however, that it overlooks serious disparities in resources and wealth that have only grown in recent decades in France, making some families far less able to look out for their younger members than others. Youth who end up being labeled *en difficulté*, they insist, hail disproportionately from disadvantaged backgrounds.

My discussion above contributes to this debate by offering another explanation for why young people have been excluded from the RMI. Although the social service professionals I interviewed in Limoges were conscious of the external forces driving social and economic change, they tended nevertheless to attribute one of the most common consequences of this change—increasing unpredictability—to the young people who passed through their offices. Rather than interpret their clients' behavior as a rational response to the instability they encountered in everyday life, they often framed it as a lack of discipline at best, and an expression of unwelcome individualism at worst. Indeed, for many providers, young people's tendency not to follow through on their projects, despite their own (the providers') best efforts to help them, amounted to nothing less than a refusal of the social contract, a denial of *solidarité*. In this view, at-risk youth were not only held at least partially responsible for the exclusion they faced; they were also considered a threat for the rest of society because of the danger of social disintegration that their perceived lack of commitment to collective life was thought to pose. It is in this light, it seems to me, that the primary form of assistance directed their way—the litany of employment policies that have passed across French legislators' desks over the last several decades—is best understood. More than mere efforts to help disadvantaged youth find work, these measures constitute above all a concerted effort to discipline what are held more widely in France to be unruly bodies. The *insertion sociale* for which they call becomes in this sense a coercive process whereby *jeunes difficiles* (risky youth) are to be recast into "good" or "responsible" citizens. By contrast, the RMI was not nearly as forceful in its demands of recipients. Under the original legislation, the terms of the *contrat d'insertion* were to be drawn up on a case-by-case basis by a social worker, who generally had considerable latitude in assigning responsibilities to beneficiaries, many of whom reported never having even heard of this obligation (Clegg and Palier 2014, 206).

What did young people themselves have to say about this situation? What did they think of the social assistance they received? And how might answering this question illuminate their worldview, especially their commitment to individualist or collectivist values?

Growing up *Assisté*

Despite the widespread belief that France's *banlieues* are cut off from the rest of society, many of the young people I came to know in the outer city of Limoges had almost daily contact with at least one social service provider; some met regularly with more than one.[18] Besides the interaction schoolgoers had with guidance counselors and school therapists, the net of social service support extended far beyond the school system in the outer city, including family counselors, psychologists, social workers, case managers, employment counselors, neighborhood educators, and association personnel.[19] Véronique's experience offers a particularly striking example of the reach of this kind of support. Véro, as her friends called her, grew up in the Val de l'Aurence, Limoges's largest housing project. Because of family problems—she told me her stepfather sometimes became violent at home—a social worker visited the family frequently. At age thirteen, Véro was transferred into foster care and was assigned a caseworker. When I first met her she was just a few months shy of eighteen and was preparing, with the help of her caseworker, to move from her foster family's home into an FJT. Having left school at sixteen with a CAP in plumbing, Véro was on the job market. She regularly met with a counselor at the *mission locale* and had completed a number of programs and trainings there. She also attended weekly meetings of a support group for unemployed youth organized within JOC. It was at one of these meetings that I initially connected with her.

Véro, like many other young people in Limoges's housing projects, spoke in acronyms when listing the social service support she received.

During our first conversation I struggled to keep up as she rattled off a veritable alphabet soup of abbreviations, from ASSEDIC and CAF to SNC and CIVIS to ALSEA and BTG.[20] When asked, Véro did not always know or, for that matter, seem to care much to know what these abbreviations and the many others I encountered during my discussions with her and her peers in the housing projects stood for, even if everyone could easily describe the kinds of services linked to each. This reflects both a common experience and a common perception. Deeply immersed in the world of social service support that permeates the housing projects, these young people tended nonetheless to be ambivalent about the assistance they received. On the one hand, they demanded a right to special attention because of the difficulties they faced—difficulties they recognized not everyone in France had to grapple with.[21] On the other hand, they discursively distanced themselves from this attention, whether by refusing to learn (or not admitting to know) what the abbreviations of the organizations and programs they benefited from meant, by suggesting that these organizations and programs were somehow unimportant or ineffective, or, as we will see below, by assigning shame to the status of *assisté*, a shorthand used by youth to designate someone who receives social assistance.

During a meeting of the support group for unemployed youth she regularly attended, Véro explained that she had very little money left to buy food. Some of the group's members asked if family could help, suggesting that her older sister, who lived nearby, float her a small loan to tide her over until her next government check arrived. At the time, Véro was enrolled in a pilot program at the *mission locale*. Although she was unemployed, it provided a modest income during periods of inactivity, as long as she met regularly with her *mission locale* counselor and participated in the trainings he recommended. Véro objected to the group's suggestion, however, reminding everyone that her sister was a single mother who struggled to make ends meet. At this point in the conversation, the group's *accompagnatrice* intervened. After reminding everyone of the importance of establishing and adhering to a strict monthly budget, she asked Véro if she had considered the soup kitchen. "I could never go there," Véro protested hotly. "I'm not a beggar like the homeless people on the streets." As some attendees nodded their approval, Matthieu, a twenty-year-old who had just come off a state-subsidized short-term contract, chimed in:

> That's the fear, the fear of falling so low. It's a slippery slope. You see, there are a lot of *assistés* in my neighborhood. Now I'm not saying that social assistance doesn't have a purpose, but look at what it does to people. Take all the associations out there. Associations for little kids, they're all right, but afterward there are associations that are pointless. [Addressing me specifically now:] In France, there are associations that help you everywhere. You become dependent. You end up having to rely all the time on others because you don't learn how to do anything yourself. It's like you never grow up.

Matthieu went on to contrast the idea of *assisté* with that of *débrouillard*. Whereas *assistés* were complacent in their infantilized state, *débrouillards*, Matthieu asserted, were resourceful. They strategically used the social services at their disposal, and in the end they—not the social service providers who worked with them—were in charge of their fate.[22]

For some young people in the housing projects, being *débrouillard* meant taking advantage of the welfare system. Some recounted how they or their friends timed the short-term jobs they worked so that they would be able to collect unemployment benefits over the summer months. Although receiving unemployment benefits required continued proof of an active job search, they said they feigned this until the fall. In reality, the feasibility of this scenario seemed questionable. According to the regulations in place in 2005 and 2006, someone would have had to work full-time for at least six months (the equivalent of 910 hours) to be eligible for unemployment insurance. Few of the young people I knew who were employed enjoyed full-time status, and although I spent a good portion of two summers in Limoges during my yearlong fieldwork period, I never talked directly to anyone who had been able to achieve this arrangement.

More often, young people described being *débrouillard* as jumping at every opportunity to work and thus support themselves. Nineteen-year-old Thomas, for example, was a self-proclaimed *débrouillard*. Although he finally "earned" a full-time position stocking shelves at a local pharmacy, he told me that this job had been a long time coming. After dropping out of school several years back, he worked odd jobs, mostly installing insulation at local construction sites. Thomas insisted I see the paystubs from those days of grueling labor, which he kept neatly organized in a folder. For him a badge of honor, these papers were tangible proof that he had managed on his own.

What are we to make of this commitment to self-sufficiency? In chapter 1 we noted that the French state's response to the "problem" of the *banlieues* has since the mid-1980s increasingly been infused with the neoliberal logics of personal responsibility and individual accountability. In the *banlieues*, a model favoring the redistribution of resources has progressively given way to repressive and punitive tactics. As we saw above, these same logics pervade recent youth employment policies and their application. Not only have young people under twenty-five been barred from the RMI, but they are pushed to look within themselves to find solutions to the social and economic problems they face. Are we to conclude that these values have trickled down and now shape the worldview of such young people as those living in Limoges's outer city? If so, what are the consequences for the French ideal of *solidarité*? Is it being supplanted by a more inward-looking, individualist, and self-serving ethos? If so, what might this mean for French society more generally?

Writing in 1967, the French sociologist Henri Mendras was preoccupied with similar questions, albeit in relation to a different segment of society. Focusing on France's countryside, he argued in *La fin des paysans* that the increasing adoption of modern farming techniques during the 1950s had driven the French peasantry to the "vanishing point" (1970, viii). As Susan Carol Rogers has pointed out, in France the figure of the peasant has at various times in French history been imbued with meanings, both positive and negative, beyond the simple referent of the farmer. "Dominant images vary over time," she writes, "but the peasant as brutish, ignorant, or backward lout is no less meaningful than is the peasant as noble savage, salt of the earth, wise keeper of the French patrimony, or authentically French Everyman" (1987, 57). Mendras presented the peasant as one of the last guardians of "traditional" values such as family, community, and civic engagement. As a result, he argued, the peasant's demise would have profound effects not only in the countryside but also across all of French society, particularly in relation to the ideal of *solidarité*. In a later book, Mendras pursued this line of thinking, arguing that during the *Trente glorieuses*, that period of unprecedented economic expansion following World War II, French society underwent a "second revolution" (Mendras 1988). Its class structure, including the peasantry but also the working class and the bourgeoisie, he submitted, was subsumed by a nebulous American-style middle-classlessness, as individualist attitudes and behaviors replaced collective subjectivities and engagement in local and national institutions.

Nearly forty years after Mendras's initial prognosis, most of the young people living in Limoges's housing projects I came to know refused class labels. In conversations with me or among themselves, the idea of class seldom came up naturally, one of the rare exceptions being reflections on the bygone and, in their estimation, "golden" days of the working class that previous generations had experienced.[23] When pressed on how they would identify themselves, my interlocutors tended to claim membership in *la moyenne* (middle or average), which they defined as *comme tout le monde* (like everyone else). Does this disavowal of class identity constitute further evidence, along with my interlocutors' emphasis on their own resourcefulness (being *débrouillard*), of a refusal of *solidarité*, a rejection of the social contract? The answer to this question may not be as straightforward as it first seems.

Early during my field research I distributed a questionnaire to young people living in Limoges's outer city. The survey, which asked respondents to reflect on media portrayals of outer-city areas in France, was not designed to produce generalizable knowledge. Rather, I hoped it would help me make initial contact with local youngsters by raising questions about which I assumed they would have a lot to say. In all, 112 youths aged fourteen to twenty-three participated. The very last question on the survey asked respondents to contemplate what values were most important to them in their everyday lives. Among the responses recorded, three words appeared the most frequently: family (94 percent), friendship (91 percent), and work (84 percent). If these answers suggested concern for interpersonal relationships and collective life more generally, this finding was confirmed during subsequent conversations when interlocutors in the outer city overwhelmingly declared a commitment to the ideal of *solidarité*, even if many claimed regretfully that the expression of this value had greatly diminished in French society in recent decades.[24] How can we reconcile these results with the discussion above? Answering this question, it seems to me, requires reflecting on the meanings the term *solidarité* may hold in France today.

Solidarité and Its Perceived Opposite, *Exclusion*

Although commonly translated as "solidarity," the French notion of *solidarité* tends to encompass meanings not readily conveyed by this word, at least not in American English. To begin, *solidarité* is used in a great deal more contexts in France than "solidarity" is in the United States. It finds its way into discussions and debates about such seemingly unrelated topics as the viability of the country's agricultural smallholders, gay rights, and globalization.[25] Moreover, the meaning and significance of the word appear to have shifted over time. Whereas in the past *solidarité* may have been most readily contrasted with the idea of individualism, this is no longer necessarily the case. The emergence of *solidarité* as an important reference in French public life can be traced back to at least the end of the nineteenth century, when Third Republic reformers, drawing on organicist conceptions of social life grounded in positivist biological theories (think Durkheim and his definition of organic solidarity based on the idea of complementary forms of difference), began to deploy the word in an attempt to carve out an ideological space between market liberalism and socialism (e.g., Bourgeois 1896).[26] Although the term lost much of its political punch at the beginning of the twentieth century as the intellectual movement out of which it developed lost steam, it has beginning in the 1980s made a remarkable comeback. Today, French politicians, journalists, and other social commentators frequently invoke the concept, and as we saw above, it has often found its way into the narratives describing recent youth employment policy. Writing on these uses of *solidarité*, Daniel Béland (2009) asserts that the term is endowed with more humanistic qualities than in the past, notably the ideas of citizenship and participation. In other words, the kind of difference underlying today's dominant understanding of *solidarité* has been reduced to one fundamental sort: inclusion in the polity versus exclusion from it.

Béland's assessment resonates strongly with my own observations in Limoges's outer-city housing projects, and helps, I think, to solve the puzzle laid out above. On one level, my interlocutors' scorn for the label *assisté* may be interpreted as a denunciation of the state's attempts, however veiled, to discipline them. On another level, though, it may be seen as a refusal to be labeled as already *exclus* (excluded), as members of an underclass, stripped not only of most basic rights because of their lack of resources, but also stripped of their very dignity, since, as we have seen above, their misfortune was at least partially construed by the state, by social service providers, and perhaps by society more broadly as a result of personal defect, a consequence of an absence of motivation to better themselves. That they rejected any class label, claiming instead to be *comme tout le monde*, and therefore not excluded, supports this second interpretation, while not necessarily invalidating the first. In this view, being *débrouillard* was not a disavowal of collective life; rather, it was the expression of a firm commitment to it.

Tracing the shifting meanings of such a potent logic as that of *solidarité* in France helps illuminate the dynamic interaction of local and extralocal forces in processes of cultural adaptation and adjustment. Although conventional wisdom suggests that the increasing reach of neoliberal ideologies across the globe today is resulting in an erasure of cultural difference, this French example provides evidence that this is not always the case. The concept of *solidarité* in France has perhaps taken on a neoliberal inflection since its revival in the 1980s, but it remains nonetheless an important signpost in contemporary French life. The real danger, I would argue, is the potential for this new understanding of *solidarité* to mask inequalities beyond the simple included/excluded binary on which it is founded. Although the young people I came to know insisted they were no different from anyone else, when push came to shove their chances for success in the job market were slimmer than most. How did they explain the difficulties they experienced when looking for work? Beginning with their reactions to the riots that ripped through France in fall 2005 and then moving on to the CPE protests in 2006, the next two chapters will attempt to answer this question.

4 Burning *Banlieues*

Race, Economic Insecurity,
and the 2005 Riots

During the eight o'clock evening news on November 14, 2005, after seventeen consecutive nights of rioting in outer cities across France, President Jacques Chirac finally addressed the nation. Uncharacteristically bespectacled and noticeably haggard, he projected a profound sense of dismay. The riots, Chirac proclaimed, signaled a "crisis of meaning," a "crisis of reference points"—in sum, a "crisis of identity." It was common knowledge that local outrage over the electrocution of three teenage boys in a poorer city neighboring Paris had triggered the unrest. Chirac offered his sympathy to the victims and their families. However, he suggested that there were other, underlying causes for the disturbance. Residents of France's disadvantaged *banlieues*, he acknowledged, live in "rough" neighborhoods, with fewer resources than other areas; they are plagued by "violence," "illegal drugs," and "out-of-control unemployment"; some are "over their heads in debt," and many lack the basic education needed to find good jobs or, frequently, any jobs at all. For them, the president concluded, the risk of "exclusion" is great, and this undoubtedly rouses frustration.

In the face of such crushing difficulty, what could be done? Chirac replied by insisting that putting France's outer-city youth to work was "essential." Although he recognized that this would mean addressing the thorny question of "diversity" in the workplace, he rejected affirmative-action-type programs as a means to do so. "We cannot," he asserted, "let ourselves be ensnared by a logic of quotas, which, in a way, points the finger at those who benefit from them and is unfair to those who do not." Rather, Chirac stated, giving "equal opportunity" to all young people, regardless of their origin, was his administration's top priority, and should be society's as well.[1]

To be sure, Chirac's stance reflects the French Republic's long-standing commitment to race neutrality. In France, an aspiration to transcend human difference is grounded in the universalist ideals of the French Revolution. At that time, concern about the influence wielded by the Catholic Church over the monarchy led revolutionaries to redefine membership in the polity as a matter of individual consent, not a question of religious affiliation. Thus, in 1789 during a debate on whether or not Jews could be French, the deputy Clermont-Tonnerre famously declared, "One must refuse everything to the Jews as a nation and grant everything to Jews as individuals" (qtd. in Bleich 2004, 167). In other words, as Mark Ingram writes, "French 'republican universalism' is the idea that the preservation of the Republic depends on its being composed not of distinct communities and diverse cultural identities but on individual citizens equal under law and linked directly to the state without intermediary representation" (2011, xxi). More than a century and a half later, following the atrocities of Nazi Germany and guilt over the complicity of France's Vichy regime in deporting Jews to concentration camps, the French government officially banned the collection and computerized storage of race-based data. Today, "color-blind" France gathers no census or other statistics on the race or ethnicity of its citizens, and employers are forbidden to do so as well.[2]

Yet the president's reference to diversity—even if he did not clarify what he meant by that term—and his explicit repudiation of policies aimed at helping minorities suggest that race is a potential marker of difference in contemporary France, even if it is not officially recognized as such by the state. In fact, some commentators on the riots did attribute the unrest to racial and ethnic difference. Although few denied the centrality of the problem of unemployment, such well-known figures as Tzvetan Todorov (a renowned literary critic), Hélène Carrère d'Encausse (permanent secretary of the French Academy), and Gérard Larcher (France's labor minister at the time) suggested that the "deviant" or "asocial" practices, especially polygamy, of various immigrant groups were a root cause of the disturbance. Such behavior, these public figures asserted, essentially rendered outer-city youth "unemployable."[3] Although these remarks incited a great deal of indignation in France, since the riots a growing body of scholarship has broken with French republican tradition by vaunting the benefits of thinking through the disturbance—and life in France's fractious *banlieues*, more generally—in racial terms. That work suggests that the riots represented a return of the repressed; they were a long-overdue wake-up call for France to address its bottled-up racial tensions (e.g., Lagrange 2010; Durpaire 2006, 2012; Ndiaye 2008).[4]

My aim in this chapter is to sort through the implications of the rise of race as a potentially meaningful category of distinction in France. Enthusiastically applauded by some who see it as a positive first step to righting the wrongs of France's colonial past, this turn toward a racialized reading of social life has been just as vehemently denounced by others who fear that it will open a Pandora's box of identity politics, ultimately cleaving French society into warring ethnic factions.[5] Rather than take sides in this debate, I take a step back to ask what meanings race may hold for those using the term in France today. I focus on claims of racism made by my interlocutors in the outer city of Limoges during the 2005 riots and at other times before moving on to consider these young people's own uses of race in the working out of everyday life. Noting that some of the young men and women I came to know looked to the black American experience for inspiration, I ask if for them race was about forging an oppositional consciousness, as it has sometimes been said to function in the United States. It appears, however, that what these young people called racism had a lot more to do with their perception of dwindling *solidarité* than any demands for the right to difference. In the end, their uses of the concept of race, I contend, were above all efforts to make sense

FIG. 12. One of my first entry points into the Val de l'Aurence neighborhood, Interval was conceived to serve as a youth information and activity center. I later learned that it had a bad reputation among some residents of the housing project, who feared the "gangs" of unemployed young men who routinely gathered outside its doors.

of the diminishing possibilities and increasing limitations they faced in the new economy.

Riots and Race

In early November 2005, I joined a group of young men at Interval, the "dry bar" in the Val de l'Aurence housing project that serves as a local youth hangout. I had been invited by Fabrice, one of Interval's coordinators, to attend the "hip-hop" workshop he holds there once a week. It would be a great opportunity for me to get to know some young people from the neighborhood, he had suggested during an initial meeting. Interval was housed in an abandoned shopping mart, atop a knoll overlooking the serpentine-shaped cement apartment blocks of the development's lower south side. Although, by day, young people could usually be seen congregating in front of the center's entrance—"holding the walls," as locals said—by the time I arrived night had fallen and the familiar figures had dispersed (fig. 12).[6] A haze of cigarette smoke hung in the stale air of the dimly lit main room, where four young men sat playing cards around a Formica-topped table. The cool flickering glow of a television screen danced behind them. Fabrice ushered me into the back room, where another group of young people were hunched over a lone computer, which during the day, I had learned during a previous visit to Interval, was meant to be used for searching for job ads and drafting application materials. The "hip-hop" workshop, I discovered, amounted mostly to surfing the Internet for music videos while shooting the breeze. Topics of discussion ranged from the latest neighborhood gossip to predictions for the next sports matchup.[7]

About a half hour after my arrival, a burst of indignation erupted in the main room. Although the rapid-fire speech was hard to make out from where I was sitting, I caught the words *bouffons* (fools) and *journalistes*. The interjection was enough to catch the attention of my companions, too, who left their computer station to see what all the commotion was about. In the main room, the four card players had turned their attention to the grainy television screen, where a discussion was taking place among three white, suit-clad men and two dark-skinned teenagers, both wearing jeans and hoodies. The dialogue, I learned, was being broadcast from Paris, the epicenter of the 2005 riots. In addition to the journalist who was moderating the show, the other participants included a municipal politician, a sociologist, and two *jeunes de quartier*, one of whom was described by the moderator as being of "Maghrebi" (North African) descent and the other of "Sub-Saharan" origin. The discussion's focus was the ongoing unrest in France's troubled *banlieues*.

The politician and the sociologist did most of the talking, but now and then the moderator asked the two young men to comment. Each time they opened their mouths, my companions at Interval became increasingly irritated by what they saw as the media's tendency to paint the problem of the *banlieues* in excessively broad strokes. Pointing accusatively at the screen, Ousmane, a regular at Interval, insisted that journalists seek out the least-articulate, least-productive youth they can find and then broadcast that image to all of France, and even the rest of the world. "What are people going to think?" he asked. Addressing me, he continued: "How are people in the United States going to perceive France's *banlieues*? They're gonna say, 'What savages live there!' They're not gonna realize how we really live inside. It's the same in France, in Limoges. People who don't live here think that the Val de l'Aurence is really dangerous, that you'll get your throat slit here. For them, it's the same as Brooklyn or the Bronx!" "News reports on the *banlieues* always show the same thing," Rachid, another frequent face at Interval, said. "You're gonna see a guy who's black or Arab, with a Lacoste cap pulled down over his head. He's wearing a track suit and sneakers, he listens to rap, drives around in a big car, and doesn't work." Ousmane nodded in agreement. "In the end, maybe we'd be better off in Brooklyn or the Bronx," he remarked. "At least there everyone acknowledges that racism is a problem. Here in France, people are hypocrites. They'll tell you race doesn't matter, but that's just not true. The French are racist!"

The exchange was striking. What began as frustration over the media's perceived propensity to peddle alterity in general quickly turned into a discussion focused on race. To be sure, skin tone was one form of difference highlighted in the televised debate. Whereas the journalist, the politician, and the sociologist were all white, the young men from the outer city who had been invited to share their perspective had darker complexions. But other markers of difference, including dress, education, and employment status, were equally salient. These forms of distinction, which in France have historically been associated with social class (Bourdieu 1984), did not escape the attention of my companions at Interval, as Ousmane's comments demonstrate. Yet, drawing on assumptions about how race works in the United States, they brandished them as proof of racism in France.

The discussion at Interval was not an unusual event. During the riots, but also at other times, young people in Limoges's housing projects complained, sometimes bitterly, about racism. Nicolas Sarkozy, who at the time was serving as minister of the interior, was a popular target. On October 26, 2005, the day before the electrocution of three teenagers of immigrant descent outside Paris ignited the riots, the eight o'clock evening news reported on an impromptu visit made by Sarkozy to a housing project in Argenteuil, a Paris suburb. Filmed in haste, the images that make up the news segment are shaky.[8] The first scene is of Sarkozy at night, surrounded by police officers, as he walks down what appears to be the neighborhood's main thoroughfare. The camera pans out. Along the streets, throngs of agitated youth chant in unison: "Sarko, on t'encule! Sarko, on t'encule!" (Sarko, up yours!). Then the camera jerks to refocus on the minister of the interior as he ducks to avoid something. The news commentator explains that the angry mob is throwing rocks and other objects at Sarkozy. Aides rush to his side, protecting his head, first with a briefcase, then an umbrella. In the next scene, police officers scan the crowd. "Over here," one yells into a walkie-talkie while pointing at a group of hooded adolescents fleeing down a dark alley. The segment ends by returning to Sarkozy, who, looking up, presumably at a resident in one of the bleak cement high-rises, comments, "You've had enough, huh? You've had enough of this bunch of *racaille* [street thugs]? Well, we're going to get rid of them for you."

As rioting erupted the following week, first on the outskirts of Paris and then in *banlieues* across France, Sarkozy's "little phrase," as it came to be known, was not forgotten. Minister for Equal Opportunity Azouz Begag publicly denounced it and other comments made by the minister of the interior in reference to outer-city youth, especially Sarkozy's avowed desire to "pressure-wash" France's urban peripheries, a measure Sarkozy deemed necessary to remove the *voyous* (hoodlums) he held responsible for the degradation of these areas.[9] The leftist newspaper *L'Humanité* called his commentary a "deliberate provocation" (Kesselman 2002). Despite this and other opposition, Sarkozy remained hardnosed.

On November 8, during a question-and-answer session at the National Assembly, he announced instructions to prefects to expel from France any foreign-born individuals found guilty of participating in the disturbance, whether or not they held valid residency cards. The measure proved highly controversial, inciting protest from members of the left, some of whom called for Sarkozy's immediate resignation, and from various human-rights groups.

The controversy surrounding Sarkozy during the 2005 riots did not escape my interlocutors in Limoges's outer city, many of whom expressed anger over what the minister of the interior had said. In early November, shortly after the riots began, a message appeared on the metallic shutters of Beaubreuil's *maison des jeunes.* "Fuck Sarkozy, him and his mother! Fuck the French!" the red scrawls declared defiantly. Then, in early December during a hip-hop concert organized by adolescents in the Val de l'Aurence housing project, performers rapped about Sarkozy, including in their lyrics the other "little phrase" heard in Argenteuil the previous October: "Sarko, up yours!" When I later asked one of the participants about the performance, he explained matter-of-factly, "Sarko, he's a dirty racist."

As minister of the interior, Sarkozy was responsible for police services.[10] Both during the riots and at other times, my interlocutors in Limoges levied charges of racism against the police force in general, arguing that it was guilty of racial profiling. Nearly everyone I knew in the housing projects could tell me how the riots had started. On October 27, 2005, a group of teenagers from Clichy-sous-Bois were returning home after spending the afternoon playing soccer when someone spotted them loitering at a construction site and called the police. As a squad car approached, the teenagers fled. Although some were apprehended, three managed to evade the police by ducking into a nearby electrical substation. This game of cat-and-mouse soon turned deadly when these three adolescents were electrocuted. Two died instantly; the third, badly burned, managed nonetheless to make his way back home, where word of the incident spread quickly. That night, young people descended into the streets of their neighborhood, smashing bus-stop shelters, torching cars, and launching rocks and other readily available projectiles at the police called in to quell the disturbance. Despite riot squad reinforcements, the unrest escalated in the following nights, eventually engulfing more than 270 French cities.

Malik, a twenty-four-year-old of Algerian ancestry who lived with his parents in the Val de l'Aurence, was outraged by the events in Clichy-sous-Bois. He insisted that the teenagers had fled the police, not because of any wrongdoing on their part, but to avoid being subjected to an identity check. Furthermore, he was certain the police had intentionally left the adolescents to die in the power station, despite the officers' claims that they had lost sight of them during the pursuit.[11] Many young people in Limoges's housing projects complained that the police routinely performed identity checks, targeting youth *de couleur* (of color). If found without proper identification, these youngsters risked getting hauled off to the local police station until their parents were able to retrieve them, which could take hours, depending on whether or not their parents were at work.

In late December, Malik recounted his most recent run-in with the police. The previous week, he had been chatting with friends in the lobby of an outer-city high-rise when a woman and two husky men approached the group. Flashing badges, the trio asked Malik and his friends for identification. Malik had left his identity card at home, but "luckily" the plainclothes officers accepted his debit card as proof instead. They then searched the youths' pockets, presumably for drugs. Although the officers left empty-handed, they reminded Malik and his friends that congregating in the building's lobby was illegal. Malik remarked that two other "white" adults and a child were also talking in the lobby, but the police did not bother them. "It's always the North African kids," he protested.

The young Limougeauds I came to know did not limit their charges of racism to high-profile political figures (such as Sarkozy) or the police. Many told me, for instance, that shopkeepers regularly followed them down store aisles because of the darker color of their skin. Some insisted that finding decent housing was more difficult for those who were not "Franco-French." They argued that immigrant families were allotted the least-desirable apartments in public housing and suggested that private landlords hesitated to rent to non-whites. For example, Souad, a twenty-three-year-old university student of Moroccan descent, said her application for a city-center studio was passed over in favor of a "white" friend who happened to be vying for the same unit.

Most often, though, interlocutors complained of racism in the job market. During a roundtable on youth employment held at city hall, a narrative about a young Parisian named Mohamed was read aloud. Although of North African descent, Mohamed, the audience learned, was born, raised, and educated in France, and he possessed French citizenship. He had earned a bachelor's degree yet was still unable to find full-time, long-term employment. To get by, Mohamed attempted to string together short-term contracts, but he complained that each time he entered a temp agency, he was asked to show his identity papers. Following the reading of Mohamed's story, Limoges's deputy mayor, an invited discussant at the roundtable, expressed sympathy for the young man's plight but stated that she could not comprehend his objections to how he was treated in the temp agencies he visited. "It's only normal that candidates be asked to prove their eligibility to work in France," she argued. This assertion exasperated a number of young people in the audience. Véro, a young woman I knew from a support group for unemployed youth, rose to her feet and vehemently countered the deputy mayor's claim, insisting that Mohamed was only asked to show his papers because he was not "white." As someone of Franco-French origin, she had never been asked for identification when looking for work, she maintained. Following the roundtable, I joined a small group of young people who had gathered in the parking lot. When I asked them about the tension surrounding the deputy mayor's comment, Mouloud, whose parents emigrated from Algeria, responded: "The thing is, the deputy mayor is right. Everyone should have to provide identification before being interviewed. The problem is that's not how it works in real life."

These anecdotes represent only a small sampling of the complaints of racism I encountered in Limoges's housing projects. For many of the young people living there, racism pervaded everyday life. How are we to make sense of this claim? Could we be witnessing the birth of a racial consciousness in France, similar to what is said to exist in the United States?

America in France?

In February 2006, several months after the riots had subsided, French rapper Diam's released her third studio album. Titled *Dans ma bulle* (In my bubble), it went on to sell more copies in France that year than any other French-language LP. This semi-autobiographical album recounts the rapper's personal journey and experiences. The daughter of a French mother and a Greek Cypriot father, Diam's arrived in France when she was four and was raised by her mother. Although she grew up in a middle-class neighborhood south of Paris, she claims to have interacted considerably with outer-city youth and affirms in the album that she raps as much for the *cités* as for the *pavillons*.[12] Diam's has been mistaken for a *beurette* (a girl of North African descent, usually understood to be from the housing projects).[13] In 2008 she converted to Islam, and in 2009 the tabloid *Paris Match* published a photograph of her wearing an Islamic headscarf.

In much of *Dans ma bulle*, Diam's addresses some of the difficult social and political issues surrounding France's fractious *banlieues*. The song "Ma France à moi" (My France) is a biting critique of what the artist calls *la France profonde*. According to Diam's, *la France profonde* is vulgar: it "scratches its balls at the dinner table" while listening to lowbrow humorist Laurent Gerra. It is also mired in ridiculous traditions. She points out that it celebrates the yearly arrival of Beaujolais Nouveau, despite the fact that this cheap, early-to-market wine is not particularly good. But above all, for the rapper *la France profonde* is "hypocritical." It "reeks of racism," she proclaims, but then "pretends to be open." The proof, according to Diam's: despite the Republic's lofty goals of universal inclusion and equality, *la France profonde* "venerates" the law-and-order hard-liner Nicolas Sarkozy and votes for the far-right, xenophobic National Front party, claiming that it got "screwed" by the arrival of immigrants. Diam's contrasts this ugly, "lying" France, which might be glossed as "traditional" or even "backward," with another, younger, technologically savvy, struggling yet hopeful, infinitely more honest, multiracial and multiethnic France. This "rainbow" France, she declares, is the one to which she swears allegiance. Playing on a well-known verse of "La Marseillaise," France's national anthem, Diam's concludes the song by calling on the members of this new, diverse France to "stand up to" *la France profonde* until it "respects" them.[14]

At the small liberal arts college where I teach, I regularly include discussion of "Ma France à moi" and the music video that accompanies it in one of my upper-level courses.[15] By that point in the semester, students are familiar with France's "color-blind" rhetoric. Upon hearing the song, their first reaction tends to be to point an accusatory finger. "Aha!" someone invariably says. "The French claim to be antiracist, but this song is proof not only that racism exists in France, but also that the French are hypocrites!" From there, students often begin making comparisons with American society. Noting the multitude of references in the song's lyrics to American companies and products, from KFC, MTV, and Foot Locker to McDonald's and Coca-Cola, some students have argued that France is increasingly dominated by the influence of American culture—including, perhaps, ideas about race and racial difference. The France Diam's describes as her own, they contend, looks an awful lot like widely circulated American ideals of multiculturalism.[16]

There is no denying the influence of American culture in France, even when it comes to ideas about race. In Limoges's housing projects, many young people told me that they drew inspiration from the American civil rights movement. Rosa Parks, Martin Luther King Jr., Malcolm X, Birmingham, Montgomery: these were people and places that came up in conversations with them.[17] One explanation for this could be my status as an American researcher. When I described the focus of my project in Limoges, people sometimes assumed (erroneously) that I was an expert on race relations in the United States. Evoking the black American experience could have been for them a way to situate me and my study. But I came to discover that these references were more than polite conversation starters; they proceeded from a general fascination with the fight for racial equality in the United States. Despite this, if we are to take seriously the intellectual labor that has gone on in anthropology and other social sciences regarding the dynamism of culture, it seems imprudent to argue that American notions of race have simply been grafted onto French society, that racial minorities in France are at long last, fifty years after their American counterparts, discovering their own racialized identities. Building on Stuart Hall's theory of race as a "floating signifier"—that is, a distinction whose meanings shift, depending on their context—I argue below that the idea of race was deployed by young people in Limoges in ways that were locally meaningful. Ultimately, their understandings and uses of the concept were far more compatible with what have been described as French universalist values than might at first appear.

Stuart Hall was a Jamaican-born sociologist and cultural theorist who grappled with the question of human diversity and how it gets worked out in the social world. Early in his career he moved to the United Kingdom, where, along with Richard Hoggart and Raymond Williams, he founded what came to be known as British cultural studies. This field went on to be influential in how American anthropologists view and define culture. According to Hall and his colleagues, culture is not a bounded, fixed entity. Rather, it consists of sets of values and practices continually interacting and changing. In 1994, Hall delivered the W. E. B. Du Bois Lecture at Harvard University. Building on this conception of culture, he offered a theory of race. Race, like culture, Hall maintained, has no inner nature or essence. Instead, the meanings people attribute to race only make sense in relation to other meanings produced in the same context. Shifts in context, either spatial or temporal or both, thus are always accompanied by shifts in the meanings race holds for people. It is for this reason that Hall described race as a "floating signifier": race is relational and is always subject to appropriation and redefinition in different cultural and social settings and at different moments. Understanding race in this way is crucial, Hall insisted, because too often it is understood as self-evident and stable. Building awareness of its culturally and socially constructed nature is the first step to combatting the ways race has been and continues to be used to rationalize inequality in the world.

Since Hall delivered that lecture on race more than twenty years ago, the temptation to view race as something fixed and objective has perhaps grown even stronger. In our era of "liquid modernity" characterized by heightened uncertainty, there is a tension between the need for mobility and flexibility and the desire to anchor identities (one's own identity, the identity of other people) in something—anything—concrete (Bauman 2000, 2007). At the same time, ever-increasing flows of people and ideas across the globe mean that today visitors to even the farthest flung corners of the world are apt to be met with a sense of familiarity. That some of the young men and women I came to know in the outer city of Limoges were eager to discuss the American civil rights movement with me offers just one case in point. Yet, as the anthropologist Susan Carol Rogers argues, this sense of familiarity is often an illusion, and a dangerous one at that since "the potential for misunderstanding resulting from complacent assumptions of similarity may be more insidious than the pitfalls generated by obvious difference" (2015, 208). What exactly did young people in Limoges mean when they evoked the idea of race and what place, if any, did race occupy in their understanding of who they were? The rest of this chapter is devoted to sorting through these questions. To begin, thinking about how these young men and women positioned Limoges on the national stage during the riots offers some important clues.

Limoges-as-Haven, Limoges-as-Hole

On November 7, after more than a week of rioting, the national daily *Le Monde* published a map of France, indicating with small fire bursts cities across the country that had been touched by the violence.[18] Although Limoges received a fire burst, I never witnessed any rioting there, and while the local press did report on a number of acts of vandalism in the area beginning October 30, these incidents rarely received more than passing comment, usually in the news-in-brief section of the local papers. Table 2 summarizes incidents in and around Limoges reported by the local press between October 30 and November 16, the last day of rioting before a "return to normalcy" was declared by the national police.[19]

TABLE 2. Vandalism reported in and around Limoges,
October 30–November 16, 2005

October 30

Three adolescents are detained in Panazol (an eastern suburb of Limoges) after setting a trash container on fire (*L'Écho de la Haute Vienne*, November 2, 2005).

November 6

Car is torched on the rue du Chinchauvaud, not far from the Gare des Bénédictins; flames spread to a second vehicle, parked nearby, damaging it (*Le Populaire du Centre*, November 7, 2005).
"Several" cars are torched in La Bastide (*Le Populaire du Centre*, November 7, 2005).

November 7

Car is torched in La Bastide, not far from the neighborhood police station; another car parked nearby is also damaged (*Le Populaire du Centre*, November 8, 2005).
Cars are "vandalized" in the Val de l'Aurence (*Le Populaire du Centre*, November 8, 2005).
Five trash containers are set on fire in the Val de l'Aurence (*L'Écho de la Haute Vienne*, November 10, 2005).
Swimming pool complex is torched in nearby Saint-Léonard de Noblat (*Le Populaire du Centre*, November 9, 2005).

November 8

Stolen car is torched in the Val de l'Aurence (*Le Populaire du Centre*, November 9, 2005).
Four adolescents throw a firecracker and a stink bomb into an operating city bus in the Val de l'Aurence; one youth is found to be in possession of marijuana (*Le Populaire du Centre*, November 10, 2005).

November 10

Molotov cocktail is thrown at the police station in Beaubreuil, starting a
small fire (*Le Populaire du Centre*, November 10, 2005).

November 11

Car is torched in Sablard neighborhood (*Le Populaire du Centre*, November 12, 2005).
Motorcycle and bicycle are torched in La Bastide (*L'Écho de la Haute Vienne*,
November 14, 2005).

November 12

Molotov cocktails are thrown at trash containers in the Val de l'Aurence,
but because of rain they do not ignite (*Le Populaire du Centre*, November 14, 2005).

November 16

Adolescent sets trash containers on fire near the Val de l'Aurence; he tells
police that he wanted to reproduce what he "saw on TV" (*Le Populaire
du Centre*, November 18, 2005).

The majority of these incidents were framed by local news outlets
as "isolated" and "without relation" to the urban violence occurring
elsewhere in the country. For example, a news-in-brief bulletin about a
torched car found November 8 in Limoges's Val de l'Aurence neighborhood emphasized that the occurrence was not linked to the riots but was,
instead, an attempt by would-be thieves to destroy evidence of their crime
("Une voiture partiellement incendiée" 2005). Similarly, an account about
another car set ablaze on November 11, this time in the Sablard housing
project, blamed the event on a "dispute between two people" ("Voiture
incendiée" 2005), and a report concerning the torching of a bicycle and a
motorcycle in La Bastide during the same night suggested that "individuals
[were] taking advantage of the current situation to pass off their settling
of scores as the work of organized gangs" ("Limoges" 2005). In fact, out

of all the short bulletins published during the riots, I only came across one that admitted a link with the unrest raging in other French cities. The brief account explained that on November 16 a seventeen-year-old apprentice baker had been detained by the police after he was observed setting fire to two trash containers not far from the municipal stadium. When questioned about his motives, the youth replied that he was trying to "reproduce what he had been seeing on TV" ("L'incendiaire" 2005).

In the end, whether or not these incidents can be linked to the 2005 riots is of little interest. What seems significant, by contrast, is the way the local press consistently attempted to disassociate them from that violence. In doing so, they painted Limoges and the surrounding area as a sort refuge, immune to the dangers of the outside world. Even the last bulletin mentioned above supports this vision of Limoges-as-haven. The apprentice-baker-turned-trashcan-arsonist could hardly be considered much of a threat compared to the frightening images of marauding, rock-throwing, car-burning hoodlums being broadcast at the same time from some of Paris's outlying neighborhoods.

In addition to these brief bulletins, a number of longer articles appeared in the local press describing vandalism in the area. They too tended to portray Limoges as far removed from the urban violence plaguing other cities. One story that received multiple-article coverage was the torching of an abandoned municipal swimming complex in Saint Léonard de Noblat, a small town about twenty kilometers east of Limoges. There were no witnesses, but authorities concluded that arson was likely the cause of the fire, since electricity to the building had been cut off for over five years. Despite the timing of the incident at the height of the 2005 riots, the region's leading papers all but ruled out any connection to the disturbance. "Authorities suspect local causes," *Le Populaire du Centre* reported, "and believe that this incident has nothing to do with the urban violence currently happening in France" ("Ancienne piscine incendiée" 2005). "It seems," *L'Écho de la Haute Vienne* suggested in a similar manner, "that the crime ought not to be associated with the upsurge in violence that has shaken the country for over a week" ("La piscine désaffectée"

2005). Beyond these remarks, however, neither paper offered much reason why not to envision a link with the riots.

Another story that made headlines in Limoges during the riots concerned a young Limougeaud suspected of taking part in a murder outside Paris. It too supported the image of Limoges-as-haven. On October 27, the same day as the Clichy-sous-Bois electrocutions, Jean-Claude Irvoas, an employee of a lighting company based in Le Havre, traveled to the poorer neighborhood of Ogremont in Épinay-sur-Seine, a city located in Paris's northern suburbs. He was to photograph a recently installed streetlamp for his firm's catalog. A neighborhood surveillance camera recorded the scene that followed. While taking the picture, Irvoas was approached by a group of three young men, who motioned for him to surrender his camera. When he refused, a scuffle ensued. Irvoas tried to escape his aggressors but was knocked to the ground by one of them, who forcefully kicked him in the head. Irvoas's wife and daughter, who witnessed the assault from the family car parked nearby, called for help. Having suffered multiple fractures, Irvoas was transported to a local hospital where, later that night, he succumbed to his injuries. Thanks to the surveillance video, two of the assailants were identified and detained within forty-eight hours of the incident; the third youth, who had a hood pulled over his head during the attack, remained at large. Irvoas's brutal beating sent shock waves through the national media. Though separate from the riots, in the following weeks his murder came to symbolize the apparent savagery of France's outer cities, where it appeared youth would kill for something as insignificant as a camera.

On November 8, *Le Populaire du Centre* reported in a half-page article that the national police were actively seeking twenty-three-year-old Limougeaud Benoît K., whom the two suspects already in custody had identified as the third assailant in Irvoas's beating. According to the article, the police believed that Benoît had retreated to his native Limousin following the incident. Officers had already performed a search of his parents' home, located in Limoges's outer city, but did not find the young man there. The article went on to note that although Benoît had a criminal record, it only included misdemeanors, such as the theft of a scooter. The author concluded by stating that Benoît's reasons for being in the Paris region the day of the attack were unknown (Lagier 2005b).

Two days later, a front-page article announced that Benoît had turned himself in to a local police captain, his childhood soccer coach. Though the article recognized that the young man had resorted to crime in the past, it questioned if he really was involved in Irvoas's death. Noting that the two other suspects had cast all the blame on Benoît, the author suggested that they would now have to "face his version of the facts." Regardless of the outcome of the case, the article concluded by emphasizing the "relationship built on trust" between Benoît and his former coach, remarking happily that it had facilitated a swift and nonviolent resolution to the affair (Lagier 2005a).

Although the articles about Benoît K. that appeared in the local press contained only passing mention of the riots, they functioned in much the same way as news reports on the disturbance insofar as they drew a clear line between Limoges and larger urban centers. The tone was one of shock and disbelief. That a Limougeaud could be caught up in a high-profile murder such as that of Jean-Claude Irvoas prompted doubt and questioning. The authors seemed to suggest that Benoît's thin police file in Limoges was proof of his innocence, but if he was in fact responsible for the murder, it was because the big city had corrupted him. Furthermore, the self-congratulatory concluding remarks about trust established between Limoges's police force and area youth painted a far more harmonious picture than the one the media cast of Paris, where violent conflict between youth and law enforcement seemed to be the norm.

The idea that Limoges was impervious to the urban violence plaguing other French cities in the fall of 2005 was made explicit in a half-page article titled "Here in my housing project, people say hello" (Spiriet 2005). Focused on Limoges's Bastide neighborhood, this "investigative report" consisted primarily of excerpts from interviews with a longtime resident identified as "Annie P." By and large, the article painted an image of a racism-free utopia where the aromas of exotic cuisines intermingled, youth danced hip-hop together, and neighbors strengthened social ties. The built landscape, the article suggested, promoted and supported such harmony thanks to its ample public lawns, "normal" public school, and recently renovated buildings. La Bastide was, according to this account, the polar opposite of Paris's seething, outer-city ghettos.

Against this image of Limoges-as-haven, I found that most Limougeauds' opinion of where they lived was far more ambiguous. It is no secret that Limoges suffers from a bad reputation in France, beginning with its name. The verb *limoger*, which means "dismiss" or "fire," was first used during World War I to refer to the experience of officers who were judged incompetent by their superiors and consequently relegated to Limoges. Today, the term is synonymous with disgrace (Troyansky 1996). It was thus with a snicker that friends in Paris told me "You've been *limogé!*" when they learned that I would be spending a whole year in the capital of the Limousin. But the perceived undesirability of Limoges goes deeper than semantics. As John Merriman has reported, seventeenth- and eighteenth-century visitors often described the city in unflattering terms, criticizing its "narrow," "dark," and "dirty" streets and its "disgusting" and "overwhelming" smell (1985, 5–6). Little progress toward improving the city's image was made in the nineteenth century. In 1821, and again in 1825, when city officials applied to the king for the designation of *bonne ville*, an honorific conferred on a number of provincial cities at the time, their requests were politely albeit firmly denied, even as a number of smaller French cities earned the rank. For the municipal council, Limoges was "a humiliating exception" (Merriman 1985, 9). Even Merriman admits that he did not like the city much when he first arrived in the 1970s to undertake his dissertation research; he recalls complaining about "horrible Limoges" and "dreary Limoges" to friends back home (1985, xviii). The repulsiveness of the city and surrounding region does not appear to be entirely imposed from the outside. Anthropological scholarship investigating rural tourism has suggested that locals are equally critical of where they live: they are quick "to recite the deficiencies of the area . . . [and] have difficulty imagining that anyone would choose to come there" (Rogers 2002, 483).

The Limougeauds I came to know generally shared this perspective.

Whenever I made a new acquaintance, he or she would invariably ask me what someone from New York could possibly be doing in an out-of-the-way place like Limoges. "You must be so bored here," a young woman from Beaubreuil sympathized. "Limoges isn't like New York. There's nothing exciting to do." For my interlocutors, the location of Limoges was undesirable; this *trou* (hole), as they called it, was too far removed from anything of interest, such as the beach or the mountains. Furthermore, they complained that the city lacked any sort of nightlife and was "dead" on weekends. The region's climate was also the subject of much contempt. During a particularly cold, rainy stretch in March, one interlocutor informed me that Limoges had the highest suicide rate in the nation. "People just can't take this miserable weather," he explained.[20]

Despite this, when young people in Limoges's outer city discussed the 2005 riots, they tended to paint a much more positive picture of their city compared to larger urban centers, especially Paris. "The news about the riots, they're making it out to be a civil war," Jonathan commented. "Maybe that's true in the big cities," he continued, "but here in Limoges, it's peaceful. If I lived in Paris or Toulouse, in a housing project, I wouldn't necessarily be able to say that." Others echoed this perspective. "Limoges's outer city is really open, not at all like Paris or some other places," Souad asserted, adding, "There's not that sense of insecurity here." "People get along pretty well," Rachid maintained. "Everyone's cool, there's not too much racism, or discrimination like that. Limoges is a good place to live." Paris, by contrast, was described as extremely dangerous. "Some of Paris's outer cities, rescue crews can't even go into them," Rachid went on to say. "When firefighters arrive, they're done for! This never happens in Limoges," he assured me, "only in Paris." Hanan offered an equally alarming depiction of Paris's *ban-lieues*. "If you're walking in Seine-Saint-Denis and look at somebody the wrong way, you'll get a bullet in your head, or if you don't have a pack of cigarettes to offer your aggressors, they'll slit your throat," she conjectured. "Here in Limoges," Hanan continued, "it's not dangerous. It's nothing compared to Paris."

These comments bear a striking resemblance to the local press's reaction to the riots. What seems significant in both cases is not so much *that* Limoges was contrasted favorably with larger urban centers, but rather *how* this contrast was achieved. Commentators, both in the local newspapers and the outer city, underscored the maintenance of social ties to support their vision of Limoges-as-haven. In other words, they saw *solidarité* as a remedy for the social ills that made Paris and other major French cities susceptible to violence. Whereas *solidarité* was, according to them, still a defining feature of life in Limoges, it seemed to have eroded elsewhere in France, leaving gaping holes in the social fabric that were precipitating disorder and conflict. In this view, racism, which, as we saw earlier in this chapter, some young people in Limoges's housing projects identified as the principal trigger of the riots, did not result from belief in inherent, irreconcilable difference, as race has sometimes been understood and mobilized in other contexts, particularly the United States; rather, it was perceived as proceeding from an absence of *solidarité*. That is, racism was viewed as the product or symptom of a generalized lack of engagement in collective life.

In the end, the message delivered by Diam's in "Ma France à moi" is perhaps not too far off from this perspective. The subtext of the song, often overlooked by my American students upon a first analysis, is a plea for greater *solidarité*. Diam's rejoices in the interconnectedness of her France (despite or perhaps because of its diversity), while condemning the corrosive individualism of *la France profonde*. Her France fights to protect family, stays connected using the latest technology, and "spends its nights on the phone"; *la France profonde*, by contrast, "lets poor people die" and "puts its own parents in nursing homes." The lack of "tolerance," of "respect" displayed by *la France profonde*—in other words, its "racism"—is, in her estimation, a consequence of its members' retreat from collective life. This linking of racism to *solidarité*—or rather an absence of *solidarité*—deserves further consideration. In the following section, I turn to the everyday uses of the concept of race, and the idea of difference more broadly, in outer-city Limoges.

The Uses of Race and Difference in Everyday Life

At the time of the 2005 riots, a number of articles appeared in the national press debating the merits of blind résumés (résumés containing no identifying information about the job applicant, such as name and address) as a potential way of combating higher than average unemployment rates in outer-city areas. "It's incredibly hypocritical!" exclaimed Rachid. "What does that mean, a 'blind' résumé? I'll tell you what it means. It means that you have to hide the fact that your parents or grandparents are Algerian or Moroccan just to get a job. What hypocrisy!" Yasmine held a similar view. Linking blind résumés to other practices meant to favor particular groups, she pointed to *discrimination positive* (positive discrimination), the French term for the more euphemistic "affirmative action." "It's like the example of positive discrimination in the United States," Yasmine told me. "I don't care if it's 'positive,' it's still a form of discrimination." This perspective, which was shared by many young people in Limoges's housing projects, would seem to result in an impasse: How could racism possibly be overcome if remedial measures, such as blind résumés and affirmative-action-style policies, were systematically refused by the very people they were supposed to help?

Writing about the group she calls "Muslim French," whose members she describes as "women and men committed to practicing Islam as French citizens and to practicing French citizenship as pious Muslims" (2014, 13), anthropologist Mayanthi Fernando tackles this question, arguing that for her interlocutors a radical shift in how identity is defined and managed in France is the only solution. Ultimately, she explains that unlike the United States where demands for the right to difference are often expressed when questions of diversity arise, Muslim French demand *the right to indifference*—that is, the right to have racial and cultural markers go unnoticed in the working out of everyday life. "Importantly," Fernando states, "this political ethic fundamentally unsettles existing configurations of identity and difference, majority and minority, center and periphery." According to her, the French republican model, although purportedly founded on the principle of universalism, draws in fact a distinct line between French *identity*, which it places at its center, and Muslim or other minority *difference*, which it relegates to the periphery. In this system, identity and difference are construed as essential, immutable characteristics. By contrast, the logic of indifference called for by minority groups, Fernando asserts, is not based on any relationship to a center. In fact, with it the center disappears entirely, and all that remain are "crosscutting constellations of heterogeneous identities." As a result, difference takes on new meaning. Echoing Stuart Hall, she states that it is "always relational and constantly shifting, never essential" (98).

This framework, where diversity becomes variation instead of deviation, helps to an extent to make sense of my interlocutors' own understandings and uses of the notion of difference, whether racial or cultural, in the negotiations that make up everyday life. Yet, it also raises an old sociological question that in France preoccupied the likes of Durkheim and before him Rousseau: Amid the great range of human diversity, how or even why do people choose to come together to form a society? What, in other words, is the glue that binds them to each other? Anticipating this problem, Fernando suggests that for the Muslim French she studied, "finding commonalities across differences" (97) was essential. As an example, she relates how one of her interlocutors disapproved of extending the right to marry to same-sex couples but could support the fight for equal treatment between men and women. This concession, however, raises the question of tolerance, which in turn reintroduces the opposition between center and periphery. After all, who gets to decide to be tolerant and who is forced to be so is a matter of power, and in this respect not all individuals are equally endowed. Even if, as Fernando suggests, demands for the right to indifference disaggregate traditional definitions of French citizenship—that is, citizenship that has been embodied as white, bourgeois, Christian or secular, and, at times, male (Scott 1997)—under this alternative model individuals approach everyone else's difference from the vantage point of their own difference, and the perception of commonalities is not guaranteed or even necessarily particularly likely. I would argue that in a given context and at a given moment some forms of difference are bound to command greater attraction than others—some "constellations," to use

Fernando's word, will shine more brightly than the rest. I have suggested that in France in the last decades of the twentieth century and the first decade of the twenty-first the notion of *solidarité* has held considerable sway. In the examples that follow, I demonstrate how, amid calls for the right to indifference, in Limoges the idea of *solidarité* was made to function both as a glue for holding like-minded individuals together and as a filter for excluding all those thought not to share or uphold this value.

"Have you met Papy yet?" an *éducateur de rue* who worked in the Val de l'Aurence housing project asked me shortly after my arrival in Limoges. "You know," he continued, "the tall, muscular black guy who hangs out at Interval all the time. You have to meet him, he'll have a ton of interesting things to tell you!" The term "black," as well as "Arab," "Asian," and "white," came up in similar circumstances: people used these labels pragmatically to describe the array of human physical difference that characterizes the inhabitants of the housing projects.[21] These terms were sometimes replaced by labels designating ancestral national origin (e.g., *le Français, le Congolais, l'Algérien, le Vietnamien*), despite the fact that nearly all of my interlocutors, even those whose parents or grandparents hailed from another country, were born in France and held French citizenship. Such labels could be linked to specific cultural practices. For example, I overheard a conversation among high school students at the homework help center where I volunteered that focused on their favorite ethnic dishes served at home. Furthermore, conversations on any range of topics could be peppered with foreign words and expressions (most often from Arabic), even when people with deep roots in France participated.

On occasion, such talk took the form of teasing. One day after Saïda, whose parents emigrated from Algeria, made an inaccurate reference to a well-known sitcom, Dahlia, whose parents hailed from Morocco, remarked in a deliberately haughty tone, "Well, as everyone knows, Algerians are not the smartest people." Dahlia's comment to Saïda was not meant to be hurtful, and it was not taken by Saïda as an insult: she laughed it off, but not before firing back an equally barbed quip about Moroccans' deplorable fashion sense. Such teasing, however, had little to do with race, at least if we are to think of race as something that is "hard-wired" or biologically transmitted. Rather, here intelligence and taste in fashion were associated with particular national ancestry. There are similar patterns with regard to French regions and their inhabitants: Auvergnats are cheap, Bretons are drunks, Limousins are inhospitable, and so on. Such claims are familiar to those groups, and references to them as a form of teasing may be acceptable (or even funny) among provincials, while they could be offensive in other contexts. Among my interlocutors in Limoges's housing projects, such banter functioned in much the same way: it was a means of expressing connectedness among individuals viewed as possessing equally different difference.

The dependence on context here, it seems to me, cannot be overstated. Outside of the housing projects, difference was also used, but the kinds of difference evoked changed to match the environment. Consider for example the series of murals produced by "at-risk" youth participating in a program overseen by Limoges's *mission locale*. The initiative consisted of hiring out-of-work youth from the outer city to "beautify" municipal walls and fences. In exchange for designing and painting murals, they received a modest stipend and, most importantly, at least according to the *mission locale* counselor I talked to about the project, structure in their lives. When I returned to Limoges in the summer of 2012 for a follow-up visit, I photographed two murals, both completed after my departure in 2006. One, located in the Val de l'Aurence housing project, features brown-skinned individuals in ethnic dress (fig. 13). The other, painted on a cement fence near the city center, depicts elements from Limoges's past, regional specialties, and the emblems of Limoges's basketball, soccer, and rugby teams (fig. 14). Difference, as represented in both of these murals, is in no way abnormal or deviant but is instead a reality of everyday life. Rather than brush difference off as insignificant or pretend that it does not exist, these murals suggest that it constitutes a reservoir of references that may be used to forge a common sense of belonging. The choice of which references to evoke depends on the context.

FIG. 13. Completed by twelve "at-risk" young people as part of a back-to-work program, this mural in the Val de l'Aurence vividly depicts the wide range of racial and ethnic difference that characterizes life in the outer city of Limoges. The mural was officially inaugurated by Cécile Duflot, Minister of Territorial Equality and Housing, when she visited Limoges in June 2012.

For the young men and women I came to know in the outer city of Limoges being "French" was not about race or even about a single, shared culture. Instead, their definition of Frenchness was elastic, stretching to encompass a multiplicity of differences, including difference in skin color. What mattered to them was the pursuit of shared references. But I would argue that finding common ground across diversity was not the end goal; it was the first step to building a common life based on each individual's dedication to advancing collectively, to promoting the common good. In sum, a commitment to *solidarité* was at the heart of how they defined membership in society.

This understanding of what it means to be French is reflected in a conflict I observed during my fieldwork. In June 2006, the tutors I

FIG. 14. Although strikingly different from the mural in the outer city, this mural near the city center also focuses on difference—just difference of a different sort. Completed by twelve "at-risk" young people in 2007, it provides an inventory of what makes Limoges and the Limousin region distinct, from a representation of the historical figure of the *blanchisseuse* (washerwoman) who used to labor on the banks of the Vienne to images of the city's traditional timbered architecture, a porcelain factory, cattle, a *clafoutis* (cherry tart), apples, and chestnuts. The emblems of Limoges's main amateur and professional sports teams also figure prominently.

worked with at the homework help center held a barbecue to cele-brate the end of the school year. A picnic area to the north of the city was selected for the event. Although the park was vacant when we arrived, other revelers soon appeared to take advantage of the pleasant, early summer evening, including a group of dark-skinned men, who, from the look of their dusty overalls, had just left a construction site. Before settling at a picnic table not far from our own, these newcomers pulled their rusty, beat-up van as close as possible, rolled down their windows, and began blasting pulsating Arabic music from the van's radio. "Algerians," Saïda muttered. "And from the looks of it," added

Yasmine, "they're fresh off the boat." As the evening progressed, the music became louder and the tutors' patience seemed to wear thinner. "You wouldn't even know we were in France anymore," objected Samira. Following this remark, Dahlia looked conspiratorially at her fellow tutors and then began to chant, "Ainsi font, font, font," a traditional French nursery rhyme. The other tutors quickly joined in the singing and followed the first song by another, "À la claire fontaine," and then another. With each song, their voices became louder, soon overtaking the workers' music. The episode ended with all of the tutors bursting into wholehearted laughter. Although the tutors' disapproval of the construction workers could be interpreted as a patent rejection of racial and cultural difference, it seems more likely that they reacted the way they did because they understood the workers' actions to be an assault on collective life, on the bonds of *solidarité* that they held necessary for society's well-being. For my interlocutors, difference, racial or otherwise, was not necessarily incompatible with membership in the French polity, *as long as that difference did not threaten or undermine the cohesiveness of the collective whole.* By blasting their music in a public area, the construction workers seemed not to share—or worse yet, not to care about—this communal ideal.

It is in this light, it seems to me, that the use of the term "Franco-French" by young people in Limoges's housing projects is best understood. The label "Franco-French" was most often employed by young people when complaining about racism to refer to either putative offenders or friends or acquaintances who supposedly did not face this form of discrimination. They tended to use it interchangeably with another label, *blanc* (white). A comment made by Yasmine, who was of Algerian descent, illustrates this practice: "You see, my skin and eyes are very light. I can pass for Franco-French." Franco-French was the only hyphenated identity I encountered during my fieldwork. None of my interlocutors described themselves as "Franco-Algerian" or "Franco-Moroccan," for example, preferring instead the unmarked categories "French" or "Algerian" or "Moroccan," as described above.[22] I would argue that they avoided hybrid labels because, unlike the designation "Franco-French," these suggest a rigid cultural duality that conflicted with their understanding of the elasticity and fluidity of identity. Or this kind of hyphenation might also potentially imply a kind of biological (permanent) dimension to identity—culturally French but biologically Algerian—that would be equally inimical to their ways of thinking about who they were. For my interlocutors, being French was not a biological fact, and one could claim Frenchness whether or not one was white, but to do so meant unequivocally upholding the principle of *solidarité*. In the end, "Franco-French" for them was just one way among others of being French, the other ways being just plain French.[23]

When all is said and done, young people in Limoges's housing projects, like Fernando's research subjects, hoped for a society in which difference, whether in skin color or in habits of mind and body, did not mean one was automatically classified as "different" and thus excluded. Observing infinite variations of difference all around them, whether in their own multiracial and multiethnic neighborhoods or in French society more generally, they maintained that difference should be unremarkable because, quite simply, everyone is different in some way or another from everyone else. In their estimation, difference therefore could not function as a basis of inclusion in or exclusion from society. That is not to say that they did not define *any* criteria for membership in the polity. What did matter, they maintained, was a commitment to building a collective life, to *solidarité*. That these young men and women relegated difference to a secondary position vis-à-vis citizenship built on the ideal of *solidarité* perhaps best reflects a truly universalist conception of the nation and helps to explain why they so vehemently rejected claims made by others that they were not fully French, such as calls during the 2005 riots for the "integration" or "assimilation" of outer-city youth or, worse yet, their expulsion from France as a solution to the violence. "But we are French!" was their resounding reply.

Why Race? Why Now?

From the preceding it seems clear that the notion of race was not used in Limoges's housing projects to forge any sort of racial consciousness, at least not by the young people I came to know. That the French rapper Diam's expresses something similar in her lyrics suggests that this finding may be generalizable to French society more broadly. By contrast, in the United States the idea of race has, at least sometimes, been called upon to shape and define identities.[24] This difference has been constitutive of and reflected in formal state policy in the two countries. Whereas in the United States, racial segregation was enforced by law well into the second half of the twentieth century and continues to have consequences today, as we saw in chapter 1, France's official stance, especially following World War II, was one of "integration" or "social mixing." Fearful of the potentially deleterious consequences of the segmentation of French cities and towns into distinctive ethnic enclaves, where individuals' particularistic concerns could risk superseding those of the local or national collectivity, planners of the *banlieues* argued that lodging immigrant families, in the right doses, alongside French families would facilitate foreigners' assimilation to French culture and ultimately avoid ethnic conflict.[25] In France, notions of shared culture—not race—have been fundamental to dominant conceptions of what it means to be French (Beriss 2004).

This observation is important for at least two reasons. First, it suggests that we must be careful not to overestimate the similarities between France and the United States, especially when it comes to discussions about the influence of American culture on French society. As we have seen, assuming that race functions in the same way in both countries risks obscuring the cultural mechanisms of adaptation and appropriation specific to each. Yet we must be equally cautious about representing each society as fixed or bounded. By arguing that France and the United States are entirely different and culturally distinct, we lose sight of the links between the two, and "nothing ever happens in France [or the United States] except the eternal return of Frenchness [or Americanness] and its confrontation with history" (E. Fassin 1995, 454). In other words, "French culture" and "American culture" become an explanation for everything. My data suggest that in Limoges at least there is an American influence when it comes to talking about race, but this influence was translated into locally meaningful terms.

This leads to an as-yet-unanswered question: Why were some young people in Limoges's housing projects seduced by the American civil rights movement? What exactly did this page of U.S. history mean to them? Anthropologist Beth Epstein (2016) offers a possible response. During fieldwork in a northern Parisian *banlieue* with a rough reputation, she was struck by an educational project organized by a local collective of artists, activists, and teachers. It consisted of engaging secondary students, mostly of "immigrant origin," in theatrical renderings of excerpts from Toni Morrison's racially charged novel *The Bluest Eye*. The aim of this initiative, one of the collective's founders told Epstein, was to help these young people explore questions relating to identity and make sense of their experience growing up in a troubled *banlieue*. Linking her observations in this outer city to the surge in racialized debates in France that followed the 2005 riots, Epstein asks what has made discussions about race possible at this particular moment in French history. "If nothing else," she asserts, "the very tenaciousness of a French republican social model that has so long resisted a more explicit differentialist reading of social life in order to protect against the more egregious consequences of racialized forms of thinking should give us pause: why is this shift toward a racialized reading of social life happening in France, and why is it happening now?" (170). Ultimately, Epstein turns to the history of the *banlieues* for answers. Although the *banlieues* were conceived to serve as a tool of social and cultural integration and a trampoline for upward social mobility for native French and immigrants alike, since the oil crises of the 1970s, their story, Epstein maintains, has been one of "integration gone awry" (177), as reduced social spending and a lack of job prospects have relegated residents to the ranks of the dispossessed. Against this backdrop of diminishing possibilities and increasing limitations, Epstein interprets contemporary French interest in race in general and in the black American experience in particular as "reflect[ing] efforts to grasp at readily identifiable sources of inequality and disenfranchisement when the far less comprehensible reasons for a lack of opportunity have moved, literally, off-shore, radically altering the meaning of local life and politics, and undercutting the sense of promise the *banlieue* once held" (187). In other words, according to her race functions in the *banlieues* as a term to name new inequalities whose origins, linked to global economic change, are so complex and abstract that they defy easy identification and classification.

My analysis of the meanings and uses of race in the outer city of Limoges adds another layer of evidence in support of Epstein's conclusions. It seems significant to note that no one I met in Limoges recognized the conflicting approaches and beliefs that emerged during the American civil rights movement. Despite the radically different views held by such figures as Martin Luther King Jr. and Malcolm X, my interlocutors presented the struggle for racial equality in the United States as a single, cohesive narrative. And ultimately for them, this narrative was one that inspired hope. It was a story of triumph and uplift in the face of crushing adversity. Racism, they recognized, still existed in the United States, but legal segregation had been overcome, and this, they maintained, was thanks to the *collective efforts and collaborative engagement of the entire black community*. In the end, racism for these young Limougeauds was the opposite of *solidarité*. It was a breakdown of the obligations of mutual respect and communal support that they held necessary for the greater good and the well-being of society. In short, it was a particularly corrosive form of individualism. And yet the neoliberal reforms underway in the *banlieues* have put a positive spin on individualism. Since the mid-1980s, young people living in France's outer cities have increasingly been exhorted to demonstrate personal responsibility and self-empowerment, particularly when it comes to building a productive future for themselves. This goal is however out of reach for many, as stable job opportunities continue to evaporate and precarious forms of employment fill the gap. Claiming racism, it seems to me, was above all an oblique way of pushing back against this particular contradiction. In the final analysis, my interlocutors' distortion of the American race story reflects a complex interplay of global flows, shifting economic conditions, pragmatic concerns, and ideological constraints. Could this condition give rise to new collective identities? Are France's *banlieues* birthing representatives of what some are calling the "precariat"? These questions are the focus of the next chapter.

5 Precariat Rising?

Articulating Social Position
around the 2006 CPE Protests

On Sunday, March 12, 2006, Prime Minister Dominique de Villepin made a special appearance on TF1's eight o'clock evening news to defend the CPE. This easy-hire, easy-fire employment contract, designed to spur employers to take on young people safe in the knowledge that they would not be bound by France's rigid employment laws, had already provoked weeks of protest, including walkouts by high school and university students and no less than two days of general strikes across France. Recently, upwards of three hundred students had staged a sit-in at the prestigious Sorbonne, ending during the early hours of the morning of March 11 with their forcible removal. Shaky footage broadcast by the news media that afternoon showed out-of-control student protestors clashing violently under cover of night with helmeted, baton-wielding, tear-gas-canister-throwing riot squads. Responding to these troubling images, Villepin pled the CPE's case and, in the process, attempted to portray the student opposition as misguided. The CPE, he argued, was not intended for them; "at-risk youth" from France's troubled *banlieues* were its target. "So you mean to say," Claire Chazal, the weekend news anchor, probed, "that you're not addressing these university students whom we've seen demonstrating?" Villepin responded,

> [The CPE] is meant for those who have the most trouble finding employment, those who go from short-term job to short-term job, from periods

of training to periods of temporary work, those who are unable to find stable jobs for years at a time, those who aren't offered any jobs at all. We had a crisis in our public housing projects, we're quick to forget, a crisis in our public housing projects, several months back. Unemployment among outer-city youth is between 40 and 50 percent. What's our response to those young people? That's the question that we have to answer this evening. Listening to what some people have said, you'd think that everything was fine, that we needn't change a thing. Youth unemployment is at 23 percent, 40 percent among those who lack degrees. So, confronted by this *précarité*, what should we do? Do we stand with our arms crossed, like we've done for so many years? Do we look the other way? Or, do we seek solutions? I've proposed the CPE.

Chazal agreed with the prime minister about the concern of *précarité* but disputed the distinction he had drawn, cautioning that outer-city youth felt as if they were being "put into a particular category," which, she insisted, "causes unease." For her, the threat of *précarité* was not limited to outer-city youth. Describing the CPE as a "gash" (*entaille*) to France's social model and a "violation" (*entorse*) of France's tradition of state welfare, she argued that rather than reduce *précarité* for a few, the measure would increase it for many.[1]

Chazal's comments that evening reflected widespread anxiety in France over the expansion of *précarité*. As the well-known sociologist Robert Castel put it in a piece he penned for the national daily *Le Monde*, for many in France the CPE was just "the tip of the iceberg." Secure employment, he maintained, was no longer the rule; it was becoming the exception (Castel 2006). "*Précarité* for all, the norm of the future," echoed a headline that appeared in *Le Monde Diplomatique* (Lefresne 2006). For some, the expansion of *précarité* meant the erasure of social classes, as what was once seen as the fate of only society's most destitute members was now becoming a common experience (Le Boucher 2006).

The idea that *précarité* constitutes a major concern today is hardly limited to France. British economist Guy Standing (2011) has pointed to recent bouts of unrest across the globe, from the 2005 riots in France to the Den Plirono protests in Greece to the Arab Spring in parts of the Middle East to the international Occupy movement, arguing that increasing employment insecurity in the global market system of the twenty-first century is yielding a troubling new category of people—a group he dubs the "precariat." This class-in-the-making, Standing suggests, is dangerous because it is, as yet, devoid of a collective consciousness and therefore voice. Both angry and anxious, its members are liable to turn from "strugglers into deviants and loose cannons prone to listen to populist politicians and demagogues" (2011, 132). The only way to rein the precariat in, the only way to prevent it from becoming a "monster," Standing asserts, is to draw it into the political process by helping it to become a class for itself.

My aim in this chapter is to interrogate this notion of a precariat, which, in France at least, garnered a great deal of attention during the CPE struggle and has since attracted widespread popular and academic interest (e.g., Autain 2012; Castel 2011; Chabanet, Dufour, and Royall 2012). By examining how my interlocutors in Limoges's housing projects interpreted the proposed employment contract and the series of rallies and demonstrations it generated, beginning in February and stretching into April, when the measure was finally repealed, I attempt to disentangle what exactly claims of a swelling precariat meant to them. Curiously, most of the young people I knew in Limoges's outer city distanced themselves from the massive street protests the CPE provoked. Why was this case? Surely they more than many in France had a stake in staving off employment insecurity. Answering this question, I argue, raises others about the rise of the so-called precariat. Namely, in what ways might this term conceal or obscure other, long-standing structural inequalities?

The Contrat Première Embauche

The Contrat première embauche, announced by Villepin's administration in mid-January 2006 as part of the Loi pour l'égalité des chances (Law for equal opportunities) and scrapped the following April in the face of massive protests, can be seen as both a continuation of past employment policy and a departure from it. Like previous initiatives, the CPE aimed at easing access to work for unemployed youth, especially those defined as being "at-risk."[2] However, it was not a subsidized contract. The CPE promised neither tax breaks nor salary support to employers, as earlier programs had.[3] Instead, in the hopes of spurring job growth the CPE took direct aim at France's rigid labor regulations, proposing to ease restrictions concerning employee termination.

As explained in Article 8 of the Loi pour l'égalité des chances, the CPE was to resemble a traditional CDI, the permanent employment contract, but with several notable exceptions.[4] It would be limited to firms in the market sector with at least twenty-one employees, and it could only be used to hire young people twenty-five or under.[5] In addition, the CPE would stipulate a mandatory "consolidation period" (*période de consolidation*) of two years, during which time employers could terminate the contract without having to provide justification. This was the point that proved most contentious.

Making sense of the controversy surrounding the CPE's consolidation period requires some familiarity with French labor law. In the postwar years the French government adopted numerous measures aimed at securing workers' rights. These included, among other things, the requirement that employers provide notification well in advance of letting employees go, that they base dismissals on strictly objective grounds, and, in the absence of employee fault or misconduct, that they provide severance pay (Howell 1992; Gaudu 1996; Bobbio 2007). Today, all employment contracts in France provide for a probation period during which employers can dismiss new hires and not be held to these requirements. In the case of a CDI, the trial period is optional. When implemented, it can vary in length, usually from a few days for unskilled workers to up to six months for high-level executives (Serverin 2007).[6]

The CPE's consolidation period was similar to the trial period of a traditional CDI. In fact, during the CPE protests the term *période d'essai* (trial period) was widely used both on the streets and in the news media in reference to it. There were, however, important differences. After the first month of employment, the CPE would have required employers to give two weeks' notice to employees they planned to let go. After six months of employment, the length of notice would have increased to one month. The CPE's consolidation period also differed in terms of severance pay. If, after four months of employment, employers decided to back out of a CPE, dismissed employees would have been entitled to compensation totaling 8 percent of pay earned since the beginning of their contract. They would also have been able to collect a fixed allowance of 490 euros per month, paid by the government for the next two months. Table 3 provides a comparison of the CDI and the CPE, indicating, among other characteristics, overviews of their respective probationary periods.

TABLE 3: Comparison of the CDI and the CPE

Sources: For CDI, http://lexinter.net/Legislation5/contrat_travail.htm; for CPE, http://www.assemblee-nationale.fr/12/projets/pl2787.asp.

Sector

CDI: Market or non-market
CPE: Market only

Size of Business

CDI: All businesses
CPE: Businesses with more than twenty employees

Eligible Employees

CDI: All employees, regardless of age
CPE: Employees under age twenty-six

Length of Contract

CDI: Open-ended
CPE: Open-ended

Probation Period

CDI: Not mandated; can last from two weeks to six months

CPE: "Consolidation period" of two years; apprenticeships, internships, or CDDs completed at same place of employment are subtracted from two years

Termination

CDI: Employee can be terminated at any time; dismissal must be justified by "real and serious" cause; the employer must first meet with employee to disclose reasons for dismissal; notification of termination must be sent by certified mail

CPE: During consolidation period, employee can be terminated at any time without justification; employer must notify employee of termination by certified mail; employee cannot be dismissed because of pregnancy, personal convictions, or matters relating to private life; union representatives have additional guarantees

Notification of Termination

CDI: Between one and two months depending on length of time worked

CPE: After one month, notification period is obligatory and increases with time worked: two weeks for one to six months worked, one month for more than six months worked

Severance Pay

CDI: Excluding termination due to gross employee misconduct, employee is due compensation equaling 10 percent of gross annual salary; additionally, employee is due 10 percent of daily pay for each vacation day not taken

CPE: If contract is broken, employer owes employee compensation equaling 8 percent of total gross salary paid since start of contract; additionally, employer must pay 2 percent of same salary to UNEDIC (French agency that manages unemployment benefits)

Unemployment Benefits

CDI: Employee is eligible for unemployment benefits if having worked six months within the last twenty-two months; benefits are calculated based on earned income

CPE: If employee is not already eligible for unemployment benefits, after four months of service is eligible to receive a two-month, fixed daily allowance of EUR 16.40, financed by the state

Training Eligibility

CDI: Employee has right to seek professional training after first year of service

CPE: Employee has right to seek professional training after first month of service

Renewal

CDI: Not applicable

CPE: If CPE is canceled before end of consolidation period, a new CPE may be signed between the same employer and employee after a waiting period of three months

---

In some respects, the consolidation period of the CPE was more protective of workers than the trial period of a traditional CDI. It proved controversial, however, because of its proposed two-year duration, which far exceeded the normal six-month maximum length of the CDI's trial period.[7] Although during those two years employees hired under a CPE and then subsequently let go would have been able to take their employers to court, the onus would have rested on the employees to prove that their termination was unjustified.[8] Critics consequently claimed that the CPE represented a violation of French labor law.

Anxiety over the possibility the CPE seemed to offer employers to fire new employees at will during the consolidation period fueled broad public opposition.[9] Such job insecurity, the measure's detractors argued, would translate into broader forms of *précarité*, including increased difficulty renting housing and obtaining bank loans. The government was quick to respond to such criticism. Villepin insisted that all employees holding a CPE would be eligible for a government-sponsored housing loan program, which could be used to finance the security deposit required by most landlords. Villepin also met with the umbrella organization of France's banks, the Fédération bancaire française, which, following their discussion, issued a memo to lending institutions urging them to treat the CPE like any CDI when reviewing loan applicants' files.

These actions were not enough to muzzle the CPE's critics. There was also the problem of insurance, they pressed. Most private landlords in France take out insurance in case of nonpayment of rent. Their ability to obtain this insurance and the attractiveness of the terms offered to them depend largely on prospective tenants' creditworthiness. Similarly, most banks require loan customers to acquire insurance to protect against unexpected loss of income. The willingness of insurers to provide this type of security is determined by an applicant's job history and the likelihood of his or her continued employment. Because no agreements had been reached with France's insurance companies, opponents of the CPE argued that employees would face almost certain *précarité* during the two-year consolidation period. Landlords would prefer tenants holding a traditional CDI, because such leases could more easily be insured, and banks would not lend to young people with a CPE if they were unable to secure their loans.[10] Widely seen as targeting an entire generation, the CPE thus tended to be perceived as the materialization of decades-old fears in France about the generalization of *précarité* and the creeping expansion of social exclusion.

The CPE Protests in Limoges

Limoges, like most other French cities, witnessed a flurry of activity during the CPE protests. On February 7, the first of the major rallies, organized by labor unions, political parties on the left, high-schoolers, and students from the University of Limoges's Faculté des lettres and Faculté des sciences, brought together an estimated five thousand demonstrators who marched through the streets of the city chanting derogatory slogans about

FIG. 15. During the first demonstration against the CPE held in Limoges on February 7, 2006, high school and university students marched down the Boulevard Gambetta from the Place d'Aine to city hall brandishing a makeshift banner reading, "On n'est pas la Kleenex génération! [We are not the Kleenex generation!]." Along the way, they chanted, "Villepin, salaud, le peuple aura ta peau! [Villepin, you bastard, the people will have your hide!]."

Prime Minister Villepin, brandishing makeshift banners denouncing *précarité*, staging sit-ins at major intersections, and lighting firecrackers and blowing whistles.[11] This first demonstration was followed by a number of others, each attracting increasing numbers of supporters, before Villepin finally withdrew the CPE in April. According to local newspaper estimates, between ten thousand and fifteen thousand people turned out for the next major demonstration, held on March 7; another fifteen thousand to twenty thousand protestors took to the streets on March 18; approximately thirty thousand demonstrators turned out on March 28; and upwards of forty thousand Limougeauds clamored against the CPE on April 4 (fig. 15).[12]

Although the demonstrators varied in age, the "anti-CPE movement," as the series of rallies, protests, and marches against the proposed employment contract came to be known, found particular support among young people, especially high school and university students. The local press highlighted this detail, one article noting that "students, and especially high-schoolers, were the force behind the demonstration" (Ruiz 2006). According to another report, "high school and university students led the march, chanting slogans henceforth known by all" (Marmain 2006a). These accounts confirmed my own impression that few "at-risk" youth participated in the demonstrations. In fact, although I attended all of the major marches and rallies, I only came across two young people I knew from the outer city. Given the size of some of these gatherings, especially as the movement gained momentum in late March and early April, it is, of course, possible that I failed to notice others in the throngs. But few of my interlocutors told me they had taken part in the demonstrations, either.

In addition to these major marches and rallies, a number of smaller demonstrations marked the anti-CPE movement in Limoges. On March 16 roughly six thousand people, primarily students, gathered at the Gare des Bénédictins, where they barricaded the tracks leading into and out of the city for more than two hours (Lavallée 2006a). Other disruptive acts followed: on March 30 approximately one thousand demonstrators, mostly high school students, formed a human chain across the four-lane road bordering the Vienne leading to the A20 highway, the main artery connecting Limoges to points north and south (Marmain 2006b); on April 6 about fifteen hundred students occupied some of the city's major intersections and bridges, including the Pont Neuf and the recently inaugurated Nouveau Pont, which has since been named the Pont du Clos-Moreau (Lavallée 2006b); and on April 7, student demonstrators blocked the entrance to the board of education's regional offices on the rue François Chénieux ("Lycéens et étudiants" 2006).

As in many other French cities, the movement in Limoges included widespread student strikes and, in some cases, the occupation of schools. On March 8, students from the University of Limoges's Faculté des lettres went on strike, followed on March 10 by students from the Faculté des sciences and the Faculté de droit and on March 15 by students attending the local Institut universitaire de technologie, a technical school granting

FIG. 16. Like other unions, Jeunes CGT, the youth collective of the CGT, plastered city walls and signposts with flyers denouncing the CPE and *précarité* and calling for participation in the protests.

associate degrees. On March 13 the first high-schoolers, from the Lycée Raoul-Dautry and the Lycée Gay-Lussac, went on strike; by March 17, students at eight additional local high schools were also refusing to attend classes.

Local chapters of some of France's principal labor unions were heavily involved in the planning and implementation of the demonstrations in Limoges, as some of the flyers plastered on buildings and signposts across the city at the time attested (fig. 16).[13] A voluminous body of scholarship has documented an overall decline in participation in the organized labor movement in France since the mid-1970s, especially among the younger generation (e.g., Andolfatto and Labbé 2009; Amadieu 1999; Mouriaux 1998; Touraine, Wieviorka, and Dubet 1984), and some research has indicated that today's youth are hostile toward it (e.g., Beaud and Pialoux

1999, 355–74). Could the unions' presence during the CPE protests signal a renewed interest in the labor movement?

A week before the February 7 demonstration, I attended an organizational meeting, held by Jeunes CGT, the local youth collective of the Confédération générale du travail (CGT; General confederation of labor). Despite a call sent out to the area's high schools and the University of Limoges, no students showed up for the event. In fact, only four individuals (besides me) attended. I learned that they were all longtime members of the collective and, with but one exception, were all over twenty-five.[14] Before the meeting began, I turned to Sandra, my contact within the group, to ask how many young people belonged to the collective. She sighed and told me that membership had plummeted in the last decade or so. This decrease in participation mirrored a decline in resources. Because of reduced funds, the group could no longer afford to maintain a permanent office, she explained, but instead shared meeting space with various neighborhood associations. As I scanned the painted cinderblock walls of the vacant Beaubreuil apartment where we were seated, I spotted several notices bearing the familiar red, white, and yellow logo of the CGT, but these were besieged by a multitude of other flyers. One announced an evening of "painting and good humor for babies, parents, and artists." Another promised "guidance and support" for recently arrived immigrants. Still others spoke of a tenant advocacy group, or called for volunteers to help "beautify" the neighborhood by joining forces to "pick up trash, mow grass, and trim hedges." A testament to the collective energies and efforts of at least some residents of Beaubreuil, the hodgepodge of papers splashed across the cramped room's beige walls betrayed the lack of resources of any single initiative.

Discussion during the meeting centered on how best to rally local youth against the CPE. "This contract is garbage," Sandra began. "We need to get young people involved." This charge was met with familiar criticism about the supposed deficiencies of today's youth.[15] "They're disinterested, they're not politically engaged," one attendee opined. "They can't see beyond the end of their noses," another concurred. Earlier, Sandra had told me that she held the older generation at least partially responsible for young people's disengagement from the labor movement. At thirty-two years of age, Sandra was a full-time postal worker and a union delegate. She explained that she had struggled for many years, bouncing from one short-term contract to another before finally "winning big" with her current CDI. Sandra recalled how her grandfather, who labored most of his adult life in one of Limoges's shoe factories before it went under in the 1970s, used to tell her stories about his participation in collective acts of resistance against the factory's management. "He's my inspiration," she confided. "The problem today," she continued, "is that not many young people have the same reference. My grandfather was a representative of a dying culture. Our own parents did not teach us anything about activism. They assumed things were getting better on their own, that social advancement was real. Well, they were wrong. Now, unemployment and *précarité* are gobbling all of us up, including them." Drawing on this understanding, Sandra appealed to the collective's members, asserting that it was their shared responsibility to "educate" the younger generation. "If we don't show them that together we can make a difference," she insisted, "no one will."

"Where do we begin?" asked Sandra's companions. Since time was short before the first planned day of protests, the group decided to start small by targeting Interval, the youth hangout in the Val de l'Aurence housing project.[16] They planned to "plaster" the center's walls with anti-CPE flyers and hold an information session and rally the day before the general strike. The objective was to convince the mostly out-of-work youth who spent their time there to join in the protests the following day. Despite the enthusiasm these concrete plans seemed to generate among the collective's members, in the end nothing came of them. The director of Interval, although "personally opposed" to the CPE, denied the collective's request, arguing that because Interval was partially subsidized by the government the center could not be used to protest state initiatives.

"All United against the CPE"?

The CPE attracted a great deal of attention in the national media. Indeed, *Le Monde* alone published well over four hundred articles about it between the day the measure was first presented in mid-January and April 10, when Villepin finally announced that it would be retracted.[17] All of the major television networks spent considerable time discussing the proposal, whether during regular newscasts or specially organized roundtables, debates, or interviews, and countless radio broadcasts were devoted to it. Alongside these more traditional forms of media, the Internet also served as an important vehicle of information. Over the course of the CPE struggle, myriad blogs and message boards appeared in which people debated the measure and frequently planned actions against it.[18]

Although the CPE struggle was a national movement, coordinated by various umbrella groups and organizations, including labor unions, student unions (especially the Union nationale des étudiants de France [UNEF]; National union of students of France), and leaders of the political left, the protests took place at the local level—literally on the streets of cities and towns. In Limoges, local media outlets provided considerable coverage of the struggle. This reporting tended to focus on the theme of *solidarité*. With headlines such as "All united against the CPE!" ("Tous unis" 2006) and "All together against the CPE!" (Catus 2006b), the local press suggested that universal condemnation of the proposed contract had forged social cohesion.

The idea of solidarity implies a union of individuals or groups, which many news accounts of the CPE struggle went on to identify. An article on the city's first major anti-CPE demonstration published in *L'Écho de la Haute Vienne*, the region's left-leaning daily, offered the following description of the protestors:

> The [high school students] gathered in large numbers at the Place d'Aine to contest the pertinence of a governmental measure that would turn them into an underclass began heading toward city hall at 10:15 a.m., loudly making their dissatisfaction known along the way. After occupying the Place Léon-Betoulle and the Carrefour Tourny, they stopped in front of the Préfecture [municipal police headquarters], where employees, united under the banners of [various labor unions and political parties], awaited them. . . . Given this impressive turnout,

a new itinerary was chosen, which led the crowd through the Place Denis-Dussoubs to the Avenue François-Chénieux, where university students . . . joined their voices to this procession that clearly wanted all to take notice. ("La mobilisation" 2006)

Lines drawn in the article were based on activity (e.g., students, employees) but also life stages, suggesting cooperation across generations. *Le Populaire du Centre*, the other daily widely read in the city, made this point even more explicit. In block letters across the paper's front page the day following the February 7 demonstration, the headline echoed the protestors' banners: "We are not the Kleenex generation!" It was immediately preceded by another title in slightly smaller but still imposing type: "All generations stand up to the 'institutionalization of précarité.'" The article that followed stressed that high school and university students had not marched alone; there were also "hundreds of workers and union members . . . and hundreds of retirees, reaffirming their commitment to *intergenerational solidarity*" (Bourgnon 2006a; emphasis added).

If this article insisted on the goodwill of older generations toward the younger one, other reports suggested that young people were equally concerned about their elders. Summarizing a demonstration organized by retirees toward the end of March to protest a government initiative seeking to reform the state pension system, an article titled "A breath of solidarity, Rue de la Préfecture," recounted, for example, how a procession of high school and university students joined in to support the protesting seniors. "This was," according to the author, "a moment of *intergenerational convergence to challenge neoliberal policies*" (Davoine 2006b; emphasis added).

The idea that the CPE represented a significant step away from France's model of social welfare toward a more liberal style of capitalism—many accounts used the word *neoliberal* to describe the measure—was widely embraced by the local press, which unambiguously denounced Villepin's proposal, suggesting that it would without doubt make the problem of *précarité* even worse. Some of the more mocking nicknames for the CPE, such as "Contrat première embûche" (First obstacle contract), "Contrat précarité exclusion" (Contract for precarity and exclusion), and "Contrat poubelle embauche" (Junk job contract), used liberally by the local media at the time, are illustrative of this stance.[19] As the movement gained momentum, the media in Limoges and beyond cast the struggle in decidedly ideological terms: the protestors were portrayed as tireless warriors, fighting the good fight against the threat of *précarité*, while the government, and especially Prime Minister Villepin and President Jacques Chirac, were represented as bungling bureaucrats, out of touch with the anxieties of the masses. Consider the following passage from an article published after Chirac announced during a televised address to the nation that he planned to pass the Loi pour l'égalité des chances, including the amendment instituting the CPE, with minor revisions:

> After the poor televised performance of a president frequently off-topic, the high school students understood that it is important to be mobilized now more than ever. . . . Resolved to choose the world in which they want to live, these young people are also expressing, beyond the question of the CPE, a desire to take on, at least symbolically, the notion of *précarité* . . . . Outspoken and determined to act to put pressure on an administration deaf to its demands, this youth has also demonstrated imagination and enthusiasm. It is too bad that citizen action is not part of the *baccalauréat* exam. If it were, it is sure that our inept President of the Republic and his political cronies would fail to impress the examiners. (Davoine 2006a)

Other news stories appearing during the CPE struggle made similar claims about the protestors and the government. One of these announced "No, the street will not yield!" (Muia 2006), and another told of a government that "bullied through" legislation in order to pursue its "labor-code-breaking" agenda ("Sept mars" 2006).

The local media's suggestion that the CPE, if allowed to pass into law, would undeniably create more victims of *précarité* was unambiguous; much less obvious was exactly who those victims would be. Some accounts argued that "the CPE heralds the weakening of the employment contract for all workers" ("Sept mars" 2006). Most news coverage, however, suggested that the proposed employment contract would primarily affect young people. Significantly, few of these stories further distinguished among members of the younger generation by taking into account factors such as social background or level of education. Instead, by and large the press suggested that all young people would be at equal risk of *précarité* if the CPE passed.[20]

The media's frequent use of the catchall term *jeunesse* (youth) is illustrative of this tendency. One news report in Limoges suggested that the CPE constituted a form of "discrimination" against "la jeunesse" ("FO: Appel" 2006), and another explicitly warned that the CPE would "doom la jeunesse to [a life of] précarité" ("Sept mars" 2006). As the anti-CPE movement gained momentum, the term *jeunesse* was sometimes used interchangeably with more precise labels, such as "high school students" or "university students," to designate the protestors, thereby not only suggesting that these young people had one voice but also that this single voice represented every young person's voice, including the voices of youth who may not have participated in the protests at all. One news headline trumpeted: "La jeunesse replies, 'Resistance!'" The report that followed, however, concerned a vote held the previous day by *university students* to continue striking, even after Villepin had promised to retract the CPE (Catus 2006a).[21] By presenting young people in Limoges—and, by extension, the rest of France—as a homogeneous category, news coverage of the anti-CPE movement effectively obscured any possibly meaningful social distinctions among them. For the young men and women I came to know in Limoges's housing projects, this perspective proved particularly troubling.

Initial understandings of the CPE among my interlocutors varied, though reactions to it were almost always the same: on the whole, they expressed concern over the measure, although not necessarily outright hostility toward it. Before the demonstrations got under way in early February, none of the young people I knew brought up the CPE spontaneously. Instead, I had to introduce the topic, as I did, for example, at Interval in mid-January. Sitting at the bar, I was talking with several regulars when, during a lull in the conversation, I happened to glance down at *Le Monde*, which, along with *Le Populaire du Centre* and the sports daily *L'Équipe*, was always on hand. A fairly lengthy front-page article addressed Villepin's new employment project. It turned out that most of my companions were already aware of the measure, and they tended to think it was a bad idea. "It's the same bullshit. That CPE is basically the same as a CDD," Ousmane maintained. "It just means more *précarité* for us." Although Ousmane complained about the CPE's consolidation period, insisting that employers would fire new employees "whenever" and "without remorse" right up until the end of the two-year trial period, he did not think it was much different from previous programs—he even went on to compare it to the Emplois-jeunes initiative, of which his older brother had been a beneficiary.[22] I heard similar comments elsewhere: youth I knew in the housing projects were more or less familiar with the terms of the CPE and related it to the state-aided contracts that they, family members, or friends had held in the past.

That these youth likened the CPE to past government initiatives seems significant. Recall that Villepin's proposed measure marked a rather substantial departure from previous youth employment policy in France insofar as it, unlike any of the state-subsidized contracts that came before it, did not promise employers financial support in the form of tax breaks or salary subsidies but instead sought to create jobs by loosening regulations on employment termination. This was the point that proved so controversial—the rallying cry of the anti-CPE demonstrators. For my interlocutors, however, this difference seemed to matter little, at least before the movement gained momentum.[23] Mostly longtime participants in past employment schemes, which generally functioned on the basis of generating short-term contracts, they had become accustomed to a relative lack of job security and consequently saw the CPE as a continuation of, not a shift in, familiar government policy.[24] As such, my interlocutors understood the CPE as being geared specifically toward *young people like themselves*, that is, the "at-risk youth" of France, who struggle to find stable work, or often any work at all. As "at-risk youth," they tended to see *précarité* as being distinctly *their* problem. This perception is perhaps not all that surprising. After all, many of these young people met frequently with social service providers, some since early childhood. As we saw in chapter 3, during these encounters they were regularly reminded of their "fragility" and "vulnerability." This view was further reinforced at school and in the job market, where they tended to accumulate failures. Faced by homogenizing messages about *précarité* and media images of protesting high school and university students during the CPE struggle, they tended to have strong reactions. Examining these against their own experiences helps us to flesh out not only their perspectives on the notion of *précarité* but also, more generally, what they viewed as their social destiny compared to the possibilities they imagined to be available to other groups.

Toward mid-March, when the anti-CPE movement was in full swing, I sat down with Thomas during his afternoon break in the atrium of the outer-city shopping center where he worked as a stock boy. A resident since birth of the surrounding neighborhood, composed mostly of low-income public housing, Thomas dropped out of school at age sixteen. For the next three years he strung together odd jobs, mostly in construction, before finally landing a full-time position in the pharmacy located in his neighborhood. I had met Thomas the previous fall through a social worker who handled his case when he was looking for work. According to her, Thomas was a real "success story." Generally affable, on this sunny March afternoon he was uncharacteristically irritated. "I just don't get it," he complained, gesturing ambiguously toward the large glass entranceway of the shopping center, which looked out onto a road leading toward the city center. "Those students protesting," he continued, "they don't work, they don't have any experience in the real world. So why are they so concerned about the CPE?" Thomas explained that earlier that morning, while running errands in the city center, he got stuck for over an hour at a protestor-mounted roadblock and as a result was late for his afternoon shift. Fariba, who also lived in Limoges's outer city but who, unlike Thomas, continued to struggle to find work since dropping out of high school three years earlier, echoed Thomas's resentment of the protestors: "Those high school kids and university students, they have it so easy. What do they know about work or *précarité*? Let them walk a day in my shoes!"

Although some young people in the housing projects avowed their incomprehension over student involvement in the protests, others offered possible explanations; fighting *précarité* usually was not one, however. Jonathan, like many of my interlocutors, did not support the CPE and was happy that so many people across France were standing up to Villepin, but he questioned the student protestors' motivations. "When you see all those high school kids on strike, even some of the university students, I really don't agree," he told me. Prodded to explain, he stated that when he was a student, sometimes strikes were called but he and his classmates did not always know (or care to know) why. "We just wanted to skip class. We just wanted to have a good time." Jonathan suspected similar motives among the CPE protestors. "The thing is, it's springtime. The weather is getting nicer. You don't want to work when you're in high school, so the CPE was a good excuse to go on strike." Rachid, who held a part-time job as a monitor in the city's central high school, had similar doubts about the student protestors' sincerity. "Most of those bourgeois kids in the school where I work, they couldn't even tell you what the CPE is," he maintained, adding, "They went on strike because they were looking for an excuse to be outside, to skip classes." Jonathan and Rachid, like many other young people in Limoges's outer city, believed that the middle-class youth who participated in the CPE protests were motivated far less by a commitment to *solidarité* than by the pursuit of individual pleasure.

Although the majority of my interlocutors in the housing projects told me they did not participate in the protests, a few said they had become involved. Yanis, an eighteen-year-old living in Beaubreuil, took part in all of the major demonstrations and even made a trip to Lyon (a distance of four hundred kilometers) to attend a regional organizational meeting. Working on a BEP (*brevet d'études professionnelles*; vocational training certificate) in hotel services, he told me that he had tried, unsuccessfully at first, to convince his classmates to join the demonstrations.[25] "They weren't interested," he sighed. "They told me the CPE wouldn't affect them."

Yanis's participation in the anti-CPE movement and his account of his classmates' lack of concern over it muddy the water somewhat. One would expect that students attending a vocational high school would feel at least somewhat threatened by *précarité*. Yanis certainly did. When asked to explain, he pointed to a hierarchy of academic degrees. Whereas he was completing a BEP, which is usually earned after successful completion of two years of courses beyond junior high school, many of his classmates were working on a *baccalauréat technologique* (vocational high school degree) with the expectation of continuing on to a *brevet de technicien supérieur* (BTS), a senior technician certificate. They would be in school for at least another two years, many of them more, and by then the law could have changed, Yanis explained. Furthermore, according to him, many of them believed, perhaps naively, that a BTS would translate into a stable, good-paying job. It was after all a postsecondary degree, and this was more than most of their parents had achieved. As for Yanis, he confided that he was not sure he would even finish his BEP. "School's not really my thing," he admitted. Instead, he dreamed—rather unrealistically, he confessed—of operating a cruise ship on the Mediterranean. "I've just gotta win the lottery first!" he added with his characteristic grin.

Yanis's participation in the anti-CPE movement suggests he was worried about *précarité*. However, it does not necessarily indicate that he felt a connection to the other protestors. His comments about the movement's leadership are illuminating in this regard:

> You know, that guy, I can't remember his name, he's the head of the national student union, he was on TV all the time. Well, he's just like the politicians. He was there to be seen, to advance his career, end of story. He doesn't give a damn about *précarité*, he doesn't give a damn about young people like me. When they retracted the CPE, he was there, all smiles in front of the cameras, patting himself on the back. But *précarité* still exists! That guy, he doesn't care about our problems. It really disgusts me.

As the anti-CPE movement gained traction, Bruno Julliard, the president of UNEF, became the student opposition's most visible spokesperson. Yanis's comments suggest that he did not believe that the student protestors, whose interests Julliard was supposed to represent, much less France's political elite, really understand the difficulties he and his peers faced. Rather, in his estimation both groups acted in calculated self-interest.

If Yanis appeared to be genuinely concerned about *précarité*, other outer-city youth, I was told, participated in the anti-CPE movement for far less ideological reasons. In the housing projects, some young people, it was explained to me, attempted to arrange CDDs and CTTs strategically. In France, following six months of employment (the equivalent of 910 hours) an individual is entitled to monthly unemployment benefits totaling 80 percent of his or her average monthly salary until finding new employment or for six months, whichever period is shorter. Some youth, I was told, worked during the winter months to claim unemployment benefits in the summer. Since the CPE was a long-term contract, it would have effectively put a stop to this practice. According to some of my interlocutors, if young people from the housing projects participated in the anti-CPE movement, it was likely because they hoped to ensure the continuation of a system they had learned to manipulate to their advantage, however small that advantage may have been.[26]

The Specter of the *Casseur*

Although in general during the anti-CPE movement media outlets presented youth as a homogeneous category (*la jeunesse*), at times, and especially when demonstrations became violent, some reports drew a distinction by invoking a familiar opposition: *casseurs*, these accounts suggested, lurked among the "genuine" or "real" protestors. The figure of the *casseur* as it is commonly recognized in France today emerged in the last decades of the twentieth century. The term is derived from the slang word *casse*, meaning "break-in" or "robbery." In fact, until the end of the 1960s a *casseur* was most often understood to be a burglar (Pierrat 2003). In 1970 the French government passed an "anti-*casseur*" law. This new legislation had nothing to do with theft but instead aimed at criminalizing the activity of the semi-anarchist groups that emerged in the wake of the May 1968 student and worker revolts. Anyone found near a smashed store or car window (the verb *casser* means "to break") during a protest risked detention.[27] Since the 1970s the term *casseur* has become strongly associated with gratuitous violence during protests, and it delineates two sets of youth. One is disciplined, nonviolent, and organized around a common rallying call; its members are viewed as legitimate protestors. The other, composed of "hoodlums" and "troublemakers," is seen as irreverent, uncontrolled, and uncontrollable; its members' sole purpose, it is thought, is to loot, destroy, and antagonize agents of law and order. The *casseur* is widely presented as an illegitimate presence at demonstrations (Gaubert 1995).[28]

At about 3 p.m. on March 23, a massive, student-led protest headed down the Boulevard du Montparnasse in central Paris toward the Esplanade des Invalides, where an anti-CPE rally was to take place.[29] This vast lawn extending northward from Napoléon Bonaparte's final resting place, the Hôtel des Invalides, to the Seine had been deliberately chosen by the student leadership in consultation with the police. The absence of stores and parked cars—in other words, potential targets—would lessen the appeal of the demonstration to *casseurs*, or at least that is what was hoped. But trouble struck swiftly. Before the throngs of protestors reached the Esplanade, plainclothes officers and UNEF members stationed in the crowd began signaling attacks. *Casseurs*, they reported, were beating down demonstrators and stealing their cellphones, MP3 players, and cameras. According to one account, the *casseurs* moved like tornadoes, banding together to participate in an assault only to break apart a few moments later; they repeated this cycle the length of the Boulevard du Montparnasse and the Boulevard des Invalides, before pouring onto the Esplanade, where they took aim at the police positioned around the lawn's perimeter (Dufresne 2013). By 7 p.m., when the "Battle of Les Invalides" ended, cars had been torched, stores and restaurants had been pillaged, and more than sixty people had been injured, including twenty-seven officers. That evening, all of France's major news networks devoted considerable coverage to the "shocking" and "disturbing" events that had transpired in the heart of Paris.

Just who were these *casseurs*? According to an article published in the national daily *Le Figaro*, the answer was obvious. "It's a rematch!"

opened the report on the events in Paris. The author went on to argue that the *casseurs* were primarily youth from Paris's outer city. They had infiltrated the students' demonstration, according to him, not to protest the CPE but rather to finish what they had started the previous fall during the riots that rocked cities across the country (Leclerc 2006). France's special police forces seemed to reach the same conclusion. Before the next major demonstration, on March 28, they stationed officers along the commuter rails serving the capital's outer-city neighborhoods, with the hope that frequent identity checks would dissuade would-be *casseurs* from joining the protests.

That the category *casseur* became virtually synonymous with that of *jeune de banlieue* during the CPE protests reflects a more general trend. Scholarship by Ivan Jablonka (2009) has demonstrated how this term fits into a long list of labels used in France to describe juvenile delinquents living on the fringes of society, from the *enfants révoltés* (rebellious children) of the end of the nineteenth century, to the *Apaches* of the Belle Époque, to the *blousons noirs* (black jackets) of the 1950s or the *loubards* (hoodlums) of the 1960s and 1970s. The difference between the term *casseur* and these other designations, Jablonka posits, is that in today's postcolonial context the word *casseur* has become "saturated with ethnicity." That is, today's young troublemakers from the margins are no longer just juvenile delinquents; they are also characterized as "black" or "Arab" (2009, 163).

In Limoges, the regional press tended to distinguish between local protests and those in larger cities, especially Paris, which were presented as far more violent. Declared a March 28 article in *Le Populaire du Centre*: "Is this a miracle specific to Limoges or to the countryside? Here, in any case, people demonstrate massively—like yesterday, in record numbers—but without ever boiling over into violence. This determination, this resolution . . . is never really given the credit is deserves" (Marmain 2006a). The few reports of violence or deviant behavior that received attention in the local press were usually minor, such as the account of the fifty-four-year-old man who exposed himself to a female student during one of the demonstrations, or the story about a group of teenagers who lit a firecracker and inadvertently burned an eighty-year-old woman at another rally. Such incidents tended to be described as "marginal."[30]

The reference to the countryside quoted above seems significant. It suggests that the violence witnessed in Paris was the result of underlying urban problems; Limoges, as a smaller, provincial city, did not suffer from this sort of trouble. In other words, even if Limoges may have an outer city, it has not experienced the same level of urban decay and ghettoization as Paris's periphery. As a result, its outer-city youth have not (not yet, at least) turned into *casseurs*. If they had participated in the protests—and the frequent use of the term *jeunesse* discussed earlier in this chapter suggests that local news professionals believed they had—they had done so with "determination" and "resolution." As we saw in the previous chapter, the local press similarly cast Limoges's peripheral neighborhoods as models of social integration at the time of the 2005 riots.

As for the young people I knew in Limoges's housing projects, they were less apt during the anti-CPE movement to contrast Limoges with larger urban centers. Instead, they argued that for the most part media representations of the *casseurs* were reductionist, even essentializing. Some interlocutors distanced themselves from the *casseurs*. "I hate to admit it, but a lot of those *casseurs* were from the outer city," said Thomas in reference to the Paris incident. He continued: "You have to understand. For some young people, it's their only way of getting noticed, of making a statement. It's their only recourse." However understandable he found them, Thomas did not approve of the *casseurs'* violent approach: "They'll tell you the system's against them, that it's not their fault." Reminding me of his own struggle to find work, he added, "If you get yourself motivated, if you're willing to accept the really tough jobs, the really dirty jobs, the ones no one else wants, you'll find work."[31] In Thomas's estimation, the *casseurs* did not share the same values as he. Other youth similarly condemned the violence but asserted that outer-city youth were not solely responsible for it. "All those *casseurs* in Paris were hooded," Mouloud noted, suggesting that anyone could have been hiding underneath their clothing. Still others insisted that violence has a legitimate place in protest; for them, linking these outbursts to specific groups was nonsensical.

Yanis, who spent considerable time participating in local demonstrations, offered the following description of his experience: "We exploded! We were so into the movement, we were so determined to revolt. We needed to express our anger. The police were right there. We didn't care if we got arrested. We had to break things!" As for Souad, she appealed to historical precedent: "The media shouldn't have singled out outer-city youth like that. Maybe they weren't doing anything. Maybe they were demonstrating like everyone else. Besides, a CPE protestor isn't necessarily someone who's especially peaceful. I won't go into May '68 with you, but whether you like it or not, France is a country that likes to break things. So, you can't just split a group into two parts like that and say that those people over there, they're just here to cause trouble." Souad pursued this idea by noting that at the local university where she was a student a number of classmates had reproached her, arguing that she, as a *jeune de quartier*, should have taken a special interest in defeating the CPE. Souad, who, in addition to her coursework held a part-time job at McDonald's, told me she did not have time to take part in the demonstrations. "I've had it with that distinction," she objected flatly, adding, "We're all the same, we're all struggling youth, we're all at risk of *précarité*. People shouldn't put others in boxes like that, all neatly tied up."

Compared to their commentary on the homogenizing accounts of *la jeunesse* circulating during the anti-CPE movement, my interlocutors' reactions to media coverage of the *casseurs* appear to be at odds. Generally, they claimed difference, arguing that they, as "outer-city" or "at-risk" youth, faced greater obstacles than other members of their generation when it came to finding and keeping good jobs. Yet when confronted by reports associating outer-city youth with the *casseurs*, they refused to be pigeonholed, asserting instead that they were no different from other young people, whether from the housing projects or not. How might this contradiction be explained?

Thinking about how the notion of *précarité* and the closely associated concept of *exclusion* are understood and explained in France is useful in this regard. As we saw in previous chapters, for the French, *précarité* is about more than just employment insecurity; it is considered a threat to society itself, because it is viewed as a cause and a consequence of an undoing of *solidarité*. When members of the media and other social commentators claimed during the anti-CPE movement that all youth were equally at risk of *précarité*, that an entire generation was sinking into a swelling precariat, my interlocutors took issue. Not to have done so would have meant accepting not only the denial or trivialization of the real social inequalities they faced day in and day out but also, possibly, their own relegation into an underclass. Indeed, if the middle-class student protestors were facing a social downgrading, my interlocutors interpreted this as meaning that those situated beneath them, such as themselves, would be pushed even further down, potentially into a position of *exclusion*. Their claims that they were the same as everyone else when confronted by media representations of the *casseurs* can be viewed as proceeding from the same logic. For them, the media unfairly associated all outer-city youth with these troublemakers, and because the *casseurs* were seen as already the victims of *précarité*, as already socially disqualified, their association with them suggested, in turn, their own social exclusion. Refusing to be thought of as *exclus*, my interlocutors disassociated themselves from the *casseurs* or attempted to contextualize their violent behavior. In either case, they contested what they saw as the tendency of members of the media to efface meaningful social difference through excessive generalization.

On another level, this discussion has demonstrated the mutability of the meanings people attach to social categories. Doubtless, few would challenge the idea that these meanings may shift over time. The example of the category *casseur* has provided a useful illustration of this. Perhaps less obvious is the variability of meanings across contexts. Whereas my interlocutors claimed the label "outer-city" or "at-risk" youth to counter the generalizations about young people produced during the anti-CPE movement, they rejected this same designation when it was associated with the negatively charged category of *casseur*. In both cases, their acceptance or refusal of the term was strategic. That is, it was always aimed at achieving a particular, desired result. In the end, we must admit that social categories such as these, but also other labels describing such constructs as race, ethnicity, or national origin, have no intrinsic meaning or value outside of the contexts in which they are put to use.

A Tale of Two Contracts

The sky was a curtain of gray, and a cold dampness, not unusual for the season, but certainly unwelcome, hung in the air on May 1, when I set forth with Véronique from underneath the naked plane trees lining the southern perimeter of the Place de la République to take part in the annual Labor Day march.[32] Despite the event's early hour, Véro had insisted that "loads" of kids from Jeunesse ouvrière chrétienne would be in attendance this year. "We're going to be out in record numbers to celebrate our victory over the CPE and to fight for the retraction of the CNE," she had declared confidently.[33] Even the poor weather that morning did not seem to dampen her spirits. Although Véro was alone when I arrived at the designated meeting point to help distribute handouts to passersby, she adamantly maintained that more Jocistes would show up. Only Lelia did, but, offering up some excuse about needing to help her mother, she left a few minutes later, before the march got under way.

The Contrat nouvelles embauches (CNE; New jobs contract) was seen as a "big brother" of sorts to the CPE. Instituted in the summer of 2005 by the newly appointed Villepin administration, this employment contract specified the same two-year consolidation period as the CPE, during which employees could be dismissed without justification. There were, however, two important differences: first, unlike the CPE, which was restricted to businesses with over twenty employees, the CNE was limited to companies counting twenty or fewer employees; second, it carried no age limitations, so any job applicant of legal working age, whether twenty-five and under or not, could be hired with a CNE.

The local press, like Véro, had anticipated a particularly strong turnout for the May First demonstration. "A May First more united than ever," proclaimed *Le Populaire du Centre* (Bourgnon 2006b); "A unified May First from the ashes of the CPE," heralded *L'Écho de la Haute Vienne* (Lavallée 2006c). According to these articles, the momentum witnessed during the CPE struggle would propel demonstrators onto the streets. "Workers of all ages, high school students and university students [will march] arm-in-arm on Monday," *Le Populaire* predicted. "This May First will have a particular flavor, a flavor of union victory . . . victory of having forged unity with the younger generation," asserted *L'Écho*. And while both papers recognized that demonstrators would march for a number of different causes, including education reform and immigration policy, "in the crosshairs [would be] the CNE" (Lavallée 2006c). Despite these projections, the local press reported the following day that only about two thousand people participated in the march—a far cry from the roughly forty-thousand-strong turnout registered in Limoges at the last of the major anti-CPE demonstrations.

This observation raises a question: Why did the CPE face so much opposition, while the CNE went relatively unchallenged?[34] According to some, the answer could be found in the timing of each bill's announcement. Unlike the CPE, which was presented to the public in January, the CNE was announced quietly and voted into law in August, when much of France was on vacation. Mobilizing people against it, critics argued, thus proved far more difficult. Others insisted that the academic calendar got in the way. The students who fought the CPE would have continued to strike until the CNE was also repealed, they maintained, but impending end-of-term examinations distracted them from this goal. Both of these explanations undoubtedly hold some measure of truth. However, the analysis offered in this chapter suggests a third explanation.

To begin, it seems unlikely that the limitations placed on the size of a business made the CNE any less offensive than the CPE. In the first decade of the twenty-first century, small businesses made up over 95 percent of all private firms in France (excluding agricultural production and certain financial institutions) and employed more than six million people, representing 35 percent of the country's workforce in private industry (Cadin and Trogan 2006). By contrast, the age-based restrictions that the CPE imposed did seem to matter. I have argued above that assumptions about social destiny underlay the CPE struggle. At issue was the question of who exactly was and should be affected by *précarité*. Most of the time, the news media suggested that the CPE would lead to a spread of this undesirable condition. Indeed, according to many local news articles all young people—*la jeunesse* in its entirety—would succumb to *précarité* if the measure passed. Although some news reports distinguished among youth, usually only a line was drawn between outer-city youth, labeled *casseurs*, and other members of the generation coming of age, who were cast as "real" demonstrators. These articles did not necessarily contradict those accounts suggesting that the CPE would spell *précarité* for all young people; rather, they implied that the *casseurs* were simply the first fatalities, a hint at what social life would be like more generally if *précarité* was not kept in check. Although during and after the CPE struggle, union leadership warned that the CNE would also generate *précarité*, the CNE was not distributed based on age *but potentially according to a person's position in society*. My analysis suggests that the middle-class students who contested the CPE deliberately ignored the CNE because they believed it would not affect them. The expectation was that its use would be limited to lower social strata, those with less educational capital. *Précarité*, along with the risk of social exclusion, would remain the destiny of the less fortunate.

This tale of two contracts, the CPE and the CNE, ultimately supports Loïc Wacquant's observation on the impossibility of the precariat:

> The precariat is a sort of *stillborn group*, whose gestation is necessarily unfinished since one can work to consolidate it only to help its members flee from it, either by finding a haven in stable wage labor or by escaping from the world of work altogether (through social redistribution and state protection). Contrary to the proletariat in the Marxist vision of history, which is called upon to abolish itself in the long term by uniting and universalizing itself, the precariat can only make itself to immediately unmake itself. (2008, 247)

Although much talk about a swelling precariat circulated in France during the anti-CPE movement, this chapter has demonstrated that its supposed members hardly shared a collective consciousness. Rather, my interlocutors' relative absence at the protests and the student demonstrators' indifference vis-à-vis the CNE after the repeal of the CPE suggest the presence of something that resembles, at least faintly, old social class lines. Could this something constitute a rallying call, a point of identification capable of generating collective action among the less fortunate? By examining what my interlocutors called *galère* and the everyday forms of sociality this condition generated, the next chapter addresses this question.

6 *Banlieue* Blues

Grappling with *Galère*

"Action!" shouted Loïc. To his side, Matthieu trained a small digital camera on the far corner of the field where we were standing. Two dark-clad, hooded figures burst from behind a screen of brush and rushed forward. A few seconds, later a third person emerged. "Stop, or I'll shoot!" he yelled, stumbling along, but the other two had already vanished over the stone fence bordering the opposite edge of the clearing. "Cut!" Loïc barked. Although unsatisfied with the take, he declared that filming would have to cease for the day. The naked trees surrounding us were casting long shadows over the frozen landscape, as the pale winter sun sank toward the horizon. The day's shoot was the second in a long string of filming sessions I attended that would stretch into early June 2006. Loïc, with the help of Matthieu and a few other close friends, had come up with the project. Recording scenes in and around Limoges with a handheld camera, they planned to produce an amateur police thriller to be shown at the *fête de quartier* (neighborhood block party) held every year at the end of June in the Val de l'Aurence. In all, nearly a dozen young people from the housing projects participated in the film; most were unemployed.

This creative and collaborative endeavor does not fit well with the usual image of France's troubled *banlieues* as fractured and fractious places. Indeed, just the previous fall it had seemed that outer-city youth were the unruly harbingers of social death and decay, at least according to some of the more strident commentators on the 2005 riots. And even then such a perspective was hardly novel. Nearly twenty years earlier, François Dubet (1987) declared an end to the *banlieues rouges*, those working-class communities thought to be bound together by a shared workplace, trade-union activism, and common political allegiances. The disintegration of these close-knit neighborhoods with the dawn of the postindustrial era, the sociologist claimed, left gaping holes in the social fabric. Anomie, the absence of social norms and values, was now the defining feature of life in France's festering outer cities, he argued.

In this chapter I focus on everyday life in Limoges's peripheral neighborhoods. My aim is not to prove or disprove claims of social disintegration. Rather, I attempt to solve a puzzle. In general, my interlocutors agreed that social relations were breaking down, particularly in the housing projects where they lived. They complained about rampant *je m'en foutisme*, a couldn't-care-less attitude that led neighbors, and even family members, to turn a blind eye to each other's problems and needs. This erosion of social ties, they said, was part of the crushing everyday experience of a condition they called *galère*. Yet I found that *galère* as they described it often induced creative and adaptive survival strategies, such as the film project discussed above. How is it possible, I ask here, that these young men and women so readily discounted these forms of sociality, preferring instead to see the fabric of social life as coming undone? To be sure, the structural bases of the inequality they faced played a role, and I spend some time discussing this below. But I also argue that widespread assumptions and beliefs about what constitutes *solidarité* in France were equally important. That these young people's experiences did not fit within this dominant discursive frame left them with little chance of finding a collective voice to fight for greater social justice. Ultimately, this chapter is about the interplay of local and global forces in the conceptualization of personhood and social identity in the new economy.

Galère in Everyday Life

"Outer-city youth do not live, they *galèrent*," one interlocutor told me early during my fieldwork. In Limoges's housing projects, the verb *galérer* and the corresponding noun *galère* were words I heard over and over again.[1]

What did these terms mean to the young people who used them? What were the primary features and the main effects of *galère*, according to them? As we will see, their understandings of their condition cannot be divorced from the strategies they developed to cope with the challenges they encountered. To begin, examining something as seemingly mundane as their everyday uses of cell phones aids, I think, in understanding what *galère* meant to them.

Cell phones were fairly ubiquitous in Limoges's outer city, where, I discovered, they held far more value than their simple functionality. For my interlocutors they were both a reminder of the problems they faced and a means of deflecting or deferring these. Cell phones first appeared in France in the early 1990s and were already widespread by the turn of the twenty-first century.[2] However, even as the technology developed and the market opened to competition, owning and operating a cell phone has remained fairly expensive in France. Cell-phone costs depend primarily on the type of service plan chosen by the customer at the time service is initiated. Most plans fall under one of two categories: pay-as-you-go accounts and long-term contracts. While the former option requires no commitment from customers (they simply refill a drained account by purchasing prepaid cards), the latter obliges users to sign on for twelve or twenty-four months, and the longer the commitment, the less costly the plan. Generally speaking, prepaid service is much more expensive than a contract, running on average fifty cents per minute in 2005 and 2006 (compared to between twenty and thirty cents with a contract). Additionally, whereas contract customers typically benefit from substantial subsidies when purchasing cell phones (with new service, most service providers offer entry-level phones free of charge or for a token euro), prepay customers usually have to shell out full or close-to-full price for their phones, the least expensive of which ran around forty euros in 2005 and 2006.[3]

Nearly all of my interlocutors in Limoges's housing projects carried cell phones with them wherever they went, and early during my fieldwork initial contacts seemed genuinely surprised that I did not have a phone of my own, requiring me to explain more than once that I was waiting for my residency card to be issued before I got one.[4] Oddly though, or so it seemed to me at first, I rarely observed interlocutors talking on their cell phones, and when they did, it was usually only for a short period of time, each call lasting no more than a minute or two. Why did these young Limougeauds insist on having cell phones if they only rarely used them? The answer to this question has much to do with their experience of *galère*—specifically, the limits they found placed on the independence that, in their estimation, they, as young adults, should enjoy.

For these young men and women, having a cell phone, I came to understand, was about much more than easy access to untethered communication. Owning a first cell phone was seen as a sort of rite of passage, a step closer to adulthood and the achievement of greater autonomy. With a cell phone, in theory they could talk wherever, whenever, and to whomever they wanted, without having to rely on the family phone. "Having a cell phone is essential," Rachid asserted. "I'm able to stay in touch with friends and I can keep my conversations private. That's not always easy in the neighborhood's small apartments." Yasmine agreed: "I couldn't live without my cell phone. It makes me feel so much more independent." Although both were adults according to the legal definition in France, neither Rachid nor Yasmine had moved away from home, and their situation was by no means exceptional. Most of the young people I came to know still lived with their parents and often complained about the constraints this arrangement placed on their personal freedom, citing, for example, the imposition of curfews or the close supervision of their comings and goings. They used cell phones as a Band-Aid fix. Even if they could not afford to live on their own, cell phones, they explained, gave them some measure of autonomy.

As symbols of much-sought-after autonomy, cell phones were frequently displayed to the public eye. If they were not worn in a visible manner—in a belt cradle, for example—they were regularly pulled out of pockets and bags, even when no messages were registered on them and their owners had no intention of making a call. During one day of observations at Interval, the "dry bar" youth hangout in the Val de l'Aurence, I witnessed a young man remove his cell phone from his pants' pocket no fewer than ten times in about as many minutes. When asked if he was expecting an important call, he shot me a look that could have been interpreted as menacing or embarrassed (I could not decide which), but he said no.[5] For nearly all of my interlocutors, cell phones also replaced wristwatches, thanks to the digital clocks built into nearly all models. "You still wear a watch?" questioned Karim, the sharp-tongued fourteen-year-old I tutored in the Val de l'Aurence. "That's so old-fashioned," he snickered. All consideration of current fashion trends aside, using cell phones as timepieces offered one more excuse to display these prized possessions.

Because of their limited financial resources, it made sense for youth such as Rachid, Yasmine, and Karim to opt for the less expensive contract when choosing a service plan; few, however, had. Instead, they mostly chose the more costly prepaid account. This decision was usually not the result of ignorance about the cost difference, nor was it a function of a "capricious" or "hard-to-pin-down" nature that some human service providers in Limoges attributed to outer-city youth.[6] On the contrary, most young people recognized that a contract would have saved them money and told me that they readily would have chosen that option but lacked the needed steady income. In fact, although in the long run contracts are less costly than accounts, even the least expensive among them required monthly payments of about forty euros, debited directly from the customer's bank account. By contrast, prepaid cards could be had for as little as five euros. With a contract, customers also run the risk of accruing additional charges if the plan's monthly allotment of minutes is surpassed. Having a prepaid account is a way to avert this undesirable outcome. Instead of accumulating extra charges when available minutes are expended, the line is put "on hold," and the phone stops working until the account is refilled with funds.

Many young people in the housing projects did, in fact, frequently run out of minutes. More than once, interlocutors who promised to call me never did. Later, when I saw them, they almost always explained that they were out of minutes. Of course, this may have only been a pretext, their way of letting me know politely that they were not interested in talking to a foreign anthropologist. However, if I called them, they generally seemed happy to talk, often for longer periods than during the calls I observed them make among themselves. A more likely interpretation then is that they were resistant to using their own minutes, if they had any minutes left to use. Unlike the United States, where both outgoing and incoming calls are billed as used minutes, in France only outgoing calls deplete minute stores, both for prepay and contract customers. Thus, when I initiated calls my interlocutors did not consume any of their prepaid minutes.

Youth in Limoges's outer city also kept track of each other's minutes. I frequently overheard or took part in conversations during which young people explained that someone was momentarily unreachable by phone because his or her minutes were depleted. In order to avoid this undesirable outcome, they tended to send text messages rather than make calls. Text messages, costing on average ten cents each, were much less expensive than calls (which, recall, averaged fifty cents per minute for prepay accounts). Sometimes, some social service providers perceived this behavior as a sign of unwelcome individualism. "You've seen all those kids typing away furiously on their cell phones," a counselor at the *mission locale* remarked with exasperation during an interview with me. "They don't even take the time to have a normal conversation anymore. What's society coming to?" Rather than indicating that these young people were uninterested in engaging with their peers, or in collective life within their neighborhoods more generally, it seems to me that their use of text messages is better explained as a calculated move to stretch out limited financial resources.

Exploring my interlocutors' uses of cell phones has offered a small window into their experience of *galère*. As symbolic capital, cell phones functioned as a highly visible stand-in for the autonomy they expected as young adults but were unable to achieve because of chronic underemployment. Although the cost-saving contract was beyond their reach, they creatively managed the more expensive prepaid account.

Other details of everyday life, such as how they engaged in leisure activities, help to flesh out the challenges they faced. Despite frequent complaints that Limoges lacked any sort of nightlife, the city boasts at least two social hot spots, sometimes colorfully referred to by locals as *rues de la soif* (streets of thirst).[7] The narrow and sloping Rue Charles-Michels cuts through the medieval city center, and the more expansive Cours Jourdan butts up against the Champ de Juillet, near the Gare des Bénédictins. Early during my fieldwork, several city employees introduced me to the Cours Jourdan, where one evening we shared drinks and discussed potential entry points into the outer city. Interlocutors in the housing projects, I later discovered, preferred the Rue Charles-Michels. Each time I accompanied groups there the plan was the same. We would meet around 9 p.m. in the housing projects and then travel by foot to the city center. After entering one of the dimly lit bars lining the street, we would move to the back, which was generally already smoke infested. None of my companions drank, unless I offered to buy a round, and few danced, despite the mass of sweaty bodies gyrating to the deafening music that filled the cramped space. Usually with a cigarette pressed against their lips, they stared blankly at the scene. It was not unusual for such outings to last well into the early hours of the morning.

What could have possibly been the allure of these nocturnal excursions? After all, it did not appear that anyone had much fun. When questioned about this, my interlocutors usually told me they were just looking to "kill time," but they could have just as easily done this in the housing projects. Like the example of cell phones, Limoges's Rue Charles-Michels, I would argue, held symbolic value for these youth. It represented what the social theorist Jean Baudrillard (1988) has called a "dream world" of mass consumption. To experience a taste of this world, however diluted, my companions sought creative solutions. Unlike the more traditional pubs and restaurants that flank the Cours Jourdan, where one is expected to at least purchase a drink in order to occupy a table, the "lounge bars" of the Rue Charles-Michels resemble nightclubs. To gain entry, a fee is charged (usually between five and ten euros), but by arriving before 10 p.m. these young people avoided even that outlay, thanks to a sort of early-bird special most of the bars on that street offer. As a result, they could go home at the end of the evening without ever having spent a cent. In the end, these excursions to the Rue Charles-Michels, it seems to me, had far more to do with lessening feelings of social exclusion than with killing time.

For my interlocutors, managing a limited budget was an everyday affair that required constant creativity, such as sending text messages instead of making calls or slipping into nightclubs at unfashionable hours to avoid paying cover charges. Sometimes, however, some individuals loosened their purse strings. Significantly, they usually described such moments of relative abandon as being accompanied by feelings of remorse. A particularly striking example of this involved one of my interlocutors' visit to the hairdresser. At a mid-March meeting of the support group for unemployed youth I frequently attended, Chloé, a regular participant, arrived sporting a stylish new haircut, complete with professional highlights. Her fresh look drew murmurs from the crowd; one young man even whistled in approbation. As for Chloé, she had guilt painted on her face. "I went crazy this week," she said with a sheepish grin. According to her, she had been to the unemployment office, but no job announcements corresponded to her profile.[8] The counselor she met with proposed writing practice cover letters nonetheless. "What good are cover letters if there is no one to send them to?" Chloé protested. Feeling frustrated and depressed, she left the unemployment office and entered the first salon she came across. Chloé's response to her peers suggests that she recognized that certain kinds of nonessential, conspicuous consumption, such as a professional haircut and highlights, were likely to set her apart from the group. However, by justifying her actions as a response to the poor job market and the employment counselor's seeming indifference toward her plight, she placed herself squarely back in their world, a world they knew to be dominated by galère.

That according to Chloé it was ultimately a sense of hopelessness that pushed her to splurge at the hair salon points to a characteristic of galère reported by many young people in the housing projects: a feeling of being stuck. As one interlocutor put it succinctly, to experience galère means to be acculé. Acculer translates as "to corner" or "to trap." It is what hunters do to game, what predators do to prey. In the context of galère, it can be taken to mean being stripped of agency, of the possibility of projecting oneself into the future. In other words, galère was seen as a state of paralysis. It equated to putting adult life—what my interlocutors called "real" life—on hold, without any foreseeable improvement. For Rachid, the effects could be as far-reaching as stunting proper masculinity. In his early twenties, Rachid was preparing a teaching certificate at the University of Limoges. He was also engaged to the daughter of a family friend. He considered himself an exception. "Most young guys in the neighborhood, kids I grew up with, kids I was friends with, they have no sexuality," Rachid told me. "These guys," he continued, "don't have work, they've never been in a relationship, they don't have plans for the future. You see them every day in the same places, with the same people, doing the same things. That's not what a man is. It's really sad." Thus, the name of the JOC support group for unemployed youth I regularly attended was "Bouge ta galère"—literally, "Get your *galère* moving." Faced by the immobilizing effects of *galère*, the group implored its members to become active, to take their future by the hand. The experience of *galère* may therefore be understood as generative. In Limoges, at least, it did not automatically equate to a social void but instead pushed those who faced it to develop collective responses, as the observations above suggest. As I explore in the following section, these responses combined to form what I call *banlieue* sociality.

Banlieue Sociality

As rioting raged in France in the fall of 2005, well-known journalist and public intellectual Thomas Ferenczi penned an opinion piece in the national daily *Le Monde*. What, he asked, could be the cause of the weeks-long stretch of violence witnessed in France's outer cities? Noting that some observers were blaming the design and development of the *banlieues*, from their concrete gigantism and suffocating uniformity to their isolation and tendency to house disproportionate numbers of ethnic minorities, he offered an alternative possibility. Linking the riots to the global spread of neoliberal doctrine, Ferenczi argued that the disturbance was a symptom of a more general disorder. France and the rest of Europe, he posited, faced mounting social disintegration. The troubled *banlieues* were for him an alarming first glimpse at society's future if preventative steps were not taken quickly (Ferenczi 2005).

Ferenczi was not the first to present such a gloomy prognosis. In his book *La galère: Jeunes en survie*, published in 1987, François Dubet argued that the widespread experience of *galère* in France's outer cities proceeds from three intertwined logics. The first, which he called "disorganization," designates a state of anomie, where there is a significant breakdown of norms and common values and understandings. In the absence of these regulations and constraints, social responsibility erodes and disorder reigns. The second logic, dubbed "exclusion" by Dubet, reinforces the first, as those experiencing *galère* progressively find themselves barred from traditional institutions of social integration, notably the school system and the labor market. Dubet described the third logic, which he labeled "rage," as "pure" or "gratuitous" violence. Frequently directed at agents of law and order but also at times nihilistic, this violence, he noted, is detached from any organized social movement (1987, 67–93). In the end, Dubet's analysis allowed him to state the central thesis of his book: *galère* is the polar opposite of industrial society, the void left behind when the social class structure of that world collapsed.

Many interlocutors in Limoges's housing projects seemed to share this perspective. "C'est chacun pour soi" (It's everyone for themselves) was a common phrase used to describe life in the outer city. This expression did not carry the sort of dog-eat-dog mentality, the idea that only the strongest or smartest succeed, that one might encounter in the United States. Rather, it designated what was perceived as a general disaffection or disinterest vis-à-vis others, manifested, according to my interlocutors, in myriad quotidian ways, from urinating or spitting in public stairwells to throwing trash from windows or tagging exterior walls, to "mooching," that is, taking without ever giving back. Despite this, over the course of my fieldwork I noted dense patterns of social relations that both constrained and enabled the agency of actors in the outer city. Why, for my interlocutors, did these networks not count as forms of social solidarity or cohesion? Attempting to answer this question requires first describing *banlieue* sociality.

I use the modifier *banlieue* to characterize the forms of sociality I observed in Limoges's outer city because these practices were intimately ascribed to space and place. David Lepoutre notes in his ethnographic account of the Cité des 4000 outside of Paris: "Whatever the negative image of these places and notwithstanding the difficulties experienced and the strategies implemented to fulfill that image, the housing projects are also, as surprising as it may seem, the places of births, of childhoods, and of memories" (1997, 42). He could have just as easily been writing about Limoges's outer city. Although the young people I came to know were quick to recite the deficiencies of their neighborhoods, often parroting negative representations of France's fractious *banlieues* that circulated in the media and elsewhere, many maintained a strong bond with the place they called home. In fact, although they unanimously reported that the outer city was "rough" and "undesirable," they did so in general terms. When it came to describing their own neighborhoods, they regularly set up sharp contrasts, arguing that where they lived was the exception that proved the rule.

Consider, for example, Chloé's reflections on her housing search. Chloé had grown up in the Val de l'Aurence, but after obtaining a state "insertion contract" she moved to a privately owned apartment near the Gare des Bénédictins. Unhappy with her new accommodations (she complained that her landlord was generally unresponsive to the problems she reported) and facing unemployment in the near future when her current contract was set to expire, she decided to return to the public housing system. Chloé hoped to be lodged in one of the newer, townhouse-style developments located nearer the city center. When I asked if she would accept an apartment in the outer city, the young woman prickled, stating that she did not want "to get mugged or worse." In the end, though, Chloé said she would return to the Val de l'Aurence, if necessary. "It's not so bad there, it's not like the other outer-city housing projects," she maintained.

Working in three different housing projects afforded me the opportunity to record many similar claims and counterclaims. Residents consistently described their neighborhood as "the best in the outer city." When pressed to justify this assessment, they tended to offer the same explanations, regardless of where they lived: their neighborhood was

FIG. 17. Until their demolition in 2010, La Bastide's Tours Gauguin, commonly referred to by locals as the "twin towers," stood on the northern edge of the city. Decried by residents of La Bastide as "ethnic ghettos," these rundown buildings were equally scorned by city-center dwellers, who complained that they were an "eyesore" and "disgrace."

"the least dangerous," "the least racist," "the most diverse," and so forth. I noted a similar phenomenon within individual neighborhoods. If their neighborhood suffered from a bad reputation, young people told me, it was not because of them but rather because of "criminal elements" living somewhere other than where they lived or where they gathered. In the Val de l'Aurence, for example, I learned several months after spending considerable time at Interval that this youth meeting place was widely viewed by residents across the neighborhood in a negative light. One older, longtime tenant told me that Interval promoted "idleness" and fostered a "gang mentality." As for the young people who frequented the establishment, they did not consider the center or themselves responsible for their neighborhood's bad reputation. Rather, "gypsies"—who, they

FIG. 18. When the twin towers were imploded, a special viewing area was set up for former residents. Although two years later the site remained vacant, plans were afoot to build a parking lot, a playground, and a multi-sports playing field.

told me, had taken over a housing tower on the neighborhood's northern periphery—were the real culprits.

Even such assignations of blame, I learned, could dissipate into nostalgia. In 2005 and 2006, interlocutors in La Bastide unanimously condemned two rundown towers that stood on the edge of their neighborhood (fig. 17). They were overcrowded, they complained; they had become immigrant ghettos, they objected. In 2012, when I returned to Limoges for a follow-up visit, I discovered that the infamous towers had been imploded two years earlier during a planned demolition (fig. 18). "You know," one interlocutor stated, "those towers were a real eyesore, but I miss them. It's hard to explain, something you live your whole life with suddenly isn't there anymore. There's a void." Former residents, she told me, regularly returned to the site, now a vacant field, to picnic or kick around a soccer ball.

Within each neighborhood I observed a range of community clubs and associations, many aimed specifically at young people. Each neighborhood had some sort of dedicated youth hangout (Interval in the Val de l'Aurence, the *maison des jeunes* in Beaubreuil, the *centre social* in La Bastide) where young people could gather informally and clubs and associations could hold meetings. Many clubs and associations functioned explicitly or implicitly along gender lines. The hip-hop workshop held weekly at Interval, for example, was in theory open to anyone, although in practice only young men participated. Similarly, the Afro-Caribbean, African, and Urban Dance Collective, also held weekly at Interval, only drew a female crowd.[9] In Beaubreuil, one association catered exclusively to first- and second-generation immigrant women. Its aim was to help this population, which was statistically at a disadvantage when it came to finding work, prepare for the job market through remedial education and vocational training.[10] Most sports clubs (soccer, martial arts, basketball, gymnastics, etc.) similarly focused on one or another gender, although I counted far more sports clubs for men than for women.

Other groups had a religious orientation. I found, for example, that the Catholic-based Jeunesse ouvrière chrétienne had a strong presence in the Val de l'Aurence. Today an international organization, JOC was founded in 1925 in Belgium to promote fellowship among young workers. Influenced by the popular education movement, it sought to make participants "actors of their own destiny" by developing and promoting their strengths and capabilities.[11] Thus JOC's motto—"See, judge, act"—reflected its mission. Jocistes were to consider their experiences collectively, pursue knowledge jointly, and work in concert to improve their condition. Since its formation, JOC has evolved in response to changing economic conditions. In the 1950s it helped establish young workers' homes; in the 1960s, it set up summer camps for seasonal workers; and in the 1980s, it formed support groups for youth facing employment insecurity.[12] Since the 1980s its focus has increasingly shifted to the challenges young people face in the job market. In 2005 and 2006, JOC commissioned a study involving the distribution of a questionnaire on employment conditions and practices to more than thirty thousand young people across France.

In the early spring of 2006, local roundtables were organized to discuss the results with community leaders.

It is arguably JOC's efforts to adapt to changing economic circumstances, particularly its present attention to the issue of *précarité*, that help explain its relevance in Limoges today. Given the city's long history of anticlericalism, I was surprised by the organization's presence in the Val de l'Aurence.[13] When questioned about this, local leadership explained that the arrival of JOC in Limoges coincided with a push by the Catholic Church in the postwar years to win back the Communist-led working classes. Other initiatives included embedding worker-priests[14] in the housing projects and building a Catholic church in the Val de l'Aurence, alongside the neighborhood's mushrooming housing towers.[15] Most, although not all, of Limoges's Jocistes were Catholic. However, as the following comment made by Coralie, the local federation's president, demonstrates, membership in JOC was about more than religious (Catholic) identity:

> We're Christian because in the beginning it was like that. Today, we accept everyone, all young people, even Muslims can join. JOC is Christian in the sense that we live according to the same belief. That is to say, although we don't necessarily believe in the same thing, we all believe that young people can advance, we all believe that we're capable of finding work, of building meaningful futures together. Some members don't necessarily want to deepen their faith, and that's okay. We respect everyone. Everyone is free to live how they want.

The idea that certain fundamental principles united (or should unite) Jocistes and, more generally, all young people struggling to find work regardless of religious affiliation was shared by Dalil, a self-identifying Muslim who sometimes attended a support group for unemployed youth organized through JOC. "I think that values, real values, what we call universal values in France, it's just a roundabout way of renaming religious values," Dalil told me during a conversation after one of the group meetings. He continued: "Solidarity, equality, respect, tolerance—these are all values promoted by religion, Catholicism or Islam. The problem today is that a lot of people seem to have lost sight of these values." According to Dalil, this support group offered a space where he and other disillusioned youth could "dispel feelings of isolation, share experiences and strategies, and act concretely."

In the end, religion itself did not appear to constitute a significant basis for *banlieue* sociality, at least not among my interlocutors. I made a point of attending mass several times in the Val de l'Aurence but never encountered any Jocistes I knew there. These young people admitted to me they were Catholic more in name than in practice. As for the young people from Muslim backgrounds whom I came to know (about half of my interlocutors), only a handful (including Dalil) said they prayed regularly. Most reported that they observed major feasts, such as Eid al-Fitr, but said this was primarily to uphold family tradition. These observations on the relative insignificance of religious practice among my interlocutors match more general trends recorded in France. In fact, despite recent claims made by politicians from the extreme right and ambitious Muslim leaders alike that a homogeneous Muslim community is fast gaining ground on the "native" French population, research points out that in France people of Muslim background hail from a wide range of nations and that the degree of self-declared affiliation with Islam among them does not differ significantly from the degree of self-declared affiliation with Catholicism among individuals of Catholic background. In both cases, only a little more than half of those polled reported regularly attending religious services (Laurence and Vaïsse 2006).[16]

The young people in my study were, of course, not representative of all outer-city youth in France or even Limoges. That the clubs and associations described above constituted important entry points for me into Limoges's *banlieue* early during my fieldwork undoubtedly skewed my results, suggesting greater participation in these types of organizations than may be the case more generally. Nevertheless, through initial interlocutors I was able to meet other young people who did not necessarily participate in any such groups. In this way, I was able to observe other dimensions of *banlieue* sociality beyond the bounds of formal structures.

One such dimension was the frequent exchange of information, especially job leads. Thomas, who stocked shelves at the local pharmacy, told me that he owed this job to neighborhood ties. His mother, he explained, was friendly with the pharmacist's wife, who, after learning that Thomas was looking for work, contacted her when a position opened up. This was not the first time Thomas's social network proved useful to him during a job search. Before being employed in the pharmacy, he held a number of odd jobs, including some in construction, which he said he found mostly through his older brother, and at least one at a local factory, which a friend recommended him for. Jonathan had a similar story to tell. Employed in the spring of 2006 in a short-term position at the electrical components manufacturer Legrand, he had previously worked at a France Télécom boutique near the city center. Jonathan explained that a friend of his who had a part-time job there knew he was good with technology and was able to convince the manager to give him a chance. Jonathan's contract at Legrand was set to expire in the fall of 2006. Before I left Limoges late in the summer of 2006, he had already begun applying to positions through the *mission locale* and the unemployment office but had yet to secure anything. Although he hoped to land a CDI, as a last resort he suspected the France Télécom store would rehire him in a short-term capacity to prepare for the upcoming holiday rush. At the Val de l'Aurence homework-help center where I volunteered several days a week, I witnessed firsthand the job networking that sometimes takes place in the outer city. The other tutors, all paid university students, had grown up in the neighborhood. Two were sisters, and many others were childhood friends. On more than one occasion I overheard some of them asking the program's coordinator if she anticipated any openings, explaining that "good friends" were looking for work and would be "ideal candidates."

Young people in Limoges's outer city not only shared information about jobs; they also routinely exchanged objects. Significantly, for the most part these included nonessentials, especially cigarettes, but also videos and music (generally downloaded from the Internet). By contrast, I rarely observed or heard of exchanges involving money or food staples. It seems to me that the explanation for this is twofold. First, as we saw in previous chapters, my interlocutors categorically refused to be considered part of *les exclus* (socially excluded people), whom they considered truly destitute. "We're not poor," they insisted; "we're not like the bums who roam the streets, who don't have anywhere to sleep at night," they maintained. Entering into exchange centered on life essentials would have meant to them that they were little better off than this category of people. That is not to say, however, that these young people did not recognize that they would likely never have the same access to certain goods as other groups. Such goods might not be required for maintaining life, but in the culture of consumption that characterizes France, as it does most other contemporary Western societies, they are associated with dominant understandings of what it means to be fully a person. In my interlocutors' eyes, it was precisely a lack of access to things like music, videos, and cigarettes—things that conspicuously give pleasure in social settings—that marked them, as a group, as different, as undeniably deficient.[17] Exchange of nonessentials helped compensate for this deficiency, concealing, albeit superficially, their difference. More broadly, it may be seen as part of a group strategy for coping collectively with an experience they shared: *galère*.

The film project I described at the opening of this chapter may be seen as one last example of a shared activity constitutive of *banlieue* sociality. In the winter of 2006, I was invited by several young people to attend shoots of a film they were working on. The project began as a sort of advertisement for JOC. Some of the local federation's adult supervisors invited the youth membership to create a "documentary" chronicling JOC's activities in the community. Things quickly took a different turn, however. Loïc, a nineteen-year-old from the Val de l'Aurence who ended up leading the project, told me that the idea of a documentary did not generate a lot of interest among JOC's members. Something more compelling was needed, he insisted. It was his idea to create a police thriller instead, and with this change in subject, he said that it was easy to recruit participants. In the end, the project was not endorsed by JOC, whose adult supervisors maintained that it strayed too far from Christian values. (Some complained to me in private that the film contained an "excess" of offensive language.) Although a core of three young members of JOC kept the project on track, the cast, which eventually swelled to eleven, included young people who were not part of the organization. Aged fifteen to twenty-three, they all hailed from Limoges's outer city. Most had grown up in the Val de l'Aurence, although the eastern Portes Ferrées neighborhood was also represented. Except for the fifteen-year-old, who was enrolled in a vocational program, they had finished or quit school but had yet to find stable employment.

Social science research has established how work offers more than an income. It also confers a status, a schedule, a social network, and a purpose.[18] Depending on the job and the position people occupy in society, all of these elements can influence, positively or negatively, their sense of self-worth and importance.[19] For the young people who participated in the film, this project became more than just a leisure activity; they treated it as if it were a *job*. Filming often spanned full days, and because the group hoped to screen the film at the block party held every June in the Val de l'Aurence, production became frenzied as this event approached. On one particularly "busy" day, customary cigarette breaks were even forgone. "We've got a job to do," one member of the cast told me, "and we're going to get it done!"

If analysis of the film's making helps illuminate how this group of young people understood and grappled with *galère*, its content is equally revealing in this regard. Written by Loïc but then recrafted with the input of the entire cast, the screenplay begins by introducing Morin, a bumbling police detective who is dispatched along with his equally inept partner by the menopausal and slightly neurotic police commissioner to investigate a local drug ring. While Morin and his partner are in the outer city harassing anyone who crosses their path, the police commissioner goes missing. Certain that she has been kidnapped, Morin launches an immediate investigation, but it turns out that the commissioner had merely been called unexpectedly to meet with her son's principal at the exclusive city-center high school he attends because he had skipped class. His instincts proven wrong, Morin is the laughingstock of the entire police brigade. But then the commissioner disappears again. Worried about being discredited a second time, Morin hesitates to open a case, despite clear signs of a struggle in the commissioner's office. When several days pass and the commissioner still does not turn up, Morin and his partner are finally convinced of foul play and set out to find her. Over the course of their investigation they arrest a number of outer-city thugs, mainly suspected drug dealers, whom they brutalize in an effort to gain information about the commissioner's whereabouts. The trail remains cold, however, until, in a bizarre turn of events, Morin discovers that it was the commissioner's own son who abducted her with the intention of delivering her to a local drug cartel in exchange for cocaine. During an animated struggle, Morin overtakes the raging adolescent and releases the commissioner. In the final scene, a beaming Morin leads the commissioner's son to prison, as his colleagues cheer him on.

Struck by the story line, I asked the group about their inspiration. They cited popular television serials, mostly American shows broadcast in France (*Law and Order*, *CSI*), but I would argue that the plot also draws on important themes in contemporary French life, especially ideas commonly associated with young people from the outer city facing *galère*. Rather than accepting these ideas as truth, however, the film turns them on their head. The plot establishes the familiar dichotomy between city center and outer city. However, instead of presenting the first space as the unequivocal location of law and order and the second as the site of criminality and social degeneration, the lines become blurred. Whereas the detectives are depicted as incompetent brutes who rough up outer-city youth for the sheer pleasure of it, the motivations of the outer-city youth remain ambiguous. Although it is suggested that some of them may be involved in drug trafficking, this possibility is never confirmed. At the film's end, the investigators are victorious, but they are unable to pin the commissioner's abduction on outer-city thugs, as they had hoped. Instead, the commissioner's own son is to blame. That mention is made earlier in the film that he attends an elite, centrally located school clearly sets him apart from the outer-city riffraff. Moreover, it turns out that he is not only a raging drug addict but also a hardened criminal, willing to sacrifice his own mother for a fix. The implications of this plot twist are obvious: the film underscores the hardships faced by outer-city youth and recasts notions of personal responsibility. Although deprivation may have pushed some young people living in the outer city to adopt a life of crime, the commissioner's son, who wanted for nothing, had done so for completely selfish reasons to the point of violating the most fundamental of social relations, that of the family.[20] Ultimately, the film invites reconsideration of neoliberal assumptions about agency and the causes and consequences of social inequality.

Toward a Collective Consciousness?

Writing on the 2005 riots, political scientist Stéphane Dufoix has remarked, "The first difficulty is to decide into which kind of frame those 'events' could—or should—find their place" (2005). Although he ultimately settled on the encompassing issue of "recognition," he rejected the idea that the unrest constituted any kind of social movement, revolt, or revolution. Dufoix was not alone in this assessment. In a contribution to the same online forum, sociologist Michel Wieviorka (2005) declared that the riots were the "very contrary" of the student and worker revolts of May 1968. "They [the riots] are not at all organized, they produce no discourse, they don't have any leader, any principle of structuration, they are typically crisis behaviours, and not at all a movement," he insisted. Other French researchers were less categorical. Sociologist Gérard Mauger (2006) argued that the rioters were actors of a "protopolitical revolt" whose principal motivation was collective indignation against illegitimate state violence, both physical and symbolic. Similarly highlighting the importance of a collective identity founded on perceptions of sharing comparable, down-trodden positions within a social hierarchy, political scientist Olivier Roy (2005) called the unrest a "youth underclass uprising." As for sociologist Didier Lapeyronnie (2006), he insisted that the conflict was fundamentally political, even if it lacked identifiable leadership. Arguing that the rioters demonstrated an intimate understanding of the mechanisms of French models of social contestation, he maintained that their "revolt" functioned as a "collective voice" that succeeded in short-circuiting inaccessible and often protracted democratic channels.[21]

Were the riots political? Were they driven by an "oppositional consciousness" (Mansbridge and Morris 2001), one born in this case of the experience of *galère*? I do not pretend to answer here questions that have provoked so much disagreement among so many French academics. However, it seems to me that my discussion of *galère* and what I have called *banlieue* sociality helps illuminate just why these questions were raised in the first place and how they relate to broader, culturally mediated concerns about social cohesion and solidarity. I have argued that in Limoges's outer city the experience of *galère* was mitigated by various collective practices, from the exchange of cigarettes to the production of a homemade film, at least among the young people who participated in my study. Yet these same young people claimed that in their neighborhoods and beyond "it was everyone for themselves," that the social fabric was fraying. Why did they not find value in the practices constitutive of the *banlieue* sociality I observed?

To be sure, structural obstacles—that is, obstacles arising from a new, flexible employment paradigm—often got in the way. The film project discussed above offers a case in point. Toward mid-April, the cast member playing the role of the commissioner abruptly stopped attending shoots. A new job (a six-month contract), I learned, prevented her from continuing in the role. In order to avoid falling behind schedule, the rest of the group rewrote the script, explaining the commissioner's absence by a kidnapping (the original plot called for Morin to be abducted). They hoped the young woman would return to film the final scene, where the commissioner was liberated from her son by the story's two unlikely heroes. She never did, however, and this plunged the group into a panic. They hastily recast the role of the commissioner and reshot all of the footage featuring her. Although, when asked, members of the cast denied harboring any ill feelings toward the young woman, she was markedly absent during the film's screening, and afterward I only saw her once with the group of friends, even though before the film she had been a regular presence whenever they gathered.

The commotion surrounding the film helps us gain perspective on the contrasting results of *précarité* in Limoges's housing projects. On the one hand, the project serves to temper some observers' claims that *précarité* unavoidably leads to social deviance and ultimately anomie (e.g., Standing 2011; Dubet 1987). On the other, it demonstrates the tenuousness of *banlieue* sociality, suggesting that differences among individuals, even temporary ones, may prevent the development of any sort of overarching consciousness, much less one capable of generating political action. In fact, even if all of my interlocutors lived in similar material conditions (the housing projects) and complained loudly about *galère*, their educational backgrounds and experiences in the job market were far from identical. Some had high school diplomas; others did not. Some had undertaken (or were undertaking) professional training; others had not. Some had completed a year or two of university coursework and then abandoned their studies; others were still pursuing university degrees. Some had been out of work for months; others shifted between temporary jobs (full-time or part-time); and still others (a very small minority) had secured long-term, full-time employment. Groups of friends, I noted, were often constituted along these lines, and sometimes changes in status provoked momentary or more long-term rifts within them.

In addition to such structural obstacles, which are likely to be present wherever neoliberal policies and practices are implemented, I would argue that cultural obstacles specific to the French context, especially ideas about what constitutes "real" *solidarité*, precluded the development of a collective consciousness among my interlocutors. "What is *solidarité*?" asked Jonathan, whose short-term contract was set to expire shortly. He continued: "Sitting on the corner and smoking cigarettes all day, is that what you call *solidarité*? Or, are you going to knock on my door and tell me to come look for work with you? That's real *solidarité*, but you don't see that today. Today, it's just a bunch of kids who are letting each other fall apart. If you want to make it, if you want to get out of here, you've got to fend for yourself. It's everyone for themselves." As this remark suggests, for my interlocutors *solidarité* was above all about *social inclusion*, which they envisioned as possible only through *employment*. Without good, stable jobs, French men and women, they insisted, had little chance of achieving full participation in the social and economic life of the nation. Although they did not necessarily discount the social and emotional support that connections with others in their neighborhoods provided, they viewed these as offering little chance of leading to long-term employment.

Such a view of *solidarité* has permeated much of the scholarship coming out of France over the past several decades investigating the "death" or "demise" of the working class. By and large, this literature has focused on how old forms of working-class organization and politics, centered on relationships developed on the shop floor, have been replaced, especially among the generation coming of age today, by general apathy at best and corrosive individualism at worst (e.g., Beaud and Pialoux 1999; O. Schwartz 1990; Terrail 1990; Renahy 2005). It is this vision, where *solidarité* through work is indisputably absent, that arguably drove French debates about the rioters' motivations in the fall of 2005. I wonder, though, to what extent the problem raised is a function of the frame of analysis used. In other words, by adopting "working class" as the most meaningful category of analysis—and this despite acknowledging its disintegration—how might this work fail to recognize the value of the everyday collective strategies deployed by such people as my interlocutors in Limoges as they grappled with their situation? The result is, in effect, the imposition of negative identities. That is, these young men and women were constantly being described, whether in scholarship, in the news, or by politicians, in terms of what they were not. It is little wonder that they internalized this perspective themselves.

Epilogue

When I returned to Limoges in the summer of 2012, change was on everyone's mind. Socialist Party candidate François Hollande had just ousted Nicolas Sarkozy from the presidency. Running under the slogan "The time for change is now," he promised to steer France in a different direction.

Leveraging the law-and-order reputation he had earned during his tenure as minister of the interior, particularly at the time of the 2005 riots, Nicolas Sarkozy had succeeded Jacques Chirac as president in 2007. Sarkozy had run as an economic liberal, promising to reform cumbersome government regulations and encourage the French to "work more to earn more." To that end, he had proposed a number of measures. He continued efforts made by the Chirac administration to weaken regulations on the thirty-five-hour workweek, effectively emptying that law of its substance (Howell 2009; OECD 2009, 50–53).[1] He instituted a "tax shield" for the wealthy, limiting the maximum tax rate to 50 percent. He froze the minimum wage beyond the legally mandated adjustment for inflation (OECD 2009, 42) and launched a debate on the extension of weekend store hours in urban and tourist areas (Roger 2008).[2] He supported a simplification of French labor law through the implementation of a single work contract, which would include streamlined procedures for layoffs ("Sarkozy veut" 2007). Finally, he called for increased pressure on the unemployed to take jobs. With this goal in mind, his administration merged the agency responsible for handling unemployment benefits with the national unemployment office, creating the Pôle emploi (Employment center). The message was clear: the jobless should no longer expect to be able to sit idly and receive unemployment checks. Going forward, all job seekers would be required to create an individualized "employment plan" in consultation with an adviser. In addition to being counseled to "moderate" expectations regarding pay and geographic location, especially if unemployed for long periods of time, those seeking work would be urged to accept any "reasonable offer of employment." Failure to do so more than twice would result in a suspension of unemployment benefits for two months, with sanctions rising for each successive refusal. In order to make low-wage and part-time work more palatable to job seekers, Sarkozy replaced the RMI with the Revenu de solidarité active (RSA; Active solidarity income), which enables recipients to combine earnings from employment with government benefits, on a sliding scale (Wacquant 2010; Greciano 2010).

The financial meltdown that began in 2008 sparked renewed state intervention in France. In his first public speech following the outbreak of the crisis, Sarkozy proclaimed that "laissez-faire capitalism was over" and called for a "new balance between the state and the market" (Guiral 2008). Concretely, his administration responded by introducing a stimulus package benefiting public infrastructure and small business, cutting local taxes imposed on businesses, increasing social spending, bailing out failing banks, subsidizing the faltering auto industry, earmarking funds for research and development, and creating a Fonds stratégique d'investissement (Strategic investment fund) for companies deemed "critical" for the competitiveness of the French economy (OECD 2009, 19–27).

Although some observers have interpreted the 2008 crisis as signaling an end to neoliberal capitalism (e.g., Kotz 2015), and in France it appeared that a new form of *dirigisme* was back to stay, at least for the foreseeable future, in 2010 Sarkozy declared in an about-face his recommitment to the neoliberal principles that had helped him secure his election as president in 2007.[3] After his party suffered a crushing defeat in the March 2010 regional elections, Sarkozy, with the help of his prime minister, François Fillon, pushed through reforms that eliminated many special pension plans for civil servants and raised the minimum retirement age from sixty to sixty-two for all French workers. Then, in 2011, working with German chancellor Angela Merkel, he announced harsh austerity measures that would slash government spending by 45 billion euros over the next three years in order to bring France's public deficit back in line with European Union standards. In addition to speeding up the implementation of the new, higher retirement age, the package of proposals included increases to the value-added tax applied to such everyday expenses as restaurant meals, books, and public transportation (Clark 2011). Observing these changes, political scientists Elisabetta Gualmini and Vivien Schmidt wrote about France, "Neo-liberalism was back with a vengeance" (2013, 368).

Since 2006 the employment picture had unquestionably worsened in France. By the summer of 2012 the national unemployment rate was nearing heights not seen since the mid-1990s (Landré 2013). Young people were hit especially hard. Unemployment among the under-twenty-six crowd jumped from 18.5 percent in 2005 to more than 21 percent in 2012 (Pech 2014). As for youth living in the troubled *banlieues*, nearly half reported they could not find work, compared to about one in three in 2005 (Zappi 2012). Although the proportion of the general population holding a CDD remained relatively stable between 2006 and 2012 (around 8 percent), in the first quarter of 2013 more than 80 percent of all new job offers were for temporary work; two-thirds specified a period of employment of less than one month (Léchenet 2013).

In an effort to distract voters from the faltering economy and to placate conservative supporters, in his last years in office Sarkozy turned his attention to the questions of immigration and law and order. He launched a national debate on French identity, featuring a controversial government website inviting visitors to contemplate, "What is French?"; he pushed through legislation banning the burka (the head-to-toe garment worn by a small minority of especially observant Muslim women in France); he proposed rescinding the citizenship of naturalized immigrants found guilty of threatening a police officer or other public official, partaking in polygamy, or practicing female circumcision; and he authorized the deportation of hundreds of Roma, or "gypsies," who had arrived in France from Eastern Europe ("Le bilan" 2012). Sarkozy also expanded minimum sentencing requirements, called for more prisons, appointed high-ranking officials as prefects in departments suffering from significant urban violence, established a police presence in "at-risk" schools, and proposed boot camps for delinquent youth (Joseph 2011; Mucchielli 2012).

Sarkozy's appeal to the far right was not enough to win him the 2012 presidential election. François Hollande entered office promising to bring an end to the austerity measures imposed by his predecessor and to tax the rich. Denouncing Sarkozy's propensity for "American-style" self-promotion and critical of what he presented as the erratic nature of his social and economic record, Hollande also claimed he would be a "normal" president. The situation he faced, however, was anything but normal (Fressoz 2012). Both of France's major political parties confronted strong voter dissatisfaction, as reflected in extreme-right candidate Marine Le Pen's score of 18 percent during the election, higher than her father had ever achieved, and the 11 percent of the vote that went to Jean-Luc Mélenchon, a candidate of the far left. Hollande was not even his own party's first choice. Dominique Strauss-Kahn, who was serving as president of the International Monetary Fund, had been considered a shoo-in for the Socialist nomination until he was caught up in an international sex scandal involving charges of rape and participation in an elite prostitution ring. Against this sobering backdrop, domestic and international problems were mounting. The political landscape at home was charged with concerns about national identity, the assimilation of minority populations, and how to reform the country's sputtering welfare system and relieve its overburdened schools. Abroad, the fate of the Eurozone loomed large. Fears about what would happen if the common currency collapsed under the weight of the financial crisis or if French banks were dragged down by the loans they had floated to other European countries were a stark reminder that France's future was tied more directly than ever to that of the world economy.

It was thus in a context of crisis and transition that I returned to Limoges. When I arrived, the city seemed shabbier than I remembered. A half-dozen empty storefronts dotted the pedestrian Rue du Clocher, one of downtown's main shopping thoroughfares. Graffiti covered the walls of several buildings surrounding the Place de la Motte, the central square where the Sunday market is held. And a number of public green spaces (the Place Jourdan, the Place d'Aine) were overgrown and strewn with litter. I also noted an increased presence of vagrant youth, what the French sometimes call *punks à chiens* (punks with dogs). Sporting dreadlocks, tattoos, and multiple piercings each, five or six sat idly near the entrance of the Monoprix at the Place de la République. As they drank beer and smoked cigarettes, their canine companions barked raucously at passersby. I discovered several more of these homeless teenagers along the walking path bordering the Vienne and found still others gathered outside the cineplex at the Place Denis Dussoubs.[4]

If these observations suggested that Limoges had been hit hard by the economic downturn and was struggling to recover, official statistics confirmed this. Between 2006 and 2012 the city's unemployment rate had jumped from 12 percent to more than 17 percent. Youth joblessness was even higher, registering at a whopping 28 percent. Poverty levels had also soared. When Hollande entered office, a little over 20 percent of Limougeauds lived below the poverty level.[5] Among people thirty and under, the figure was more than 29 percent (INSEE 2015).[6]

How had the individuals who had been part of my study in 2005 and 2006 fared in the economic storm? Had they been able to find jobs? If so, what were the terms of their work arrangements? Six years older, did they at last consider themselves to be "real" adults—that status that seemed so elusive to so many of them during my original fieldwork period? Had they started families of their own? If so, what aspirations or expectations did they have for their children? It was with these questions in mind that I reinterviewed five individuals, three men and two women. Although I had hoped to reconnect with more participants from the original study, tracking people down proved harder than I had expected. I had collected a list of email addresses before leaving Limoges but discovered that many of them no longer worked. Before returning to the city, Facebook was a valuable tool for finding "lost" interlocutors, and after my arrival word of mouth was also effective. In all, I was able to locate ten individuals. Their busy work and family schedules and at least one tragedy precluded meeting with everyone.[7] The interviews I was able to conduct lasted between two and three hours. I recorded these with my interlocutors' permission to facilitate analysis later. I cannot claim with certainty that their stories are representative of what has become of the other young people from the original study, but the range of their experiences suggests that this group is neither overly homogeneous nor excessively idiosyncratic.

I begin with Rachid, who, before I left Limoges in 2006, learned that he had failed the exam required for national certification to teach at the high school level. Originally intent on becoming a history teacher, he was unsure what his future would hold. Although he could take the exam a second time, he feared the result would be the same. Another option, he told me, would be to pursue further coursework to become a lawyer, but he said he was tired of school and was no more certain of passing the many exams a law degree would require. When I returned to Limoges, I was curious to learn what path he had taken.

Finding Rachid in 2012 proved fairly easy. Although the initial email I sent bounced back, a contact at JOC introduced me to a young man who was working as a neighborhood mediator in the Val de l'Aurence. In a happy coincidence, Rachid was his supervisor. When I phoned, Rachid readily agreed to meet with me the next day in his office. My first impression when we sat down at the large table in the studio apartment that had been reserved for the new neighborhood mediation program was that Rachid looked terribly tired. He still sported the same buzz cut, but his usually olive skin was pale, and his eyes, which I remembered as bright and inquisitive, were bloodshot and surrounded by dark circles. When I asked how he was, Rachid complained that he had just worked another all-nighter. Our discussion turned to his work history and current job.

After failing the certifying exam, Rachid decided to leave school, "at least for a while." He took an extended trip to his parents' native Algeria, where in the winter of 2007 he married the daughter of a family friend (Rachid was already engaged in 2006). Although his wife had also grown up in Limoges, her parents, like Rachid's, maintained strong ties with family in Algeria. At first the young couple contemplated making their lives in that country, but ultimately they decided to return to Limoges. "We both speak Arabic, we both have dual citizenship," Rachid explained, "but in the end," he added, "Algeria is not our home. We've only ever been tourists there." Back in Limoges, Rachid's wife found work almost immediately as a social worker at the university hospital. Although her position was temporary, it was eventually converted to a permanent contract. By contrast, Rachid has struggled to find stable employment. He was rehired as a tutor at the homework-help center in the Val de l'Aurence (the job he held when I first met him in 2005), but he was unsatisfied with the limited hours and temporary nature of that work. To supplement the income he earned tutoring, a need that became pressing after the couple welcomed a daughter in 2009, he worked as an aide in a local high school and undertook some temp work, mostly clerical jobs. Then, about two years later, Rachid was hired in a three-year position as the lead neighborhood mediator in the Val de l'Aurence.

Long used by the French government to address the problems of urban violence and decay, social mediation received particular attention in France following the 2005 riots (Stébé 2005, 2012). In the Val de l'Aurence this momentum translated into a new initiative. With a team of six mediators, including Rachid as the supervisor, this "Listen and Mediate" service focused on such everyday problems as noise disturbances and property destruction. The goal, according to Rachid, was to solve disputes among neighbors before involving the police. In practice this amounted to patrolling the neighborhood, holding office hours, and manning a hotline. Most calls, Rachid explained, were from elderly residents "complaining about something or other," but in the end it usually turned out they were "just lonely and looking for someone to talk to."

Nonetheless, Rachid sensed that the neighborhood had become "more dangerous" in recent years. Part of this impression, he explained, was influenced by a vicious murder he had witnessed five months earlier. During the early evening hours of January 26, 2012, a father and his adult son were brutally shot near the Corgnac shopping complex in the upper Val de l'Aurence, apparently as part of a settling of scores over a stolen car. Having heard the gunfire, Rachid and another mediator arrived on

FIG. 19. Interval, the youth hangout in the Val de l'Aurence that had been located in a vacant shopping mart, would soon have a new home. Scheduled to be completed in 2013, the new building, which would be entirely sheathed in vertical cedar slats, was meant to contrast sharply with the surrounding concrete high-rises. Ten local "at-risk" youths were involved in the construction as part of a ready-for-work program.

the scene before the paramedics or police. "The old man was lying on the concrete. His shirt was drenched in blood. He was making awful, guttural sounds. He couldn't talk," Rachid recalled.[8]

Rachid linked the murder to what he saw as a more general decline in social bonds in the neighborhood. Pointing out of the window of the studio apartment where we were seated to a nearby housing tower, he claimed that that building was filled to capacity with immigrant families. "It didn't used to be like that," Rachid insisted. "Before, there was more mixing, people got along, people talked to each other. Now the Val de l'Aurence is turning into a neighborhood of little ghettos." I asked about recent initiatives, pointing out that I had visited a trailer parked in the housing project as part of a nationwide urban renewal program. The trailer's purpose, I learned, was to distribute information to residents about upcoming endeavors aimed at improving the quality of life in the neighborhood. In the Val de l'Aurence this included renovating interior and exterior spaces, improving outdoor lighting, and rebuilding Interval, the youth hangout that had been an important entry point for my research in 2005 and 2006 (fig. 19). Work on the new Interval, I learned, was being undertaken as an *atelier et chantier d'insertion* (Integration workshop and project). The idea was that local "at-risk" youth would learn a trade and contribute to the social revitalization of their neighborhood while being gainfully employed. Rachid, however, scoffed at these efforts: "It's like applying a Band-Aid to a gunshot wound. The intentions are good, but in the long run what difference will it make?"

In the end, Rachid admitted that he longed to distance himself from the Val de l'Aurence. He no longer lived in the housing project. As soon as his wife's contract was made permanent, they moved to a small, rented, single-family home a few minutes away. However, every time he came in to work he felt all of the neighborhood's problems, familiar and new, pressing down on him. Beyond the scope of his job, which required confronting these problems head-on, he worked irregular hours and tended to be away from home late into the evening. This proved especially difficult ever since the family added a second child in 2011. Rachid's three-year contract was set to expire in 2013. There was talk, he told me, that it would be renewed for another three years, but he was not sure he could last that long in the job. In the meantime he was applying to other positions, mostly administrative work in the municipal government. At the same time, he was contemplating returning to school to complete his teacher certification.

Before we took leave of each other, Rachid compared his course to a boat floating on the ocean. Back when he was in school the boat's motor was working, propelling him toward a specified point on the horizon: Rachid would become a history teacher. When he failed the certifying exam, the engine sputtered and died and the boat went adrift. Despite this, Rachid managed to remain positive. "In a sense, I guess I'm lucky," he concluded. "The boat hasn't capsized yet." Still, for him the future was cloudy. "Who knows what storms may lie ahead?" he added grimly. Because of this, Rachid was thankful for his wife's job. Even if he became unemployed in the near future, his family, he surmised, would be able to make do.

I was able to reconnect with Jonathan, also a former tutor in the Val de l'Aurence, thanks to Facebook. Employed in a full-time, permanent position with the Société nationale des chemins de fers français (SNCF; French National Railway Company), France's state-owned railway operator, he was doing better than Rachid, at least in terms of employment. When I left Limoges in 2006, Jonathan was finishing up a short-term contract at the electrical components manufacturer Legrand. He told me that he had applied to over one hundred positions, which had yielded a half-dozen interviews or so but no job offers. As a backup plan, Jonathan had been in touch with the supervisor of a cell-phone boutique where he had worked in the past. It seemed likely that he would be able to get short-term work there, at least for the holiday season. But then, "by a stroke of luck" he got a call back from SNCF about a position as a train handler. It entailed ensuring that incoming and outgoing trains used the correct rails as well as removing cars for repair when necessary and undertaking general track maintenance. The work was "hard," Jonathan told me. Because his functions were mostly performed outdoors, he was constantly exposed to the elements. Furthermore, the hours were irregular, including weekend and nighttime on-call duties. "I didn't mind, though," he maintained, adding that he saw the job as "a foot in the door." Jonathan's assessment turned out to be accurate. Although the position was temporary, his contract was renewed once. Then, a permanent position as a signaling technician opened up. When Jonathan was offered this job, he was elated. Not only did it correspond better to his bachelor's degree in fiber optics and entail more regular hours, but it also meant "real stability."

Like Rachid and his wife, Jonathan moved out of the Val de l'Aurence when he was hired into the full-time position. He bought a small house outside the village of Aixe-sur-Vienne, several kilometers southwest of Limoges. When I met him there for our interview, he was in the midst of a fairly substantial renovation, involving the removal of a wall separating his kitchen and dining space. As he gave me a tour of the project, he explained proudly that he was undertaking all of the work himself.

Apart from his dog, Maquis, Jonathan lived alone. When I asked if he ever thought about settling down and starting a family, at first he sidestepped the question, joking that his mother and I must have been in communication. Later during our conversation, however, he opened up somewhat on the topic. Having devoted so much time and effort to what he called the "management of my career," he had not paid attention to the years passing by. Now thirty-two, he declared himself "too old to get married and start a family." Although Jonathan expressed regret over this, he said he was "happy overall." In addition to his home improvement projects and spending time with his dog, he had taken up running and had even competed in a few local races. Jonathan has not remained in touch with many friends from the housing project, but mentioned that he had heard Hanan (also a former tutor) had married and moved to Paris, where she now worked in marketing.

I found Chloé, who had in 2005 and 2006 occasionally participated in the JOC support group for unemployed youth, through one of that group's former leaders, with whom I had remained in intermittent contact via email. Chloé had unquestionably fared the least well of the individuals I reinterviewed. Of average heft when I originally met her, she had put on a tremendous amount of weight by 2012, so much so that I barely recognized her when she greeted me at her apartment door. When we last spoke, Chloé had just settled back into public housing after a brief stint renting from a private landlord closer to the city center. Having learned that her state-aided contract would not be renewed, she was facing unemployment, a prospect that alarmed her since she had not accumulated enough hours at her current job to qualify for unemployment benefits. Our conversation, which took place in the cramped living room of the Val de l'Aurence apartment she now occupied, was frequently interrupted by the play of her two-year-old daughter, who, Chloé complained, "loves to get into everything."

Chloé described the road she has traveled as "hard." Unable to find work after the end of the state-aided contract she held, she met with a counselor at the *mission locale* who secured "emergency funds" to help her cover living expenses and enrolled her in a sales program, combining coursework and on-the-job training. For the next six months she worked part-time in a city-center toy store. She and her boss, the only other employee and owner of the toy store, "really hit it off," Chloé told me. Upon completion of the sales program, Chloé found herself with an offer of employment—a permanent, full-time position in the toy store! Reminding me that she had completed a vocational certificate in logistics, she explained that the owner was impressed with her ability to manage inventory. This, combined with the expertise she had gained in sales, made her an "ideal" candidate.

Chloé worked at that job until mid 2009, when, according to her, "misfortune struck." As France slumped into its worst recession since World War II, many mom-and-pop businesses folded, including the toy store. Chloé had worked enough hours to collect unemployment insurance, and by then she was over twenty-five and thus eligible for the RMI. Despite this, she sank into what she described as a "deep depression." Around that same time, an old boyfriend, who had been in and out of prison, reappeared; he claimed he needed a place to sleep until he could get back on his feet. Chloé acquiesced, and before long the two had become romantically involved again. When, several months later, she announced that she was pregnant, the boyfriend left; Chloé has not heard from him since. During her pregnancy, Chloé gained far more weight than her midwife recommended, and she has been unable to shed it since giving birth. For a time, she and her daughter managed to live modestly off various state allowances, but, desirous of more income and due to a "change in government policy," Chloé went back to work around her daughter's first birthday.[9] At the time of our conversation she held a short-term contract as a retail sales associate in a city-center clothing store but was on disability leave due to back problems.

Given Chloé's familiarity with state initiatives for the unemployed, I asked her what she thought of recent policy changes. Was the government doing enough? Her answer was a resounding "no." In addition to slashing programs, access to state allowances and benefits has become more difficult, she insisted. For her, this did not make sense in a worsening job market. Chloé also claimed that not everyone in France is treated equally when it comes to the distribution of social assistance. Recounting the conditions surrounding her move to her current apartment, she suggested that "immigrants" have an unfair advantage. Chloé explained that after the birth of her daughter she was eligible for a larger apartment. As she had done in 2006, she requested one of the smaller, newer developments near the city center but ended up with another, albeit slightly more spacious, unit in the Val de l'Aurence. By contrast, "immigrant families," she maintained, were moving into those more desirable apartments "in droves." "It's enough to make you racist," Chloé concluded. I did not ask and therefore can only guess whom Chloé voted for in the 2012 presidential election, if she voted at all. The fact that extreme-right candidate Marine Le Pen received nearly 15 percent of the vote in Limoges during the first round, compared to the 8 percent her father picked up in 2007, is evidence of growing anti-immigrant sentiment in the city.[10] Chloé's experiences and perspectives suggest a link between such xenophobia and the faltering economy.

Like Chloé, Thomas, whom I found still employed at the pharmacy where he had been stocking shelves in 2006, remained a resident of the Val de l'Aurence. Whereas Jonathan suggested that he had put his personal life on hold to focus on work, Thomas had done the opposite. This is perhaps because of the stability Thomas achieved early in life relative to many of his peers. During my original fieldwork period he was one of the few young people I met who had managed to secure a full-time, permanent position, and this despite having dropped out of high school. As was our custom in the past, we met for the follow-up interview in the atrium of the shopping complex where he worked. Thomas had changed little. He was still lanky and soft-spoken; only his hair, now a little thinner, betrayed the passing years.

Because his employment situation had remained the same, Thomas told me he had little on which to update me in that regard. By contrast, there had been many changes in his personal life. Shortly after I left the field, he began "seeing" a young woman, the younger sister of his best friend, also a lifelong resident of the Val de l'Aurence. Within a year, the two were married. In 2009 their first daughter arrived, followed by another in early 2012. Thomas's cell phone was full of pictures of his children, which he showed me, glowing with pride.

Thomas's wife, I learned, worked as a cashier in what used to be Carrefour, the Walmart-like store that served as an anchor in the same shopping complex where the pharmacy was located. When, in 2011, Carrefour announced that it would be closing that site, there was a moment of panic, Thomas related. Would his wife still have a job? Although the family could make do on his salary alone, "things would be tight," he maintained, especially considering the imminent arrival of their second child. These fears were quickly allayed, however, when the couple learned that another big-box retailer (Hyper U) would be taking over the space and retaining most of the personnel, including Thomas's wife. On maternity leave at the time of our conversation, she had a job to return to.

As for Thomas, his work still consisted mostly of stocking shelves at the pharmacy, but he had taken on a few new responsibilities as well: he was involved with inventory management, helping to place and receive orders, and from time to time he lent a hand at the register, ringing up customers when the pharmacist was busy. Thomas liked this part of his job the best, because, according to him, it offered the opportunity to get to know a lot of different people, young and old, from the neighborhood. He was considering returning to school to become a pharmacy technician, which would allow him to take on an advisory role vis-à-vis customers and enable him to command a higher salary. The degree would likely take three years to complete, however. Due to his family commitments, Thomas had put this project "on hold" for the time being.

Given his continued residence in the Val de l'Aurence and his interactions at work with other residents, I asked Thomas to share his impressions of the neighborhood. Did he think it had changed in recent years? Like others in the housing project I had spoken to, he expressed alarm over the recent murder, which, he told me, took place "just steps from where I work." However, he considered that event was "an anomaly." "There have always been bad elements in the neighborhood," he went on to say, recalling how when he was a teenager a group of "thugs" followed him home one day and stole his scooter. The murder, he insisted, although more serious, was not a reflection of the neighborhood in general. "Events like that don't define life here. There are a lot of good people, too. I see them every day," he insisted. When asked if he feared for his safety or that of his family, he replied: "Let's face it, life is more and more uncertain. You never know what might happen to you or to the people you love. That's the case in the Val de l'Aurence, that's the case everywhere." For Thomas, trying to escape this uncertainty was pointless. "You must learn to live with it," he maintained. "Then, you hope for the best."

Manon, a former Jociste and cast member of the amateur police thriller discussed in chapter 6, expressed a similar sense of growing uncertainty in today's world when I reinterviewed her. Although she had stopped participating in JOC several years earlier, a contact there who remained in touch with her was able to provide a phone number. When I called, Manon happily agreed to meet with me. Our conversation took place in a city-center café, not far, she told me, from the apartment she and her partner rented. She made no mention of being a new mother, so it was to my surprise that she arrived wearing a baby sling with her eight-week-old daughter nestled inside. Clearly, there was much to discuss!

Manon began by updating me on her employment experiences. When I left Limoges, she was in the midst of completing a nursing program. Manon reported that she had failed the qualifying exam. "It was a real blow. I didn't know what to do after that," she recalled. As an alternative, she ended up pursuing certification as a visiting home aide, reasoning that this path would allow her to put to use the education and training she had already completed. That the Limousin region has an aging population also meant that there likely would not be a shortage of jobs, Manon explained. And she was right. Once certified, Manon had no trouble obtaining a temporary, but renewable, contract at a local care center. In general, Manon enjoyed her work, especially the contact she had with patients and the knowledge that she was "making a positive impact" on their lives. However, there were some aspects of her job she found challenging. Manon complained about having to work nights and weekends, especially in the beginning. She also said her work could at times be "downright disgusting," depending on the type of ailment her patients suffered from and how dependent they were on her to complete everyday tasks, such as bathing or using the toilet. Worst of all, it was emotionally draining. Working with the elderly, she told me, meant confronting death often. She admitted that she still cried every time she lost a patient.

In Manon's personal life, the most obvious change was the recent arrival of her daughter. Manon and the baby's father, I learned, had met through a mutual friend and had been together for about four years. Holding an associate's degree in physical education, he worked as a trainer at a local gym. Manon related that his position was temporary; he hoped eventually to land a civil service post in physical education, either in the school system or a municipal service, but these were coveted jobs and thus hard to come by. Manon and her partner entered into a civil partnership after living together for about a year, because of the tax advantages this arrangement offers. With the arrival of their daughter, they had discussed marriage but had not made any concrete plans. "I think we're just both overwhelmed right now, being new parents. And everything is so up in the air. We'd like to be more stable in our professional lives," Manon shared. Looking to the near future, she longed to delay her return to work. Her maternity leave would end in less than two months, but she could not imagine being ready to go back to her job. "Truth be told," she said, "I'd like to stay home with my daughter, but we're just not in a position to make that possible right now."

Despite this, Manon considered herself "fortunate" compared to many of her peers. She pointed to the example of Véro to demonstrate how different their lives had turned out. Like Manon, Véro had taken part in the amateur film project, but I had not been able to track her down in 2012. In 2006 she completed a vocational certificate in plumbing and, with the assistance of a counselor at the mission locale, was applying to sales positions at area home-improvement stores. According Manon, when none of these applications led to an offer, Véro worked off the books at a local plumbing outfit, but this arrangement was short-lived. Apparently, her boss refused to pay the hourly rate agreed upon, so Véro quit. She then bounced from one short-term contract to another, often with long periods of inactivity in between, before finally leaving Limoges.

Rumors swirled that she had taken up prostitution in the seaside city of La Rochelle and was living on the streets.

In the end, Manon attributed her own outcome to chance. Although she recognized that Véro's story was exceptional, many friends from her childhood, she told me, still struggled, still faced *galère*, and the situation only seemed to be worsening. When I asked what she thought the fate of the next generation would be, she replied, "There is no more fate. The only certainty today is uncertainty." As for her daughter, who was still snuggled up against her, Manon wished her "lots of luck."

I have chosen to conclude with these words from Manon, because they capture succinctly a sentiment expressed to varying degrees by all of the individuals I reinterviewed. Although these French men and women reported different personal and professional experiences, and some had clearly done better than others, they all attributed, partly or mostly, whatever failures or successes they had had to *chance*. How might we interpret this observation in relation to the findings presented earlier in this book, which suggested that the notion of *social destiny* constituted an important organizing principle for the youth I studied in 2005 and 2006? More specifically, what might it tell us about social inequality today and how people make sense of it?

In the preceding chapters I showed how a sense of social destiny guided the young people I came to know in Limoges's housing projects as they positioned themselves and others in society. This was particularly clear during the 2005 riots and the 2006 CPE protests. Whereas most of my interlocutors expressed empathy for the rioters, even if many condemned the violent approach they took, virtually none said they could identify with the protestors. Drawing lines on the basis of such distinctions as level of education, access to employment, income, and place of residence, they argued that the middle-class students who led the anti-CPE movement had no real grounds to fear job insecurity; in short, they did not share their social destiny. This sense of destiny, I argued, resembled in important ways long-standing notions of class identity, suggesting the continued, albeit muted or muffled, presence of a logic of social class in France. Indeed, the embeddedness of the concept of class in French culture and society undoubtedly explains in large part why the idea of social destiny held such sway over my interlocutors in the first place, whereas in other cultural settings people might not find it nearly as intuitive or compelling.

My interlocutors in Limoges did not use the vocabulary of class, however, preferring the binary included/excluded (*inclus/exclu*) to describe the marginalization they faced. Although they understood themselves to be dangerously close to the precipice of social exclusion, much more so than the student protestors, they insisted that they had not yet fallen into the abyss. This view doubtless owes much to structural changes in the economy, particularly the organization of work: the spread of neoliberal ideologies and policies in the last decades of the twentieth century and continuing today has promoted the fragmentation and casualization of the workforce, which in turn has had a hand in lessening sentiments of belonging to a working class. However, I have argued that my interlocutors' perspective was also guided by another embedded cultural logic—*solidarité*. Whereas social reformers in nineteenth-century France, drawing on revolutionary rhetoric, adopted an organicist definition of this term, whereby different social classes were vital to the "well-being" or "equilibrium" of French society, today *solidarité* in France appears to be more readily understood as a result of engagement with and participation in the collective life of the polity. Being a "good" or "responsible" citizen—a goal encouraged in much of the literature describing the state work programs for "at-risk" youth examined earlier and echoed by the social service providers I interviewed—means being included, or at least this is how the majority of the young people I came to know in Limoges's housing projects understood it. For them, the alternative—being excluded—was tantamount to renouncing French identity itself.

Much discussion in France and beyond in recent years has focused on the consequences of globalization. Although globalization may be seen as a positive force in the United States, doubtless at least in part because of the dominance American cultural exports enjoy on the world stage, in places such as France it is often described in a negative light. Globalization, critics contend, results in cultural homogenization, or the irrevocable loss of cultural diversity. As we have seen, this was a view shared by many in

France during the CPE protests: opponents of the proposed employment contract claimed that it reflected the spread of an especially dangerous strain of freewheeling American capitalism that would ravage France's "tradition" of social welfare.

No less cautionary, my analysis points to a different risk. The persistence in France of the intertwined logics of class and solidarity, even if the salience and content of these logics have shifted over time, suggests that fears about the flattening of cultural difference in the face of globalization may be overstated, at least in this specific case study. Neoliberal ideologies and practices are without a doubt present today in France, but they are understood, negotiated, and (at times, at least) contested in ways that may be described as distinctly "French." The real danger, I would argue, is the potential for these reworked logics to mask old and new inequalities. In the end, the simple binary included/excluded could not account for the diversity of experience and access that my small sample of interlocutors reported in Limoges's housing projects. How could it possibly achieve this on a larger scale? Furthermore, by wiping away the vocabulary of class, even if understandings of class difference persisted, this binary left no meaningful collective point of identification around which to rally—far from it. As we saw, the idea of a precariat could not fill this void, and while some young people in Limoges's housing projects looked to the black American experience to help explain the marginalization they faced, such efforts were largely unsuccessful. This was not because the racism they faced was not real; instead, in the French context, race continues to be widely repudiated as an irrelevant or invalid basis of social classification, much less hierarchical distinction. Indeed, even my interlocutors who complained about racism did so by insisting the French were "hypocrites." More often than not, the result was that individuals described feeling alone as they struggled to manage problems far beyond their control, or even comprehension.

That the individuals I reinterviewed in 2012 framed their experiences in terms of luck instead of destiny suggests an acceleration of this shift. In other words, it appears that any tacit expectations or assumptions about class they may have had in 2005 and 2006, which allowed them to project more or less where on the social map they would or should land, had all but disappeared by 2012. This, it seems to me, could be the result of at least two factors. First, although some observers have argued that the 2008 economic collapse would herald the downfall of neoliberal ideology and modes of governing, this was not the case in France, where, as we saw above, after a few feeble attempts at state intervention Sarkozy announced a new round of free-market reforms, and his successor, Hollande, has followed suit (Marlière 2012; "François Hollande, Liberal?" 2014). It is probable that this reaffirmation of neoliberal doctrine, with its emphasis on personal responsibility and individual solutions to complex social and economic problems, reinforced the inclusion/exclusion binary, particularly in the context of deep economic recession and skyrocketing unemployment, which further stoked fears of social exclusion. Second, life staging cannot be ignored. Whereas in 2005 and 2006 many (most) of my interlocutors did not yet consider themselves to be adults, for the individuals I reinterviewed in 2012 this was no longer a relevant question. To be sure, some had achieved traditional markers of adulthood, including steady employment, marriage (or another stable, long-term commitment), and children of their own, and this could be why they no longer expressed concern about becoming adults. But their comments also indicate that for them the definition of adulthood itself may have shifted to include greater tolerance of uncertainty and unpredictability than had been the case six years earlier. In the end, this is perhaps not surprising given that their assumptions and expectations about adulthood were realized or upset during the worst economic recession France has experienced since World War II. Weighted down by scarcity and the worries that accompany the daily struggle to stay afloat, many may have realized that they never would have the lives they had expected, much less the ones they had hoped for.

In his recent book *A Precariat Charter*, economist Guy Standing (2014) argues that the increasing casualization of labor relations around the world results in more than just vague feelings of uncertainty; it also produces "rights insecurity," turning citizens into "denizens," stripped of basic freedoms and civil liberties. Insisting that the global economic transformations responsible for this trend are inevitable, he maintains that any and all resistance is futile. Instead, Standing calls for a fundamentally new understanding of labor and self to restore human dignity and promote social justice. Work, he submits, should be treated "instrumentally" rather than as a central component of who we are. In other words, we need to get away from the mind-set that the job defines the person. Such "occupational freedom," Standing asserts, would enable policymakers to look beyond the workplace when addressing the thorny questions of inequality and insecurity. As a concrete step, he proposes a citizen's income, payable to all.

Like Standing's previous work on the precariat, this book is bound to incite controversy, especially his recommendations concerning a basic universal income, an idea that has been in circulation for some time but has yet to win widespread support.[11] Nonetheless, I find his notion of "occupational freedom" productive for thinking about new possibilities to sidestep employment insecurity and its consequences. If my study has anything to contribute to this question, it is that local ways of understanding and experiencing work and the social world more broadly may help or hinder such a shift. To be sure, across much of the West and beyond, work has come to be linked more or less explicitly to personhood and social identity, and Standing is mindful of this. "Job titles," he writes, "became social classifiers, and those without a worthy title became the objects of pity if not contempt" (2010, 248). Doubtless, this is no less the case in France than elsewhere. However, my study suggests that something else is also at play in the French context. Beyond providing a readily identifiable marker for sorting people in a social hierarchy, work, I have argued, is bound up, through potent cultural logics linking *solidarité* to inclusion, with conceptions of national identity. Any abrupt attempt to disassociate the two will likely be met with stiff resistance. That is not to say that ideologies are immutable. On the contrary, my follow-up research in Limoges suggests that cultural change is under way. Perhaps if current economic conditions persist, and nothing at present indicates they will not, the radical transformations advocated by Standing will become possible. For the time being, though, it seems probable that individuals such as those whose stories I have related here will continue to understand not only what place they hold in French society but also, fundamentally, what it means to be French in relation to employment or its absence. This, in the final analysis, is why they yearn to labor.

In a prescient afterword to the 1981 republication of *Learning to Labor*, Paul Willis took stock of the economic changes that had occurred since the completion of the original book. Noting the stirrings of a global move toward more flexible employment arrangements as well as rising unemployment rates, especially among the youngest and the least qualified, Willis issued a number of chilling warnings. Society, he predicted, would become increasingly polarized, and this, he suspected, would lead to frustration among the swelling ranks of the oppressed. Violence and antisocial behavior would increase, according to him, giving way in some cases to full-blown political and social unrest (1981, 212).

Now, more than thirty-five years later, Willis's ominous predictions have come true. From parts of West Africa, where boy soldiers turn to war in the absence of any other means of subsistence (Hoffman 2011), to India, where a shockingly high percentage of the population has too little to eat (Yardley 2010), to places closer to home, such as the American Rust Belt, where industrial downsizing has disrupted long-held notions of masculinity and self-worth (Broughton and Walton 2006), or southern Louisiana, where the petroleum industry's system of labor camps fulfills demands for a tractable workforce (Higgins 2005), across the globe an austere regime of insecurity has taken root. One deleterious consequence of this, anthropologist Marc Abélès (2010) suggests, is that today more and more people around the world are forced to turn their attention away from former goals concerning how to live harmoniously together in order to focus their energies instead on sheer survival.

Despite his predictions, Willis was unsure how much these changes would affect the internal cultural logics of the working-class community he studied. He could envision a scenario in which, rather than destroy them, they would be reinforced. Nevertheless, Willis insisted on the "*irreducibility* and *unpredictability*" (1981, 201) of such cultural logics, arguing not only that changes in the employment landscape would likely play out differently in different places, but also that the results could not be easily anticipated. My study in Limoges certainly supports this conclusion and, more broadly, makes a case for the vital importance of continued anthropological investigation of the changing nature of work. Indeed, it is only by drawing out how the global processes driving shifts in employment practices intersect with local ideologies in the working out of everyday life that we can hope to understand the struggles over work insecurity under way across the globe today; and it is only then that we will be in a position to begin to envision locally appropriate solutions. This is one of the great challenges facing anthropology—dare I say all of humanity—as we look toward the future.

Notes

Introduction

1. For the most recent figures on employment in France, see the website of the Observatoire des inégalités (Observatory of inequalities), a nonpartisan French think tank whose scientific committee is composed of a number of high-profile French intellectuals (http://www.inegalites.fr).

2. In *Le Père Goriot* (1835), Balzac wrote: "Le secret des grandes fortunes sans cause apparente est un crime oublié, parce qu'il a été proprement fait" (The secret of great fortunes without apparent cause is a crime forgotten, for it was properly done).

3. See "20 Nation Poll Finds Strong Global Consensus: Support for Free Market System . . . ," Program on International Policy Attitudes, University of Maryland, January 11, 2006 (http://www.worldpublicopinion.org).

4. See "Perceptions to Globalization across 10 Countries," IFOP, January 26, 2011 (http://www.ifop.com).

5. The term *Trente glorieuses* was coined by the economist Jean Fourastié (1979) by analogy with the "Three Glorious" days of the July Revolution of 1830.

6. Of course, *dirigisme* cannot take all the credit for this growth. The accelerated economic expansion witnessed in France during the *Trente glorieuses* was also a function of its economy's initial lag relative to these other countries.

7. For an ethnographic account of the complex interplay of forces and considerations that goes into the making of an elite "esprit de corps" at ENA, see chapter 4 of Irène Bellier's (1993) monograph.

8. Under France's system of absolute monarchy, society was organized into three distinct, ranked orders: the clergy, the nobility, and the "third estate"

(everyone else). Such hierarchy, defenders of this arrangement maintained, was essential to social well-being, and in this respect the nobility was thought to play a particularly important role, or rather roles. Nobles were (or were supposed to be) at once intermediaries between the king and his people, the kingdom's defending warriors, and, as landlords, custodians of the kingdom's prosperity. Above all, nobles were called upon to be virtuous: "Nobility, their priests warned, meant setting a Christian example of virtuous behavior, respecting the sacraments, dispensing charity, and eschewing the sin of pride to which nobles were especially prone" (Doyle 2009, 38). The expression *noblesse oblige* (nobility obliges) draws its meaning from this charge. To be noble meant to enjoy various privileges: nobles were exempt from certain taxes and duties; they could not be pressed into forced labor on the roads (in fact, it was considered illegal for any noble to undertake manual labor or engage in any type of trade); they had access to special courts where they could take their grievances; they could not be subjected to corporal punishment; and, if convicted of a capital offense, they were beheaded rather than hanged. But with such privilege came great responsibility. Nobles were expected to demonstrate honor and, if necessary, sacrifice for the general good—including, as the kingdom's protectors, the ultimate sacrifice of their own lives. This higher calling was held to generate a superior moral code, justifying nobles' privileged social status.

9. In particular, this work has built upon Foucault's (2008) notion of biopolitics.

10. Serge Audier (2012) reminds us, however, of the significant French lineage of the word *neoliberalism* and the various groups in early-twentieth-century France that declared themselves to be "neoliberal."

11. The idea that the French should tame or rationalize nature extends beyond this context, as Susan Carol Rogers (2000) has highlighted in her discussion of the perceived social functions of farming in France.

12. Figures according to the OECD Statistics Database: Total Social Expenditures (https://stats.oecd.org/Index.aspx?DataSetCode=SOCX_AGG).

13. France is not the exception in this regard. Writing on the notion of precarity, Neilson and Rossiter (2008) note that most work for most workers around the world has historically been precarious.

14. For a compelling ethnographic account of this consolidation, see Caroux-Destray (1974).

15. The term *précarité* was first used in the 1950s and 1960s in discussions about those individuals who, for various reasons, were not benefiting from the country's rapid modernization.

16. This idea is also found in some sociological writing. See, e.g., Caillé (1994) or Castel (1995).

17. Political economist and secretary of labor during the Clinton administration Robert B. Reich (2001) has, e.g., suggested that increased flexibility in employment practices can be advantageous for employees.

18. At the start of their book the authors note that one of the questions driving their research project had to do with why workers who in 1990 accounted for nearly 25 percent of the workforce had nonetheless become "invisible" in French public debate (Beaud and Pialoux 1999, 15).

19. French social historian Gérard Noiriel warns against this temptation in his synthesis of workers' experiences in nineteenth- and twentieth-century France, arguing that the "distinctive characteristic of the history of the French working class is its extreme instability" (1990, xii). Richard Hoggart ([1957] 1998), whose semi-autobiographical reflections on the British working class have gained some attention among French social scientists (Passeron 1999), is equally critical of this tendency.

20. All translations of unpublished material are my own.

21. The title alone of the Fassins's book implies this shift, even if qualified with a question mark: *De la question sociale à la question raciale?*

22. I use the adjective "blue-collar" to translate the French notion of *populaire*, even if this word does not quite convey the same meaning. Whereas "blue-collar" tends to be used to designate manual laborers in such fields as manufacturing, mining, or construction, *populaire* has a broader sense, capturing the idea of the "people" or the "masses"—in other words, individuals located toward the bottom of a social hierarchy, including, but not limited to, manual laborers. For a discussion of the meanings attributed to the term *populaire* in France, see Grignon and Passeron (1989).

23. Consider, e.g., these headlines: "Sarkozy et la banlieue: Les noces rebelles" (*L'Express*, April 4, 2012); "Melanchon: 'Pour la banlieue le mot-clé est le partage des richesses'" (*L'Humanité*, April 1, 2012); "François Hollande détaille ses mesures pour la banlieue" (*Le Figaro*, March 16, 2012).

24. On the French conception of social and cultural "mixing," see, e.g., MacMaster (1991).

25. For up-to-date income guidelines, see https://www.limogeshabitat.fr/plafonds_de_ressources_2015_1.pdf.

26. Many months later, after building a network of contacts among the city's social service providers, including a social worker at the public housing office, I learned that such long waiting periods generally only apply to some of the city's

public housing; the largest (and most rundown) developments frequently have at least a few vacant units. "Too bad you didn't know me when you arrived," the social worker said. "I could have gotten you in." I can only guess why the agent I first met turned me down. This experience demonstrates the influence local actors have over the direction ethnographic research takes and the difference between what is available if one has access to informal local networks as opposed to being an outsider, who may be held to the formal rules.

27. Although this age bracket is approximate (some of the young people I came to know were younger and others older), I chose it because, at the time of my research, sixteen was the minimum age when minors, with the approval of their parents, could leave school to work, whereas twenty-four was the last year of ineligibility for the RMI.

28. Although I have employed pseudonyms, I have been consistent in their use and have assigned a single name to each interlocutor cited in the book. Thus, the reader interested to do so can follow which comments have been made by whom with the assurance that, e.g., "Jonathan" in chapter 2 is the same person as "Jonathan" in chapter 6.

1. On Edge

1. As I noted in the introduction, many months later, after getting to know a social worker at the public housing office, I learned that this was not entirely true.

2. For example, two prominent downtown streets are named after Jean Jaurès and Jules Guesde, two stanch socialists who lectured in nineteenth-century Limoges.

3. In addition to books by Merriman and Corbin, a number of other works have scrutinized this leftist tradition. Kathryn Amdur (1987) has studied the twentieth-century trade union movement, David Wright (1991) has examined the socialists' grip on municipal control during the same period, Louis Pérouas (1979) has established the importance of anticlericalism for the city, and Laird Boswell (1998) has explored the surrounding area's communists.

4. Composed principally of small-scale farmers, the majority of the French population remained rural until the 1930s, and a "rural exodus" only really took off during the *Trente glorieuses* following World War II.

5. For a case study, see Joan Scott's (1974) fascinating account of the glass workers of Carmaux.

6. Local stocks of kaolin have since been depleted. According to an employee

at one of Limoges's last working porcelain factories, today the substance is shipped in, mainly from Brittany.

7. Merriman reports: "Tuberculosis killed thirty-six of the seventy-five porcelain workers who died in 1887; the following year twenty of thirty such workers who were examined by a doctor suffered from the disease; another survey found that 73 percent of female workers had it" (1985, 170).

8. The word *faubourg* derives from the French words *faux* (false) and *bourg* (town or village).

9. In addition to the old Viraclaud quarter, Merriman notes, prostitution was especially prevalent in the "amorous" woods near the estate of Martin de la Bastide, located beyond the northern perimeter of the city (1985, 96). The reputation of these woods seems to have changed little since the nineteenth century. An avid runner, I was delighted to find well-blazed trails in the wooded park that now occupies this space. However, I was warned by locals to avoid this area after dark. The Bois de la Bastide, as well as the nearby shores of the man-made Lac d'Uzurat, I was told, are the stomping grounds of prostitutes and transvestites.

10. In 1940s war-torn France, Limoges was the largest city near the demarcation line, situated just seventy kilometers from the occupied zone.

11. One such new industry was electrical components. The manufacturer Legrand, headquartered in Limoges, began as a porcelain factory but diversified its production to include electrical components when competition to the porcelain industry from abroad became a threat in the early decades of the twentieth century. Following World War II, Legrand turned exclusively to the manufacture of electrical wiring devices, and today it is a world leader in this area.

12. Concern over political stability in nineteenth-century France was well founded. After the Revolution, France witnessed the birth and passing of no fewer than six different regimes before the founding of the Third Republic in 1870: the First Republic (1792–1804), the First Empire (1804–14/15), the Restoration Monarchy (1814/15–30), the July Monarchy (1830–48), the Second Republic (1848–52), and the Second Empire (1852–70).

13. For an in-depth discussion of these changes, see Pinkney's (1972) classic account.

14. As Pinkney (1972) notes, this criticism was in part based on a romanticized vision of pre-Haussmann Paris, according to which members of different social classes lived next door to each other or even in the same houses. T. J. Clarke (1984) has argued that rather than create a new order of class segregation,

Haussmannization reflected above all moral and societal changes that were already under way.

15. Janet Horne writes: "The bourgeoisie's gradual appropriation of urban space can be traced from the nineteenth-century preoccupation with building sewage systems and controlling the stench of refuse and human excrement to the twentieth-century utopia of the planned city and suburbs" (2002, 267).

16. This thinking does not appear to be unique to Limoges. Kenny Cupers (2014) pursues the idea of how the development and construction of the *grands ensembles* were about more than the expansion of the welfare state. They, the author contends, were at least partially the result of intense aspirations on multiple levels in the context of growing mass consumerism.

17. For a detailed discussion of the *villes nouvelles* initiative, see Epstein (2011), particularly chapter 1.

18. In his ethnographic study of sustainable urban development in a northeastern arrondissement of Paris, Andrew Newman (2013) observed a similar emphasis on the notion of civic engagement. By pushing residents to accept responsibility for monitoring and controlling their own neighborhoods, city planners and politicians, he argues, engendered a new neoliberal subjectivity which he terms "vigilant citizenship."

19. In February 1989, Ayatollah Khomeini famously issued a fatwa calling for the death of novelist Salmon Rushdie. A month later, the Islamic Salvation Front was born in Algiers. At the same time, religiously inflected conflict raged in Lebanon. As John Bowen notes, "Religion, but particularly Islam, seemed to have crossed into politics in places very close to France" (2007, 83).

20. Tissot cites François Dubet's classic 1987 study, *La galère*, as emblematic of this body of work.

21. Limoges's three ZUSs—Beaubreuil, La Bastide, and Le Val de l'Aurence—have also been declared *zones de redynamisation urbaine* (ZRUs; Urban revitalization areas), signifying that the income base is especially low.

2. Longing for Yesterday

1. Consider, e.g., Daphne Berdahl's (1999a) discussion of *Ostalgie* in the context of German reunification. For more recent treatments of nostalgia by anthropologists, see the volume edited by Olivia Angé and David Berliner (2015).

2. There are a few exceptions to this rule, including when a CDD is used to replace an employee whose departure precedes the definitive elimination of the position he or she occupied or for fixed-term employment abroad. In each of these cases, the contract may cover a period of up to twenty-four months.

3. For a discussion of this shift, see chapter 1.

4. These are, of course, stereotypes. On the matter of religion alone, even if there has been a great deal of concern in France of late over the rise in Islamic fundamentalism among outer-city youth, such fears are largely exaggerated. For a discussion of religious affiliation in Limoges's outer city, see chapter 4.

5. "Nous, on racaille!" Karim explained. The verb *racailler* comes from the noun *racaille*, meaning "scum" or, in the context of the outer city, "*banlieue* trash." It is generally considered an insult, although in its back-slang form, *caillera*, it can take on a positive meaning in the outer city, close to that of "gangsta" or "thug." Karim's comment could therefore be approximated in English as "We thug around" or "We thug it up."

6. Carrefour serves as the anchor store in the Val de l'Aurence shopping complex, and Cora and Conforama do so in Beaubreuil.

7. For an in-depth discussion of the links between such verbal play, honor, and reputation in a French outer city, see Lepoutre (1997), especially part 4.

8. See chapter 1 for a discussion of the development of Limoges's *grands ensembles*.

9. Not everyone I met was enthusiastic about these conveniences. A few cynics suggested they were put into place to keep the outer city's "undesirable" elements out of the city center.

10. Youth continuing on to a vocational high school (*lycée professionnel*) may remain in the outer city, where several of these establishments are located. The only general-track high school (*lycée général*) is in the city center.

11. Local social workers and association leaders lamented over this trend, which, they told me, they attempted to combat by organizing regular outings to the city center during which neighborhood youngsters could visit museums, attend the theater, explore the medieval district, or participate in other "cultural" activities.

12. At the time, Jonathan was working part-time at a cell phone boutique in the city center.

13. Noureddine's choice of the fictional American character Tom Sawyer deserves attention. With it, he may have been attempting to display a certain sort of cosmopolitan knowledge not usually associated with outer-city youth. It is just as likely, though, that he had been influenced by the popular Japanese anime series bearing the same name, which aired in France during the 1980s. Consider the lyrics of the show's theme song: "Tom Sawyer . . . he knows the marvels of the forest: the roads, the rivers, and the paths. He carries in his pockets fabulous things: three lengths of string, some stones and some wood, which he shares with all his friends" (my translation).

14. As Trincaz, Puijalon, and Humbert (2011, 124) note, today the term *quatrième âge* (fourth age) has appeared to label the very elderly (and therefore dependent on those who work), as life expectancy in France, as elsewhere, has increased.

15. In ancien régime France, the word *privilèges* was used to refer to the social and economic advantages held by the nobility (for a more detailed description, see the introduction, note 8).

16. Fred Davis (1979) somewhat clumsily terms this second sort of remembrance "antiquarian feeling."

17. Hanan's position as a counselor was created with a state-aided contract. For more on these types of work contracts, see chapter 3.

18. For a lengthier discussion of the concept of *noblesse oblige*, see the introduction.

3. Jobs for At-Risk Youth

1. Students also benefited from a slight reduction in fare on public transportation (municipal bus system, tramway). In 2006 they paid just under 24 euros for a monthly pass (the full fare was 30 euros). Most of the young people at the roundtable had left the school system and therefore were ineligible for this discount.

2. In 2012, Chevènement's initial goal was finally met, with 85 percent of eighteen-year-olds earning the *baccalauréat*.

3. Whereas in 1965, 35 percent of eighteen-year-olds had left school without a degree, in 1994 this was the case for only 8 percent. By 2008 this figure had barely budged, hovering around 6 percent (Lefresne 2010, 188).

4. In 2009 the RMI was replaced by the Revenu de solidarité active (RSA; Active solidarity income). Although the age restriction was lifted with the name change, it is unlikely that many young people will qualify for this benefit. Among the conditions for eligibility, the applicant must prove that he or she has worked 3,500 hours in the past three years. Due to high rates of youth unemployment and underemployment, accumulating this amount of time worked will probably prove difficult.

5. For a discussion of the different types of work arrangements possible under French law, see chapter 2.

6. Although there is some overlap, these terms designate different levels of achievement toward the CAP or the BEP, which are vocational certificates delivered after successful completion of two years of high school study in a vocational track. *Sans qualification* indicates little or no high school study; although the individual may have begun working toward a CAP or BEP, he or she did not complete all of the required coursework. *Peu ou pas qualifié* suggests

that vocational training was undertaken, and the coursework was perhaps completed, but the individual does not possess a CAP or BEP, for lack of passing the qualifying exams. *Peu ou pas diplômé* generally refers to someone having completed a vocational program; he or she may possess a CAP or BEP, but no other academic credentials (Aeberhardt, Crusson, and Pommier 2011, 157).

7. For a discussion of the term *quartier sensible*, see chapter 1.

8. Jacques Chirac called on the French to wage a war against exclusion in 1995, when he launched his presidential campaign by suggesting that a "social fracture" separated the haves from the have-nots.

9. During the 1980s and 1990s France experienced three periods when the president's party did not control a majority in the legislature and was not represented in the cabinet.

10. For more information regarding these measures and others, see Aeberhardt, Crusson, and Pommier (2011).

11. Internship programs that have specified a professionalization component include the Contrat de qualification (Skill formation contract), the Contrat d'adaptation (Adaptation contract), and the Stage d'initiation à la vie professionnelle (Initiation to the world of work internship).

12. The TUC program was widely criticized because it conferred the status of intern rather than employee. Beneficiaries were therefore barred from a number of social protections, including the accumulation of retirement benefits and unemployment insurance. In 1990 the TUC program was phased out in favor of the CES program, which, in contrast, conferred an actual CDD (fixed-term employment contract).

13. See Schwartz (1981).

14. Consider, e.g., the names of the following programs: Itinéraire personnalisé d'insertion professionnelle (Personal itinerary for work reintegration) and Trajet d'accès à l'emploi (Pathway to employment program).

15. Close relationships between social service professionals and the young people they work with were not always positively viewed. I knew at least one street educator (for a description of this term, see following note) who was criticized by his peers for being "too close" to the youth he served.

16. The position of *éducateur de rue* developed out of the specialized prevention movement that emerged in France in the wake of World War II, when the first *clubs d'enfants* were organized. Oftentimes recruited from among outer-city residents, *éducateurs de rue* work directly with young people on the streets. In Limoges, at least, they tended to try to draw young people into neighborhood associations based on their interests. For example, one *éducateur de rue* ran

a weekly hip-hop workshop, and another organized a monthly videogame tournament.

17. FJTs emerged as part of the post–World War II response to the housing crisis (see chapter 1). Initially run either by industrialists looking to house needed labor or religious groups (particularly catholic nuns) concerned about the rise of deviance and promiscuity in cities, they have since undergone an evolution shaped by changing economic conditions. In today's labor market, they mostly house young people (under age twenty-six) working under fixed-term contracts (CDD, internship, temporary job) and thus unable to secure leases elsewhere. A number of FJTs exist in Limoges. Most are located in or near the city's peripheral housing projects.

18. The terms sometimes used to describe the *banlieues* are illuminating in this respect. In the media they have been called "excluded," "marginalized," and "relegated" since at least the beginning of the 1980s (Champagne 1993), and in academic circles they have been presented as "exiled" (Dubet and Lapeyronnie 1992) and likened to "ghettos" (Lapeyronnie 2008). The popular designation *la zone* perhaps best encapsulates the perceived isolation of these areas. Originally used during the nineteenth century to describe the military no-man's-land located just beyond Paris's city walls, today this term is routinely applied to France's urban peripheries more generally (Boyer and Lochard 1998, 45–47).

19. In his ethnographic study of the representation of immigrants in Lyon during the 1970s, Ralph Grillo (1985) traced the development of this world of intense social service support. More recently, Faïza Guène (2004) has offered a vivid account of it in a semi-autobiography.

20. Some of these abbreviations, I would learn, represented nationwide organizations or programs: ASSEDIC (Association pour l'emploi dans l'industrie et le commerce) was the agency that, until 2009, when it was merged with the national unemployment office, handled unemployment benefits. CAF (Caisse d'allocations familiales) provides social welfare family allowances. SNC (Solidarités nouvelles face au chômage) is a national, privately funded association whose members work in teams of two to assist job seekers. CIVIS (Contrat d'insertion dans la vie sociale) was in 2005 a relatively new state initiative aimed at "accompanying at-risk youth" as they searched for work. Other abbreviations were specific to Limoges: ALSEA (Association limousine de sauvegarde de l'enfance et de l'adolescence) is Limoges's "specialized prevention" agency, whose personnel include neighborhood educators and case managers, such as the one assigned to Véronique; BTG (Bouge ta galère) is a support group

for long-term unemployed youth that was sponsored by, yet run separately from, Limoges's local chapter of JOC.

21. This is the focus of chapter 5.

22. Katherine Browne (2004) and Florence Weber (1989) have noted similar adaptive strategies among disadvantaged populations, albeit in very different settings.

23. For a discussion of these reflections on the past, see chapter 2.

24. For a lengthier discussion of this perception, see chapter 6.

25. See Heller (2013) and Rogers (2000) on references to solidarity in agriculture, Poulin-Deltour (2015) on the gay rights debate, and Védrine and Moïsi (2001) on globalization.

26. Durkheim ([1893] 1984) famously defined *solidarité organique* (organic solidarity) as the result of an increasing division of labor in society.

4. Burning *Banlieues*

1. A recording of the complete address can be found at http://www.ina.fr/video/2964833001/declaration-du-president-de-la-republique-monsieur-jacques-chirac-video.html.

2. For a discussion of color-blind policy in France, see Bleich (2004).

3. See Hargreaves (2005) as well as the following newspaper articles: "Beaucoup de ces Africains sont polygames," *Libération*, November 15, 2005; "Le Ministre de l'emploi fait de la polygamie une 'cause possible' des violences urbaines," *Le Monde*, November 16, 2005.

4. This work coincides with and draws on the recent translations into French of such key texts as Judith Butler's *Gender Trouble* (1989, 2006), Gayatri Spivak's "Can the Subaltern Speak?" (1988, 2006), and Paul Gilroy's *Black Atlantic* (1993, 2010).

5. For a useful discussion of the emergence in France in the first decade of the twenty-first century of race a category of analysis, see the special issue of *Public Culture* on "Racial France" edited by Janet Roitman, particularly the contributions of Jean-François Bayart, Achille Mdembe, and Ann Laura Stoler: *Public Culture* 23, no. 1 (2011): 55–84, 85–119, and 121–56, respectively.

6. *Tenir les murs*, "to hold the walls," describes the action of (young) people who hang out as opposed to doing something productive.

7. Soccer was a favorite, and talk about this sport really picked up the following winter and spring during the African Cup and World Cup tournaments. Basketball was also a popular sport, thanks to the (mostly past) national and international successes of Limoges's professional basketball team. An

American—a certain Ed Murphy—I was told repeatedly, used to be one of the team's star players.

8. The segment can be viewed at http://www.ina.fr/video/2951569001019.

9. During a visit the previous June to the Parisian suburb of La Courneuve, where an eleven-year-old boy had been killed by a stray bullet, Sarkozy proclaimed, "The hoodlums are going to disappear. I'll get the manpower necessary, but we're going to clean up this neighborhood." A week later, also in La Courneuve, he was quoted as saying, "The term 'pressure-wash' is the right term, because we have to clean this up." For a news summary on Sarkozy's "inflammatory" language during the months leading up to the riots, see http://www.ina.fr/video/2954175001011/sarkozy-et-les-banlieues-video.html.

10. The French Ministry of the Interior is charged with maintaining public order; this includes overseeing police services, national security, and immigration policy. These functions contrast radically with those of the U.S. Ministry of the Interior, which is responsible for the management and conservation of federally owned land.

11. Immediately following the incident, there was a great deal of uncertainty about what had actually happened. In a tell-all account (Mignard and Tordjman 2006) coauthored by the lawyers of the teenage victims' families, it appears that the officers on the scene witnessed the three youths scale the walls of the electrical substation but declined to follow them, stating that they would not live long. Despite this, in May 2015 the officers were found innocent by a court of law.

12. In the song "Me revoilà," Diam's proclaims: "J'rappe pour les tess, j'rappe pour les pav'," meaning, "I rap for the projects, I rap for the detached houses." In back slang, cité becomes tess (from téci); a pavillon (pav') is a modest (two- or three-bedroom) detached home. In Limoges, most of the grands ensembles were surrounded by pavillons.

13. Diam's has said this in numerous interviews. See also Sibony (2007).

14. The track "Marine" conveys a similar message. In this open letter to Marine Le Pen, the daughter of and soon-to-be successor to National Front leader Jean-Marie Le Pen, Diam's contrasts two Frances: that of the xenophobic and racist extreme right and that of the multiethnic and multiracial banlieues. "Why are you so pale?" she asks Marine Le Pen before adding, "Come visit my neighborhood. It's colorful, it's jovial."

15. "Ma France à moi": https://youtu.be/aU0qq4_3jGY.

16. For a recent depiction of these ideals, consider Coca-Cola's "It's Beautiful" ad, which premiered during the 2014 Super Bowl. The commercial features the

familiar song "America the Beautiful," sung in a number of different languages (https://youtu.be/D4BC8zUfNhU). The immediate backlash the Coca-Cola ad received on Twitter and the company's Facebook page brings into sharp focus just how contested this vision of a harmonious, multicultural United States really is (Lee 2014).

17. As I will discuss below, interlocutors rarely distinguished between the sometimes very different stances on race and racial identity held by these American icons. Nonetheless struck by their familiarity with at least their names, I asked where they had learned about them. Responses varied, including television, especially serials such as *Law and Order* and csi where racial tensions sometimes take center stage, as well as American feature films. At least a half dozen young people had seen the blockbuster *Malcolm X*. One young man commented that as a child he had watched most of the miniseries *Roots* when it aired in France. Other young people told me they had completed school projects related to the American civil rights movement. One young woman, for example, said she had given a presentation in junior high school on Rosa Parks.

18. A reproduction of the map is available at http://www.lemonde.fr/societe/infographie/2005/11/07/les-principales-villes-touchees-par-les-violences_707204_3224. html.

19. A return to normalcy was declared based on the observation that roughly "only" one hundred cars had been burned in a single night, a figure close to the national daily average in 2005.

20. The young man was not entirely mistaken. According to a report published by INSEE in 1999, Haute-Vienne was second only to Côtes d'Armor in terms of reported suicides. For every one hundred thousand inhabitants there were thirty-four suicides in Haute-Vienne, compared to thirty-nine in Côtes d'Armor. The author of the report attributed this higher-than-average rate to these areas' aging populations, however, not their climates (Thomas 1999).

21. The word *black*, borrowed from English, tended to be preferred, although I also heard the French term *noir* and its back-slang equivalent, *renoi*.

22. As Kenneth Prewitt's (2013) work on the U.S. census suggests, this differs from common practice in the United States.

23. Daniel Sabbagh (2004) has suggested that in France, perhaps more than other places, the notions of race and ethnicity are blurred. *Ethnique*, he submits, is often used as a euphemism for *racial*, since "race" tends to be viewed as a racist term in France. My data suggest that something different is happening in Limoges's housing projects. Youth there seemed to understand race as being separate. They recognized the visible reality of physiological differences

between the categories "Arab" and "French," but they did not believe that this difference necessarily corresponded to a cultural (ethnic) difference. In other words, for them someone can be physiologically indistinguishable from "French" people (like an Italian or an American) but not be culturally French.

24. Consider, e.g., the multitude of political movements founded throughout American history on the idea of racial identity, including white supremacy movements (e.g., the Red Shirts, the White League, the Ku Klux Klan) as well as the various groups associated with the Black Power movement.

25. With regard to the idea that social cohesion would be threatened if the number of immigrants became too high in any single building or neighborhood, see MacMaster (1991) on the "threshold of tolerance."

5. Precariat Rising?

1. A complete transcript of the exchange is available at http://archives. gouvernement.fr/villepin/acteurs/interventions_premier_ministre_9/dans_ les_medias_497/intervention_journal_televise_20h_55513.html.

2. The introductory paragraphs of the text submitted by Dominique de Villepin to the National Assembly on January 16, 2006, regarding the proposed Loi pour l'égalité des chances make this distinction explicit: "Some of our fellow citizens still experience today inequalities of opportunity that are not only unacceptable in relation to the principles of the Republic but also endanger national cohesion. . . . The population living in disadvantaged urban areas (ZUSS) is proportionally younger and less educated than the national average. [This population] is therefore at greater risk of being unemployed. . . . The law presented below . . . aims to make equal opportunities a reality for all." The full text is available at http://www.assemblee-nationale.fr/12/projets/pl2787.asp.

3. For a description of some of this policy, see chapter 3.

4. Villepin used Article 49-3 of the constitution to push the Loi pour l'égalité des chances through the National Assembly, arguing that the matter was "of the utmost urgency," given the riots the previous fall (Roger 2006). The full text of the law is available at http://legifrance.gouv.fr/affichTexte. do?cidTexte=JORFTEXT000000268539&dateTexte=&categorieLien=id.

5. There were some exceptions. The CPE could, e.g., be used by a business employing twenty people or less that was based out of someone's home. Otherwise, the CNE, described later in this chapter, would apply. With regard to the cutoff age, twenty-five has been the maximum age for a number of specialized contracts initiated in France over the years to facilitate young people's access to work (see chapter 3). This is because beginning at age twenty-five, unemployed

persons became eligible for the RMI, which provided a guaranteed minimum income to the jobless who did not have rights to unemployment benefits. In 2006, RMI benefits amounted to 433.06 euros per month for individuals living alone. In 2009 the RMI was replaced by the RSA, which enforces much more strictly the obligation of claimants to find work.

6. For an in-depth description of employer responsibilities regarding dismissals, see the voluminous *Code du travail*.

7. If an employee completed an internship or held a CDD prior to being hired under a CPE by the same employer, this time worked would be subtracted from the two-year probationary period.

8. After the two-year consolidation period the CPE would become an ordinary CDI, and the onus of supplying justification for termination would revert back to the employer.

9. In theory, even under the CPE employers could only dismiss employees for "real and serious" causes, even if they were not required by law to disclose those reasons at the time of termination. If, subsequently, a dismissed employee brought a case to court, the employer would be required to defend his or her decision to terminate the contract.

10. The news media tended to support this view. Consider, e.g., the report aired March 15, 2006, as part of the *France 2* nightly news broadcast. Through an examination of the attempts by employees holding CNEs to obtain bank loans, its unambiguous concern was to determine the effects of the proposed CPE. As will be discussed later in this chapter, the CNE (Contrat nouvelles embauches) had been passed into law the previous summer. It was identical to the CPE but was limited to businesses with twenty employees or less. With hidden cameras in tow, journalists, disguised as CNE holders, applied for loans at three separate banks. They reported that in each case their request was denied after it proved impossible to find insurers willing to underwrite the loans. (In one instance, a bank suggested the loan applicant use personal property as collateral.) The message conveyed was that the CPE would result in increased *précarité*, as the CNE already did, but to an even greater extent.

11. A general assembly was held at the University of Limoges's Faculté des lettres and Faculté des sciences on January 31 to plan for the February 7 demonstration. In addition to university students, some high school students and representatives of a number of unions (AGEL-FSE, SUD, UNEF, CFDT, CGT) were in attendance. *L'Écho de la Haute Vienne* reported that five thousand people demonstrated on February 7 ("Début de mobilisation" 2006); *Le Populaire du Centre* estimated that participation was closer to four thousand ("La mobilisation" 2006).

12. These figures were reported in the local press (Bourgnon 2006a).

13. Membership from the following unions was present at all of the major marches and rallies: Confédération française démocratique du travail (CFDT; French democratic confederation of labor), Confédération générale du travail (CGT; General confederation of labor), Force ouvrière (FO; Workers' force), Solidaires unitaires démocratiques (SUD; Solidary, unitary, democratic).

14. Recall that the CPE could only be used to hire persons under age twenty-six. The people present at the meeting were therefore not directly concerned by it.

15. For a discussion of these sorts of critiques, see chapter 3.

16. In France, public contestation often takes the form of "orderly disorder" (Murphy 2011). General strikes are called well in advance, and law enforcement is alerted in an effort to maintain public order and safety.

17. A search on LexisNexis returned 459 articles containing the term "CPE."

18. In Limoges, students created a blog (http://manifestation87.skyrock.com) to plan and discuss demonstrations. Following the CPE protests it remained active, serving as a platform to protest other government initiatives. As of June 2016 the site was still live, but the last post, which concerned a demonstration against proposed budget cuts to the school system, was made in January 2009. According to my contact at the Jeunes CGT, the Internet, along with cell phones, constituted the primary means by which young people stayed in touch with each other during the struggle.

19. See, e.g., the article in *L'Écho de la Haute Vienne* on March 1, 2006, with the headline "Tous unis contre l'embauche embûche!" (Altogether against dead-end jobs!).

20. The following excerpt from an article about an early general assembly held at the University of Limoges, during which students debated actions to be taken against the CPE, constitutes one of the rare exceptions: "It remains to be seen if, with the high school students, [the university students] will be able to mobilize other secondary school students, including those in vocational programs, who, as always, will be the first victims of this Kleenex contract. If the CPE constitutes an attack on all young people, it also represents a new assault on the young proletariat, already bounced between periods of training and temp-work assignments" ("Début de mobilisation" 2006).

21. An end to the strike was called for in the Faculté des lettres, as well as in most high schools in Limoges, on April 13.

22. Launched in 1997 by the Jospin administration, Emplois-jeunes aimed at reducing

youth unemployment by heavily subsidizing positions (CDIs or CDDs) in the non-market sector. For more information on this program, see chapter 3.

23. A small minority of my interlocutors participated in the protests. I will return to this point shortly.

24. For a discussion of past employment policy, see chapter 3.

25. The general education high schools in Limoges went on strike before the vocational high schools.

26. None of my interlocutors admitted to this practice, which they presented as an abuse of the welfare system. As we saw in chapter 3, they were critical of stereotypes portraying outer-city youth as socially parasitic and attempted to prove to me the contrary. Regardless, given the difficulty many of these young men and women experienced when seeking even short-term employment, the ability of anyone to plan periods of work and leisure in this way can be reasonably questioned.

27. Passed on June 8, 1970, the anti-*casseur* law was repealed in 1981 under the Mauroy (center-left) administration, which viewed it as "repressive."

28. This negative image of the *casseur* has not gone unchallenged ("Début de mobilisation" 2006).

29. The police estimated attendance at the protest to be around twenty-three thousand; the unions reported double that number.

30. See, e.g., "Violences en marges des manifestations," *Le Populaire du Centre*; March 17, 2006.

31. Thomas told me that before being hired full-time as a stock boy at the local pharmacy, he had worked many years in construction, mostly installing insulation.

32. France, like many other countries with a history of a resident working class, observes Labor Day (La Fête du Travail) on May 1, commemorating the 1886 execution of the Haymarket workers in Chicago, Illinois.

33. Véro, unlike most of my other interlocutors, had participated in a number of anti-CPE marches. She admitted to me, though, that she had only taken part at first because the program instructor of the sales training program she was undertaking had urged her group to do so. She questioned, however, the instructor's sincerity, noting that he usually spent most of their sessions together on the phone with his girlfriend. She suspected that he had sent them off to the demonstration as a pretext for canceling class so he could go home. Caught up nonetheless in the movement after this first experience, Véro tried, rather unsuccessfully, she admitted, to persuade other youth to join in.

34. The CNE ultimately faced the same fate as the CPE, but not until 2008, after a number of French judges ruled that it violated conventions established by the UN's International Labor Organization.

6. *Banlieue* Blues

1. The word *galère* originally referred to the galley ships propelled by oarsmen—usually prisoners or slaves—from ancient times through the eighteenth century. In popular contemporary usage, the noun and corresponding verb *galérer* have retained some of their original meaning, indicating a particularly difficult albeit usually temporary situation. For example, "Quelle galère!" might translate as "What a hassle!" or "What a headache!" This was not how my interlocutors used the term. As I go on to explain, for them *galère* was a chronic condition.
2. For an overview of the development and deployment of mobile phones in France, see Poupée (2003).
3. In 2005 and 2006, EUR 1.00 traded for about USD 1.25.
4. I could have gotten a prepaid phone as soon as I arrived in France, but I preferred to wait for my residency card to sign up for the contract option in order to take advantage of the associated cost savings.
5. Recall that my fieldwork took place in 2005 and 2006, before the advent of smartphone apps such as Facebook, Twitter, or Instagram, which otherwise could have accounted for this behavior.
6. See the discussion of the concept of *zapping* in chapter 3.
7. For a discussion of locals' tendency to denigrate the city and surrounding region, see chapter 4.
8. Chloé, who held a CAP in logistics, was the recipient of a specialized state "insertion contract" (see chapter 3 for a discussion of this type of contract). She had recently learned that her position, which consisted of assembling cardboard shipping boxes in a nearby factory, would not be renewed. Because this job was part-time, she had not worked enough hours to qualify for unemployment benefits and was therefore anxious about finding new work as quickly as possible.
9. Upon an invitation from the collective's leader, I attended one of the weekly meetings but immediately felt out of place in what was clearly a female space. I did not return. Despite the collective's focus on "ethnic" dance, members came from varied backgrounds, including what my interlocutors called "Franco-French" (see chapter 4).
10. I volunteered once a week in the association by offering an English-language class.

11. Popular education, which is at the crossroads of politics and pedagogy, may be defined as an educational technique designed to raise the consciousness of its participants about how their individual experiences are connected to larger social problems. Participants are encouraged to act to effect change on the problems facing them. According to one of my interlocutors, popular education is *pour et avec* (for and with), meaning that it is not limited to the diffusion and production of academic knowledge, but instead recognizes each person's capacity to develop at any stage of life in multiple domains, including the arts and sciences, but also technical knowledge, sports, and leisure activities. In this way, popular education aims to remove elitism from the learning process. For a useful overview of the popular education movement in France, see Mignon (2007).

12. For discussions of JOC's past, see Pierrard, Launay, and Trempé (1984).

13. For a discussion of this history, see Pérouas (1979).

14. To win back France's Communist-led, largely unchurched working classes, in 1943 the French cardinals founded the "Mission to Paris." Specially trained young priests began to take jobs in factories and set up homes in the industrial suburbs to pursue their evangelizing mission more effectively. Wearing overalls, they held full-time jobs, said mass, and performed other pastoral duties during off hours. By the 1950s the program fell out of favor with the Vatican, which perceived it as favoring left-wing politics at the expense of traditional priesthood. A retired worker-priest continued to live in the Val de l'Aurence in 2005 and 2006. Very knowledgeable about the neighborhood, he became a valuable interlocutor. For an overview of the worker-priest movement in France, see Suaud and Viet-Depaule (2004) and, in English, Arnal (1986).

15. As far as I know, this was the only dedicated place of worship in the outer city. The church was sometimes presented as a bone of contention by members of the local Muslim community, who complained that no similar accommodations had been made for them. Although a mosque was under construction on the Rue Émile Zola, Muslims wishing to pray in the outer city, I was told, had no other choice than to hold services in vacant apartments or basement storage rooms.

16. Although Laurence and Vaïsse report that the age distribution of the population of Muslim origin is skewed toward youth, they caution against sweeping assumptions about a religious revival among this group. The authors note that this difference is at least in part due to an initial divergence in Muslim and non-Muslim fertility rates (2006, 22). Citing a "skyrocketing" increase in the halal market and the presence of the Tabligh, political scientist Gilles Kepel

(2012) by contrast argues that socioeconomic malaise has led to increased Muslim devotion and religiosity, especially among young people. The extent to which the results of his study, conducted in one area of the Parisian suburbs, are generalizable to wider France remains unclear. My findings in Limoges do not support such an extrapolation.

17. Jennifer Patico (2008), in her work on post-soviet Russia, notes a similar emphasis on the exchange of nonessentials as a way of promoting sociability in a shortage economy.

18. Anthropologists came curiously late to discussions about work and personhood. For an early treatment, see Jiménez (2003).

19. On the role employment can play in the construction of personhood and social identity in the French context, see Baudelot and Gollac (2003).

20. Social science research conducted in France has suggested that the family is widely seen as a fundamental building block of society (e.g., Singly 2010, 2005). In this view, problems in the family are considered to have a direct, negative impact on society. Thus, following the 2003 heat wave, during which thousands of elderly people died, some commentators linked what they presented as the neglect of younger family members to check in on aging relatives to a "crisis of social bonds." President Jacques Chirac's address to the nation offers this perspective: http://www.ina.fr/video/2372467001002.

21. Whereas the French have been preoccupied with situating the riots in terms of working-class history and consciousness, on the other side of the Atlantic, race has often been held up as the most useful explanatory frame (e.g., Schneider 2014).

Epilogue

1. In 2000, Prime Minister Lionel Jospin's administration had reduced the workweek from thirty-nine to thirty-five hours. For an overview of this law and the controversy surrounding it, see Trumbull (2002).

2. Historically, businesses are closed in France on Sundays, and those that have chosen to open have faced steep fines (Virgin Megastore, Ikea, etc.).

3. Sarkozy's return to a neoliberal agenda was doubtless just as much the result of political maneuvering as it was reflective of ideological orientation (Levy 2010).

4. The problem was not new. In the fall of 2005 a neighborhood educator (éducateur de rue) stationed in the city's central districts told me that youth homelessness was on the rise. When Limoges went on to elect a center-right mayor in 2014, the first time the city had not put a Socialist in this office in more than one

hundred years, the newcomer made this issue a priority by pushing through a controversial decree outlawing begging ("Arrêté anti-mendicité" 2014).

5. In 2012 an individual living in France was defined as "poor" when his or her income was less than 993 euros per month (http://www.inegalites.fr/spip.php?article343).

6. In 2012 Limoges consistently performed worse than national averages: on the national level in the same year, urban unemployment was 9.7 percent, youth unemployment was 21.4 percent, and the share of the population living below the poverty line was 14 percent (www.insee.fr).

7. The day before I was to meet with one woman, she phoned to tell me that her brother, who had moved to Nantes several years earlier, had just been in a serious car accident; she was leaving that evening to be by his side. I later learned through a common acquaintance that the brother did not survive his injuries.

8. The homicide and international hunt for the suspected killers made national headlines ("Limoges: Un mort" 2012; "Guet-apens mortel" 2012).

9. The "change in policy" to which Chloé was referring was probably the phasing out of the RMI and its replacement by the RSA. As noted above, in order to receive the RSA, job seekers could not refuse employment more than twice.

10. For a comparison of the 2007 and 2012 election results in Limoges, see http://www.lemonde.fr/resultats-election-presidentielle/limoges,87280.

11. For an especially virulent critique of Standing's previous book *The Precariat*, see Breman (2013).

References

Abélès, Marc. 2010. *The Politics of Survival*. Translated by Julie Kleinman. Durham NC: Duke University Press.

Aeberhardt, Romain, Laure Crusson, and Patrick Pommier. 2011. "Les politiques d'accès à l'emploi en faveur des jeunes: Qualifier et accompagner." In *France, portrait social*, 153–72. Paris: INSEE.

Allison, Anne. 2013. *Precarious Japan*. Durham NC: Duke University Press.

Amadieu, Jean-François. 1999. *Les syndicats en miettes*. Paris: Seuil.

Amdur, Kathryn E. 1987. *Syndicalist Legacy: Trade Unions and Politics in Two French Cities in the Era of World War I*. Champaign: University of Illinois Press.

Amselle, Jean-Loup. 2003. *Affirmative Exclusion: Cultural Pluralism and the Rule of Custom in France*. Translated by Jane Marie Todd. Ithaca NY: Cornell University Press.

———. 2011. *L'ethnicisation de la France*. Clamecy, France: Lignes.

"Ancienne piscine incendiée." 2005. *Le Populaire du Centre*, November 9.

Andolfatto, Dominique, and Dominique Labbé. 2009. *Toujours moins! Déclin du syndicalisme à la française*. Paris: Gallimard.

Angé, Olivia, and David Berliner, eds. 2015. *Anthropology and Nostalgia*. New York: Berghahn.

Arcand, Isabelle, and Raymond Leblanc. 2011. "Academic Probation and Companioning: Three Perspectives on Experience and Support." *Mevlana International Journal of Education* 1 (2): 1–14.

Arnal, Oscar L. 1986. *Priests in Working-Class Blue: The History of the Worker-Priests, 1945–1954*. Mahwah NJ: Paulist Press.

"Arrêté anti-mendicité à Limoges: Une 'guerre' à l'usure." 2014. *Le Populaire du Centre*, August 30.

Audier, Serge. 2012. "Is There a French Neoliberalism?" In *French Liberalism from Montesquieu to the Present Day*, edited by Raf Greenens and Helena Rosenblatt, 208–29. Cambridge: Cambridge University Press.

Autain, Clémentine. 2012. *Le retour du peuple: De la classe ouvrière au précariat*. Paris: Stock.

Barbier, Jean-Claude. 2005. "La précarité, une catégorie française à l'épreuve de la comparaison internationale." *Revue Française de Sociologie* 46 (2): 351–71.

Bartkowiak, Isabelle. 2005. "Les jeunes en difficulté de 1980 à nos jours: De représentations en réalités sociales." In *La place des jeunes dans la cité: Espaces de rue, espaces de parole*, edited by Élisabeth Callu, Jean-Pierre Jurmand, and Alain Vulbeau, 27–46. Paris: L'Harmattan.

Bauchet, Pierre. 1986. *Le plan dans l'économie française*. Paris: Fondation nationale des sciences politiques.

Baudelot, Christian, and Michel Gollac, eds. 2003. *Travailler pour être heureux? Le bonheur et le travail en France*. Paris: Fayard.

Baudrillard, Jean. 1988. *Jean Baudrillard: Selected Writings*. Stanford CA: Stanford University Press.

Bauer, Michel, and Elie Cohen. 1985. *Les grandes manœuvres industrielles*. Paris: Belfond.

Bauman, Zygmunt. 2000. *Liquid Modernity*. Cambridge: Polity Press.

———. 2001. *The Individualized Society*. Cambridge: Polity Press.

———. 2007. *Liquid Times: Living in an Age of Uncertainty*. Cambridge: Polity Press.

Beaud, Stéphane. 2002. *"80% au bac"—et après? Les enfants de la démocratisation scolaire*. Paris: La Découverte.

Beaud, Stéphane, and Younes Amrani. 2005. *Pays de malheur! Un jeune de cité écrit à un sociologue*. Paris: La Découverte.

Beaud, Stéphane, and Michel Pialoux. 1999. *Retour sur la condition ouvrière: Enquête aux usines Peugeot de Sochaux-Montbéliard*. Paris: Fayard.

Béland, Daniel. 2009. "Back to Bourgeois? French Social Policy and the Idea of Solidarity." *International Journal of Sociology and Social Policy* 29 (9/10): 445–56.

Bell, Jonathan, and Timothy Stanely, eds. 2014. *Making Sense of American Liberalism*. Urbana: University of Illinois Press.

Bellier, Irène. 1993. *L'ENA comme si vous y étiez*. Paris: Seuil.

Berdahl, Daphne. 1999a. "'(N)Ostalgie' for the Present: Memory, Longing, and East German Things." *Ethnos* 64 (2): 192–211.

———. 1999b. *Where the World Ended: Re-Unification and Identity in the German Borderland*. Berkeley: University of California Press.

Beriss, David. 2004. "Culture-as-Race or Culture-as-Culture: Caribbean Ethnicity and the Ambiguity of Cultural Identity in French Society." In *Race in France:*

Interdisciplinary Perspectives on the Politics of Difference, edited by Herrick Chapman and Laura L. Frader, 111–40. New York: Berghahn.

"Le bilan de Sarkozy sur l'immigration: De plus en plus dur." 2012. Le Nouvel Observateur, January 29.

Birnbaum, Pierre. 1977. Les sommets de l'État: Essai sur l'élite du pouvoir en France. Paris: Seuil.

Bleich, Erik. 2004. "Anti-Racism without Races: Politics and Policy in a 'Color-Blind' State." In Race in France: Interdisciplinary Perspectives on the Politics of Difference, edited by Herrick Chapman and Laura L. Frader, 162–88. New York: Berghahn.

Boas, Taylor C., and Jordan Gans-Morse. 2009. "Neoliberalism: From New Liberal Philosophy to Anti-Liberal Slogan." Studies in Comparative International Development 44 (2): 137–61.

Bobbio, Myriam. 2007. "De la difficulté de licencier." In Le contrat de travail, edited by Dominique Méda and Évelyne Serverin, 34–45. Paris: La Découverte.

Boëldieu, Julien, and Catherine Borrel. 2000. Recensement de la population 1999: La proportion d'immigrés est stable depuis 25 ans. Paris: INSEE.

Bonnevialle, Lionel. 2011. "L'activité des missions locales et PAIO en 2009: Forte hausse des premiers accueils sous l'effet de la crise." Dares Analyses 26:1–7.

Boswell, Laird. 1998. Rural Communism in France, 1920–1939. Ithaca NY: Cornell University Press.

Bourdieu, Pierre. 1984. Distinction: A Social Critique of the Judgement of Taste. Translated by Richard Nice. Cambridge: Harvard University Press.

———. 1986. "The Forms of Capital." In Handbook of Theory and Research for the Sociology of Education, edited by John. G. Richardson, 241–58. Westport CT: Greenwood Press.

———. 1996. The State Nobility: Elite Schools in the Field of Power. Translated by Lauretta C. Clough. Stanford CA: Stanford University Press.

———. 1998. "The Essence of Neoliberalism." Translated by Jeremy J. Shapiro. Le Monde Diplomatique, December. https://mondediplo.com/1998/12/08bourdieu.

Bourgeois, Léon. 1896. Solidarité. 3rd ed. Paris: Armand Colin.

Bourgnon, Yves. 2006a. "On n'est pas la Kleenex génération!" Le Populaire du Centre, February 8.

———. 2006b. "Un Premier Mai unitaire comme jamais." Le Populaire du Centre, April 29.

Bowen, John R. 2007. Why the French Don't Like Headscarves: Islam, the State, and Public Space. Princeton NJ: Princeton University Press.

———. 2010. Can Islam Be French? Pluralism and Pragmatism in a Secularist State. Princeton NJ: Princeton University Press.

Boyer, Henri, and Guy Lochard. 1998. *Scènes de télévision en banlieues, 1950–1994*. Paris: L'Harmattan.

Breman, Jan. 2013. "A Bogus Concept?" *New Left Review* 84:130–38.

Broughton, Chad, and Tom Walton. 2006. "Downsizing Masculinity: Gender, Family, and Fatherhood in Post-Industrial America." *Anthropology of Work Review* 27 (1): 1–12.

Browne, Katherine E. 2004. *Creole Economics: Caribbean Cunning under the French Flag*. Austin: University of Texas Press.

Bryant, Rebecca. 2015. "Nostalgia and the Discovery of Loss: Essentializing the Turkish Cypriot Past." In *Anthropology and Nostalgia*, edited by Olivia Angé and David Berliner, 155–77. New York: Berghahn.

Butler, Judith. 1989. *Gender Trouble: Feminism and the Subversion of Identity*. New York: Routledge.

———. 2006. *Trouble dans le genre: Le féminisme et la subversion de l'identité*. Translated by Cynthia Kraus. Paris: La Découverte.

Cadin, Didier, and Philippe Trogan. 2006. "Les très petites entreprises: Des acteurs majeurs de l'économie en France." In *PME/TPE en bref*, edited by J.-C. Martin, 1–4. Paris: DCASPL.

Caillé, Alain. 1994. *Temps choisi et revenu de citoyenneté, au-delà du salariat universel*. Caen, France: Démosthène/MAUSS.

Cameron, David R. 1991. "Continuity and Change in French Social Policy: The Welfare State under Gaullism, Liberalism, and Socialism." In *The French Welfare State: Surviving Social and Ideological Change*, edited by John Ambler, 58–93. New York: New York University Press.

Cancé, Raphaël, and Hélène Fréchou. 2003. "Les contrats courts: Source d'instabilités mais aussi trempelin vers l'emploi permanent." *Premières Informations et Premières Synthèses* 14 (1): 1–8.

Caroux-Destray, Jacques. 1974. *Un couple ouvrier traditionnel: La vieille garde autogestionnaire*. Paris: Anthropos.

Castel, Robert. 1995. *Les métamorphoses de la question sociale: Une chronique du salariat*. Paris: Fayard.

———. 2006. "Et maintenant le 'précariat': Le statut de l'emploi change et une nouvelle ère commence: Le travail à n'importe quelles conditions." *Le Monde*, April 29.

———. 2007. *La discrimination négative, citoyens ou indigènes?* Paris: Seuil.

———. 2011. "Les ambiguïtés de la promotion de l'individu." In *Refaire société*, edited by Pierre Rosanvallon, 13–25. Paris: Seuil.

Catus, Bertrand. 2006a. "La jeunesse répond: 'Résistance!'" *L'Écho de la Haute Vienne, April 11.*

———. 2006b. "Tous ensemble contre le CPE." *L'Écho de la Haute Vienne,* February 7.

Chabanet, Didier, Pascale Dufour, and Frédéric Royall, eds. 2012. *Les mobilisations sociales à l'heure du précariat.* Rennes, France: École des hautes études en santé publique.

Champagne, Patrick. 1993. "La vision médiatique." In *La misère du monde,* edited by Pierre Bourdieu, 94–123. Paris: Seuil.

Clark, Nicola. 2011. "Government of France Proposes Austerity Cuts." *New York Times,* November 7.

Clarke, T. J. 1984. *The Painting of Modern Life: Paris in the Art of Manet and His Followers.* Princeton NJ: Princeton University Press.

Clegg, Daniel, and Bruno Palier. 2014. "Implementing a Myth: The Evolution of Conditionality in French Minimum Provision." In *Activation or Workfare? Governance and the Neo-Liberal Convergence,* edited by Ivar Lødemel and Amílcar Moreira, 203–28. Oxford: Oxford University Press.

Code du travail. 2015. 77th ed. Paris: Dalloz.

Cohen, Elie. 1992. *Le colbertisme high tech: Économie des télécoms et du grand projet.* Paris: Hachette.

Cohen, Stephen G. 1977. *Modern Capitalist Planning: The French Model.* Berkeley: University of California Press.

Corbin, Alain. 1975. *Archaïsme et modernité en Limousin au XIXe siècle, 1845–1880.* Paris: Marcel Rivière.

Coutant, Isabelle. 2005. *Délit de jeunesse: La justice face aux quartiers.* Paris: La Découverte.

Cupers, Kenny. 2014. *The Social Project: Housing Postwar France.* Minneapolis: University of Minnesota Press.

DARES (Direction de l'animation de la recherche, des études et des statistiques). 1996. *Quarante ans de politique de l'emploi.* Paris: DARES.

———. 2000. *La politique de l'emploi en 1999.* Paris: DARES.

Davis, Fred. 1979. *Yearning for Yesterday: A Sociology of Nostalgia.* New York: Free Press.

Davoine, Jérôme. 2006a. "L'intervention présidentielle renforce la mobilisation lycéenne." *L'Écho de la Haute Vienne,* April 4.

———. 2006b. "Vent de solidarité rue de la Préfecture." *L'Écho de la Haute Vienne,* March 31.

"Début de mobilisation à l'Université de Limoges." 2006. *L'Écho de la Haute Vienne,* February 2.

Desbordes, Chantal. 2004. *Atlas des populations immigrées en Limousin*. Paris: INSEE.

Desforges, Michel. 2002. *Limoges: Petite histoire d'une grande ville*. Paris: Lucien Souny.

Desplanques, Guy. 2008. *Des facteurs de changement 1, Territoires 2040*. Paris: La documentation française.

Divay, Sophie. 2002. "Emplois-jeunes: La précarité au cœur des discours et des pratiques." *Agora* 28:132–46.

Diverneresse, Bernard. 1986. "Pauvreté et espace à Beaubreuil." PhD diss., Université de Limoges.

Dormois, Jean-Pierre. 2004. *The French Economy in the Twentieth Century*. Cambridge: Cambridge University Press.

Doyle, William. 2009. *Aristocracy and Its Enemies in the Age of Revolution*. Oxford: Oxford University Press.

Dubet, François. 1987. *La galère: Jeunes en survie*. Paris: Fayard.

Dubet, François, and Didier Lapeyronnie. 1992. *Les quartiers d'exil*. Paris: Seuil.

Dufoix, Stéphane. 2005. "More Than Riots: A Question of Spheres." December 2. http://riotsfrance.ssrc.org/Dufoix.

Dufresne, David. 2013. *Maintien de l'ordre*. Paris: Fayard.

Duplouy, Bérangère. 2003. *Portrait des quartiers de Limoges*. Paris: INSEE.

Durkheim, Émile. (1893) 1984. *The Division of Labor in Society*. Translated by W. D. Halls. New York: Free Press.

Durpaire, François. 2006. *France blanche, colère noire*. Paris: Odile Jacob.

———. 2012. *Nous sommes tous la France! Essai sur la nouvelle identité française*. Paris: Philippe Rey.

Epstein, Beth S. 2011. *Collective Terms: Race, Culture, and Community in a State-Planned City in France*. New York: Berghahn.

———. 2016. "Redemptive Politics: Racial Reasoning in Contemporary France." *Patterns of Prejudice* 50 (2): 168–87.

Fassin, Didier. 2011. *La force de l'ordre: Une anthropologie de la police des quartiers*. Paris: Seuil.

Fassin, Didier, and Éric Fassin, eds. 2006. *De la question sociale à la question raciale: Représenter la société française*. Paris: La Découverte.

Fassin, Éric. 1995. "Fearful Symmetry: Culturalism and Cultural Comparison after Tocqueville." *French Historical Studies* 19 (2): 451–60.

Ferenczi, Thomas. 2005. "Désintégration sociale." *Le Monde*, November 10.

Ferguson, James. 2009. "The Uses of Neoliberalism." *Antipode* 41 (1): 166–84.

Fernando, Mayanthi L. 2014. *The Republic Unsettled: Muslim French and the Contradictions of Secularism*. Durham NC: Duke University Press.

"FO: Appel à la grève interpro." 2006. *Le Populaire du Centre*, February 27.

Fogg, Shannon L. 2009. *The Politics of Everyday Life in Vichy France: Foreigners, Undesirables, and Strangers.* Cambridge: Cambridge University Press.

Foucault, Michel. 2008. *The Birth of Biopolitics: Lectures at the Collège de France, 1978–1979.* Translated by Graham Burchell. New York: Palgrave Macmillan.

Fougeras, Maurice. 2011. "Renault Défense promet des embauches à Limoges." *Le Populaire du Centre,* December 13.

Fourastié, Jean. 1979. *Les trente glorieuses, ou la révolution invisible de 1946 à 1975.* Paris: Fayard.

Fourcade, Bernard. 1992. "L'évolution des situations d'emploi particulières de 1945 à 1990." *Travail et Emploi* 52 (2): 4–19.

Fourcaut, Annie. 2004. "Les premiers grands ensembles en région parisienne: Ne pas refaire la banlieue?" *French Historical Studies* 27 (1): 195–218.

"François Hollande, Liberal?" 2014. *The Economist,* January 11.

Fressoz, Françoise. 2012. "Hollande, un 'président normal' dans une situation anormale." *Le Monde,* June 18.

Ganti, Tejaswini. 2014. "Neoliberalism." *Annual Review of Anthropology* 43:89–104.

Gaspard, Françoise. 1995. *A Small City in France: A Socialist Mayor Confronts Neofacism.* Translated by Arthur Goldhammer. Cambridge: Harvard University Press.

Gaubert, Christophe. 1995. "Badauds, manifestants, casseurs: Formes de sociabilité, éthos de virilité et usages des manifestations." *Sociétés Contemporaines* 21:103–18.

Gaudu, François. 1996. "Les notions d'emploi en droit." *Droit Social* 6:569–85.

Gautié, Jérôme. 1999. "Promoting Employment for Youth: A European Perspective." In *Preparing Youth for the Twenty-First Century: The Transition from Education to the Labour Market,* 387–418. Paris: OECD.

Gendron, Bénédicte. 2009. "The Vocational Baccalaureate: A Gateway to Higher Education?" *European Journal of Vocational Training* 46 (1): 4–27.

Gershon, Ilana. 2011. "Neoliberal Agency." *Current Anthropology* 52 (4): 537–55.

Gilroy, Paul. 1993. *The Black Atlantic: Modernity and Double-Consciousness.* Cambridge: Harvard University Press.

———. 2010. *L'Atlantique noire: Modernité et double conscience.* Translated by Charlotte Nordmann. Paris: Éditions Amsterdam.

Girling, John. 1998. *France: Political and Social Change.* New York: Routledge.

Givord, Pauline. 2005. "Formes particulières d'emploi et insertion des jeunes." *Économie et Statistique* 388–89:129–43.

Goldhammer, Arthur. 2015. "The Old Continent Creaks." *Democracy* 37 (3): 30–42.

Greciano, Pierre-Alain. 2010. "Économie: vers l'éclaircie?" In *La France en 2009. Chronique politique, économique et sociale,* edited by Frédéric Charillon, Pierre-Alain Greciano, and Patrice Liquière, 67–92. Paris: La documentation française.

Green, Nancy L. 1991. "L'immigration en France et aux États-Unis: Historiographie comparée." *Vingtième Siècle* 29 (1): 67–82.

Grignon, Claude, and Jean-Claude Passeron. 1989. *Le savant et le populaire: Misérabilisme et populisme en sociologie et en littérature*. Paris: Seuil.

Grillo, Ralph. 1985. *Ideologies and Institutions in Urban France: The Representation of Immigrants*. Cambridge: Cambridge University Press.

Gualmini, Elisabetta, and Vivien A. Schmidt. 2013. "State Transformation in Italy and France: Technocratic versus Political Leadership on the Road from Non-Liberalism to Neo-Liberalism." In *Resilient Liberalism in Europe's Political Economy*, edited by Vivien A. Schmidt and Mark Thatcher, 346–73. Cambridge: Cambridge University Press.

Guène, Faïza. 2004. *Kiffe kiffe demain*. Paris: Hachette.

"Guet-apens mortel dans une cité de Limoges." 2012. *Le Parisien*, January 28.

Guiral, Antoine. 2008. "Le laisser-faire, c'est fini." *Libération*, September 26.

Hall, Peter A. 1986. *Governing the Economy: The Politics of State Intervention in Britain and France*. Oxford: Oxford University Press.

———. 1990. "The State and the Market." In *Developments in French Politics*, edited by Peter A. Hall, Jack Hayward, and Howard Machin, 171–87. New York: St. Martin's Press.

Hall, Stuart. 1994. "Race, Ethnicity, Nation: The Faithful/Fatal Triangle." W. E. B. Du Bois Lecture, Hutchins Center for African and African American Research, Harvard University.

Hargreaves, Alec G. 2005. "An Emperor with No Clothes?" November 28. http://riotsfrance.ssrc.org/Hargreaves.

Harvey, David. 2005. *A Brief History of Neoliberalism*. Oxford: Oxford University Press.

Heller, Chaia. 2013. *Food, Farms, and Solidarity: French Farmers Challenge Industrial Agriculture and Genetically Modified Crops, New Ecologies for the Twenty-First Century*. Durham NC: Duke University Press.

Hidouci, Myriam, and Laurence Kundid. 2001. "Sur le 'retour . . .': À propos de la démarche sociologique de Stéphane Beaud et de Michel Pialoux." *Ethnologie Française* 31 (3): 497–501.

Higgins, Rylan. 2005. "Bodies for Rent: Labor and Marginality in Southern Louisiana." *Anthropology of Work Review* 26 (3): 12–22.

Hoffman, Danny. 2011. "Violence, Just in Time: War and Work in Contemporary West Africa." *Cultural Anthropology* 26 (1): 34–58.

Hoggart, Richard. (1957) 1998. *The Uses of Literacy: Aspects of Working-Class Life*. Piscataway NJ: Transaction.

Horne, Janet R. 2002. *A Social Laboratory for Modern France: The Musée Social and the Rise of the Welfare State*. Durham NC: Duke University Press.

Howell, Chris. 1992. *Regulating Labor: The State and Industrial Relations Reform in Postwar France*. Princeton NJ: Princeton University Press.

———. 2009. "The Transformation of French Industrial Relations: Labor Representation and the State in a Post-Dirigiste Era." *Politics and Society* 37 (2): 229–56.

"L'incendiaire voulait faire comme à la télé." 2005. *Le Populaire du Centre*, November 18.

Ingram, Mark. 2011. *Rites of the Republic: Citizens' Theatre and the Politics of Culture in Southern France*. Toronto: University of Toronto Press.

INSEE (Institut national de la statistique et des études économiques). 2008. "Le chômage au premier trimestre 2008: Le Limousin n'a plus l'exclusivité du taux le plus bas." http://www.insee.fr/fr/themes/document.asp?reg_id=9&ref_id=13482.

———. 2012. "Limoges: Chiffres clés." http://www.insee.fr/fr/bases-de-donnees/esl/comparateur.asp?codgeo=com-87085.

———. 2013. "Taux de chômage localisé par région: Limousin." http://www.insee.fr/fr/bases-de-donnees/bsweb/serie.asp?idbank=001515859.

———. 2014. "Portrait de territoire: Arrondissement de Limoges." http://www.insee.fr/fr/insee_regions/limousin/themes/dossiers/dossier_16/pdt_arr_limoges.pdf.

———. 2015. "Commune de Limoges (87085)." http://www.insee.fr/fr/themes/comparateur.asp?codgeo=com-87085.

Jablonka, Ivan. 2009. "La naissance du 'casseur': Délinquance et ethnicité dans la République (1981–2006)." In *Les âmes mal nées: Jeunesse et délinquance urbaine en France et en Europe, XIXe–XXIe siècles*, edited by Jean-Claude Caron, Annie Stora-Lamarre, and Jean-Jacques Yvorel, 153–64. Besançon, France: Presses universitaires de Franche-Comté.

Jancius, Angela. 2006. "The Anthropology of Unemployment." *Ethnos* 71 (2): 141–42.

Jiménez, Alberto Corsín. 2003. "Working Out Personhood: Notes on 'Labor' and Its Anthropology." *Anthropology Today* 19 (5): 14–17.

Joseph, Marion. 2011. "Délinquance juvénile: Sarkozy veut un encadrement militaire." *Le Figaro*, September 13.

Karpiak, Kevin G. 2013. "Adjusting the Police: State, Society, and the Distance of Just Violence in Contemporary France." In *Policing and Contemporary Governance: The Anthropology of Police in Practice*, edited by William Garriott, 79–95. New York: Palgrave Macmillan.

Kepel, Gilles. 2012. *Banlieue de la République: Société, politique et religion à Clichy-sous-Bois et Montfermeil*. Paris: Gallimard.

Kesselman, Mark. 2002. "The Triple Exceptionalism of the French Welfare State." In *Diminishing Welfare: A Cross-National Study of Social Provision*, edited by Gertrude Schaffner Goldberg and Marguerite G. Rosenthal, 181–210. Westport CT: Auburn House.

Kingfisher, Catherine, and Jeff Maskovasky. 2008. "Introduction: The Limits of Neoliberalism." *Critique of Anthropology* 28 (2): 115–26.

Kingslover, Ann E. 2011. *Tobacco Town Futures: Global Encounters in Rural Kentucky.* Long Grove IL: Waveland Press.

Kingston, Paul W. 2000. *The Classless Society.* Stanford CA: Stanford University Press.

Kipnis, Andrew B. 2008. "Audit Cultures: Neoliberal Governmentality, Socialist Legacy, or Technologies of Governing." *American Ethnologist* 35 (2): 275–89.

Kotz, David M. 2015. *The Rise and Fall of Neoliberal Capitalism.* Cambridge: Harvard University Press.

Kuisel, Richard F. 1993. *Seducing the French: The Dilemma of Americanization.* Berkeley: University of California Press.

————. 2012. *The French Way: How France Embraced and Rejected American Values and Power.* Princeton NJ: Princeton University Press.

Lagier, Franck. 2005a. "Benoît K. s'est livré chez lui." *Le Populaire du Centre*, November 10.

————. 2005b. "Épinay: Un Limougeaud recherché." *Le Populaire du Centre*, November 8.

Lagrange, Hugues. 2010. *Le déni des cultures.* Paris: Seuil.

Landré, Marc. 2013. "Le taux de chômage pourrait dépasser cette année son record historique de 10,8%." *Le Figaro*, June 6.

Lane, Carrie M. 2011. *A Company of One: Insecurity, Independence, and the New World of Whie-Collar Unemployment.* Ithaca NY: Cornell University Press.

Lapeyronnie, Didier. 2006. "Révolte primitive dans les banlieues françaises: Essai sur les émeutes de l'automne 2005." *Déviance et Société* 30 (4): 431–48.

————. 2008. *Ghetto urbain: Ségrégation, violence, pauvreté en France aujourd'hui.* Paris: Robert Laffont.

Larivière, Jean-Pierre. 1968. *L'industrie à Limoges et dans la vallée limousine de la Vienne.* Clermont-Ferrand, France: Presses universitaires Blaise Pascal.

Laurence, Jonathan, and Justin Vaïsse. 2006. *Integrating Islam: Political and Religious Challenges in Contemporary France.* Washington DC: Brookings Institution Press.

Lavallée, Nicolas. 2006a. "Énorme mobilisation lycéenne et étudiante." *L'Écho de la Haute Vienne*, March 17.

————. 2006b. "Limoges bloquée." *L'Écho de la Haute Vienne*, April 7.

———. 2006c. "Un Premier Mai unitaire sur les cendres du CPE." *L'Écho de la Haute Vienne*, April 29.

Lavaud, Catherine, and Geneviève Simonneau. 2010. *Le Limousin peine à retenir ses jeunes diplômés*. Paris: INSEE.

Lazzarotti, Raymond. 1970. "Limoges, capitale régionale, peut-elle devenir une métropole d'équilibre?" *Norois* 65 (1): 57–80.

Le Boucher, Éric. 2006. "Les inégalités deviennent moins visibles." *Le Monde*, May 20.

Léchenet, Alexandre. 2013. "Explosion du nombre de CDD de moins d'un mois." *Le Monde*, November 21.

Leclerc, Jean-Marc. 2006. "Parmi les casseurs, des mineurs venus de banlieue." *Le Figaro*, March 25.

Lee, Jolie. 2014. "Coca-Cola Super Bowl Ad: Can You Believe This Reaction?" *USA Today*, February 4. http://www.usatoday.com/story/news/nation-now/2014/02/03/coca-cola-ad-super-bowl-racism/5177463.

Lefresne, Florence. 2006. "Précarité pour tous, la norme du futur." *Le Monde Diplomatique*, March. http://www.monde-diplomatique.fr/2006/03/LEFRESNE/13264.

———. 2010. "Trente ans de politique de l'emploi des jeunes en France: Une tentative d'évaluation." In *Les jeunesses au travail: Regards croisés France-Québec*, edited by Christian Papinot and Mircea Vultur, 185–205. Québec: Presses de l'université de Laval.

Lenoir, Rémi. 1979. "L'invention du 'troisième âge.'" *Actes de la Recherce en Sciences Sociales* 26–27:57–82.

Lepoutre, David. 1997. *Cœur de banlieue: Codes, rites et langages*. Paris: Odile Jacob.

Levy, Jonah D. 2008. "From *Dirigiste* State to Social Anaesthesia State: French Economic Policy in the *Longue Durée*." *Modern and Contemporary France* 16 (4): 417–35.

———. 2010. "The Return of the State? French Economic Policy under Nicolas Sarkozy." Annual Meeting of the American Political Science Association, Washington DC, September 2–5.

Lima, Léa. 2005. "Justice et jugement dans les politiques de lutte contre l'exclusion professionnelle au Québec et en France." In *La place des jeunes dans la cité (tome 1): De l'école à l'emploi*, edited by Cécile Baron, Élisabeth Dugué, and Patrick Nivolle, 161–76. Paris: L'Harmattan.

"Limoges: Un mort après un vol de voiture." 2012. *Le Figaro*, January 1.

"Limoges: Véhicules incendiés à la Bastide et des cocktails qui font long feu." 2005. *L'Écho de la Haute Vienne*, November 14.

Loriaux, Michael. 1991. *France after Hegemony: International Change and Financial Reform*. Ithaca NY: Cornell University Press.

"Lycéens et étudiants bloquent le Rectorat et se mobilisent contre la répression." *L'Écho de la Haute Vienne*, April 8.

MacMaster, Neil. 1991. "The 'seuil de tolérance': The Uses of a Scientific Racist Concept." In *Race, Discourse, and Power in France*, edited by Maxim Silverman, 14–28. Aldershot UK: Avebury.

Macridis, Roy C. 1987. "Politics of France." In *Modern Political Systems: Europe*, edited by Roy C. Macridis, 75–159. Englewood Cliffs NJ: Prentice Hall.

Mains, Daniel. 2007. "Neoliberal Times: Progress, Boredom, and Shame among Young Men in Urban Ethiopia." *American Ethnologist* 34 (4): 659–73.

———. 2011. *Hope Is Cut: Unemployment and the Future in Urban Ethiopia*. Philadelphia: Temple University Press.

Mansbridge, Jane, and Aldon Morris, eds. 2001. *Oppositional Consciousness: The Subjective Roots of Social Protest*. Chicago: University of Chicago Press.

Mantsios, Gregory. 1995. "Class in America—2006." In *Race, Class and Gender in the United States*, edited by Paula S. Rothenberg, 182–97. New York: St. Martin's Press.

Marlière, Philippe. 2012. "Has François Hollande Gone from Being Mr. Normal to Mr. Neoliberal?" *The Guardian*, August 19.

Marmain, Stéphane. 2006a. "Record battu?" *Le Populaire du Centre*, March 29.

———. 2006b. "Anti-CPE: Le grand bazar." *Le Populaire du Centre*, March 31.

Marsac, Annette, and Vincent Brousse. 2005. "Les lieux de l'immigration ouvrière en Limousin." In *Un siècle militant: Engagement(s), résistance(s) et mémoire(s) au XXe siècle en Limousin*, edited by Vincent Brousse and Philippe Grandcoing, 147–86. Limoges: Presses universitaires de Limoges.

Massé, Pierre. 1965. *Le plan ou l'anti-hasard*. Paris: Gallimard.

Mauger, Gérard. 2006. *L'émeute de novembre 2005: Une révolte protopolotique*. Vulvaines-sur-Seine, France: Éditions du Croquant.

Mdembe, Achille. 2011. "Provincializing France?" *Public Culture* 23 (1): 85–119.

Mendras, Henri. 1970. *The Vanishing Peasant: Innovation and Change in French Agriculture*. Translated by Jean Lerner. Cambridge: MIT Press.

———. 1988. *La seconde révolution française, 1965–1984*. Paris: Gallimard.

Merriman, John M. 1985. *The Red City: Limoges and the French Nineteenth Century*. Oxford: Oxford University Press.

Mignard, Jean-Pierre, and Emmanuel Tordjman. 2006. *L'affaire de Clichy: Morts pour rien*. Paris: Stock.

Mignon, Jean-Marie. 2007. *Une histoire de l'éducation populaire*. Paris: La Découverte.

"La mobilisation en voie d'extension." 2006. *L'Écho de la Haute Vienne*, February 8.

Mouriaux, René. 1998. *Crises du syndicalisme français*. Paris: Montchrestien.

Mucchielli, Laurent. 1999. "Violences urbaines, réactions collectives et représentations de classe chez les jeunes des quartiers relégués de la France des années 1990." *Actuel Marx* 26:85–108.

———. 2005. *Le scandale des "tournantes."* Paris: La Découverte.

———. 2012. *Vous avez dit sécurité?* Nîmes, France: Éditions Champ Social.

Muia, Anne-Marie. 2006. "Non, la rue ne cédera pas!" *Le Populaire du Centre*, March 19.

Murphy, John P. 2011. "Protest or Riot? Interpreting Collective Action in Contemporary France." *Anthropological Quarterly* 84 (4): 977–1008.

Ndiaye, Pap. 2008. *La condition noire: Essai sur une minorité française.* Paris: Calmann-Lévy.

Neilson, Brett, and Ned Rossiter. 2008. "Precarity as a Political Concept, or Fordism as Exception." *Theory, Culture, and Society* 25 (7–8): 51–72.

Newman, Andrew. 2013. "Gatekeepers of the Urban Commons? Vigilant Citizenship and Neoliberal Space in Multiethnic Paris." *Antipode* 45(4): 947–64.

Nicole-Drancourt, Chantal. 1992. "L'idée de précarité revisitée." *Travail et Emploi* 52:57–70.

Nicolet, Claude. 1974. *Le radicalisme.* Paris: Presses universitaires de France.

Noiriel, Gérard. 1990. *Workers in French Society in the Nineteenth and Twentieth Centuries.* New York: Berg.

Nonini, Donald M. 2008. "Is China Becoming Neoliberal?" *Critique of Anthropology* 28 (2): 145–76.

OECD (Organisation for Economic Co-operation and Development). 2009. *OECD Economic Surveys: France.* Paris.

Ong, Aihwa. 2006. *Neoliberalism as Exception: Mutations in Citizenship and Sovereignty.* Durham NC: Duke University Press.

Palier, Bruno. 1999. *Réformer la sécurité sociale: Les interventions gouvernementales en matière de protection sociale depuis 1945.* Paris: Institut d'études politiques de Paris.

Passeron, Jean-Claude, ed. 1999. *Richard Hoggart en France.* Paris: Bibliothèque publique d'information, Centre Georges Pompidou.

Patico, Jennifer. 2008. *Consumption and Social Change in a Post-Soviet Middle Class.* Stanford CA: Stanford University Press.

Paugam, Serge, and Helen Russell. 2000. "The Effects of Employment Precarity and Unemployment on Social Isolation." In *Welfare Regimes and the Experience of Unemployment in Europe,* edited by Duncan Gallie and Serge Paugam, 243–64. Oxford: Oxford University Press.

Pech, Thierry. 2014. "Tous inégaux face au chômage." *Alternatives Économiques. Chômage: a-t-on vraiment tout essayé?* 99 (1): 25–28.

Pérouas, Louis. 1979. "Limoges, une capital régionale de la libre pensée à l'orée du XXe siècle." *Annales du Midi* 91 (142): 165–85.

Perrier, Antoine. 1924. "Limoges: Étude d'économie urbaine." *Annales de Géographie* 33 (184): 352–64.

Perry, Matt. 2007. *Prisoners of Want: The Experience and Protest of the Unemployed in France, 1921–45.* Burlington VT: Ashgate.

Pierrard, Pierre, Michel Launay, and Rolande Trempé. 1984. *La JOC: Regards d'historiens.* Paris: Éditions Ouvrières.

Pierrat, Jérôme. 2003. *Une histoire du milieu: Grand banditisme et haute pègre en France de 1850 à nos jours.* Paris: Denoël.

Piketty, Thomas. 2003. "Income Inequality in France, 1901–1998." *Journal of Political Economy* 111 (5): 1004–42.

Pinkney, David H. 1972. *Napoleon III and the Rebuilding of Paris.* Princeton NJ: Princeton University Press.

"La piscine désaffectée détruite entièrement par un incendie." 2005. *L'Écho de la Haute Vienne,* November 9.

Poulin-Deltour, William. 2015. "Gay Activism and the Question of Community." In *Transatlantic Parallaxes: Toward Reciprocal Anthropology,* edited by Anne Raulin and Susan Carol Rogers, 109–24. New York: Berghahn.

Poupée, Karyn. 2003. *La téléphonie mobile.* Paris: Presses universitaires de France.

Prasad, Monica. 2005. "Why Is France So French? Culture, Institutions, and Neoliberalism, 1974–1981." *American Journal of Sociology* 111 (2): 357–407.

Prewitt, Kenneth. 2013. *What Is Your Race? The Census and Our Flawed Efforts to Classify Americans.* Princeton NJ: Princeton University Press.

Price, Roger. 1993. *A Concise History of France.* Cambridge: Cambridge University Press.

Reich, Robert B. 2001. *The Future of Success.* New York: Knopf.

Renahy, Nicolas. 2005. *Les gars du coin: Enquête sur une jeunesse rurale.* Paris: La Découverte.

Richland, Justin. 2009. "On Neoliberalism and Other Social Diseases: The 2008 Sociocultural Anthropology Year in Review." *American Anthropologist* 111 (2): 170–76.

Ridet, Philippe. 2005. "M. Sarkozy durcit son discours sur les banlieues." *Le Monde,* November 21.

Roger, Patrick. 2006. "Égalité des chances: M. de Villepin choisit le 49-3, la gauche la motion de censure." *Le Monde,* February 10.

———. 2008. "Nicolas Sarkozy veut développer le travail du dimanche." *Le Monde,* November 13.

Rogers, Susan Carol. 1987. "Good to Think: The 'Peasant' in Contemporary France." *Anthropological Quarterly* 60 (2): 56–63.

———. 1991. *Shaping Modern Times in Rural France: The Transformation and Reproduction of an Aveyronnais Community.* Princeton NJ: Princeton University Press.

———. 2000. "Farming Visions: Agriculture in French Culture." *French Politics, Culture, and Society* 18 (1): 50–70.

———. 2002. "Which Heritage? Nature, Culture, and Identity in French Rural Tourism." *French Historical Studies* 25 (3): 475–503.

———. 2015. "*Faux Amis* in the Countryside: Deciphering the Familiar." In *Transatlantic Parallaxes: Toward Reciprocal Anthropology*, edited by Anne Raulin and Susan Carol Rogers, 208–28. New York: Berghahn.

Rosanvallon, Pierre. 2000. *The New Social Question: Rethinking the Welfare State.* Translated by Barbara Harshav. Princeton NJ: Princeton University Press.

Ross, Kristin. 1999. *Fast Cars, Clean Bodies: Decolonization and the Reordering of French Culture.* Cambridge: MIT Press.

Rousso, Henry, ed. 1986. *De Monnet à Massé: Enjeux politiques et objectifs économiques dans le cadre des quatre premiers plans (1945–1965).* Paris: CNRS.

Roy, Olivier. 2005. "The Nature of the French Riots." November 18. http://riots-france.ssrc.org/Roy.

Rudolph, Nicole C. 2015. *At Home in Postwar France: Modern Mass Housing and the Right to Comfort.* New York: Berghahn.

Ruiz, Olivier. 2006. "Contre le CPE: Les jeunes ont du cœur." *L'Écho de la Haute Vienne*, March 8.

Sabbagh, Daniel. 2004. "Affirmative Action at Sciences Po." In *Race in France: Interdisciplinary Perspectives on the Politics of Difference*, edited by Herrick Chapman and Laura L. Frader, 246–58. New York: Berghahn.

"Sarkozy veut un contrat unique inspiré du CNE." 2007. *Le Nouvel Observateur*, January 25.

Sawyer, Malcolm C., and Mark Wasserman. 1976. *Income Distribution in OECD Countries.* Paris: OECD.

Schneider, Cathy Lisa. 2014. *Police Power and Race Riots: Urban Unrest in Paris and New York.* Philadelphia: University of Pennsylvania Press.

Schwartz, Bertrand. 1981. *Rapport sur l'insertion professionnelle et sociale des jeunes.* Rennes, France: Apogée.

Schwartz, Olivier. 1990. *Le monde privé des ouvriers: Hommes et femmes du Nord.* Paris: Presses universitaires de France.

Schwegler, Tara A. 2009. "The Bankrupt Framework of Neoliberalism: A Bailout of Anthropological Theory." *Anthropology News* 50 (4): 24.

Scott, Joan W. 1974. *The Glassworkers of Carmaux: French Craftsmen and Political Action in a Nineteenth-Century City*. Cambridge: Harvard University Press.

———. 1997. *Only Paradoxes to Offer: French Feminists and the Rights of Man*. Cambridge: Harvard University Press.

Sedel, Julie. 2009. *Les médias et la banlieue*. Lormont, France: Bord de l'eau.

"Sept mars: FO appelle à la grève." 2006. *L'Écho de la Haute Vienne*, February 21.

Serverin, Évelyne. 2007. "Le travail et ses contrats." In *Le contrat de travail*, edited by Dominique Méda and Évelyne Serverin, 13–23. Paris: La Découverte.

Sewell, William H. 1980. *Work and Revolution in France: The Language of Labor from the Old Regime to 1848*. Cambridge: Cambridge University Press.

———. 1986. "Artisans, Factory Workers, and the Formation of the French Working Class, 1789–1848." In *Working-Class Formation: Ninetheenth-Century Patterns in Western Europe and the United States*, edited by Ira Katznelson and Aristide R. Zolberg, 45–62. Princeton NJ: Princeton University Press.

Shonfield, Andrew. 1965. *Modern Capitalism: The Changing Balance of Public and Private Power*. Oxford: Oxford University Press.

Sibony, Daniel. 2007. "Diam's." *Le Nouvel Observateur*, March 15.

Silva, Jennifer M. 2013. *Coming Up Short: Working-Class Adulthood in an Age of Uncertainty*. Oxford: Oxford University Press.

Silverstein, Paul A., and Chantal Tetreault. 2006. "Postcolonial Urban Apartheid." June 11. http://riotsfrance.ssrc.org/Silverstein_Tetreault.

Singly, François de. 2005. *Le soi, le couple et la famille*. Paris: Armand Colin.

———. 2010. *Sociologie de la famille contemporaine*. Paris: Armand Colin.

Spiriet, Thierry. 2005. "Ici, dans ma cité les gens disent bonjour." *L'Écho de la Haute Vienne*, November 8.

Spivak, Gayatri Chakravorty. 1988. "Can the Subaltern Speak?" In *Marxism and the Interpretation of Culture*, edited by Cary Nelson and Lawrence Grossburg, 271–316. Champaign: University of Illinois Press.

———. 2006. *Les subalternes peuvent-ils parler?* Translated by Jérôme Vidal. Paris: Éditions Amsterdam.

Standing, Guy. 2010. *Work after Globalization: Building Occupational Citizenship*. Cheltenham UK: Edward Elgar Publishing.

———. 2011. *The Precariat: The New Dangerous Class*. London: Bloomsbury Aacdemic.

———. 2014. *A Precariat Charter: From Denizens to Citizens*. London: Bloomsbury Academic.

Stébé, Jean-Marc. 2005. *La médiation dans les banlieues sensibles*. Paris: Presses universitaires de France.

————. 2012. "La médiation sociale au cœur de la 'crise urbaine.'" *Informations Sociales* 2 (170): 82–88.

Stewart, Kathleen. 1988. "Nostalgia—A Polemic." *Cultural Anthropology* 3 (3): 227–41.

Suaud, Charles, and Nathalie Viet-Depaule. 2004. *Prêtres et ouvriers: Une double fidelité mise à l'épreuve, 1944–1969.* Paris: Karthala.

Suleiman, Ezra N. 1979. *Elites in French Society: The Politics of Survival.* Princeton NJ: Princeton University Press.

Tannock, Stuart. 1995. "Nostalgia Critique." *Cultural Studies* 9 (3): 453–64.

Terrail, Jean-Pierre. 1990. *Destins ouvriers: La fin d'une classe?* Paris: Presses universitaires de France.

Terrio, Susan J. 2009. *Judging Mohammed: Juvenile Delinquency, Immigration, and Exclusion at the Paris Palace of Justice.* Stanford CA: Stanford University Press.

Thomas, Jean-Noël. 1999. "Les inégalités face au suicide." Paris: INSEE.

Tissot, Sylvie. 2004. "La parole et le projet comme remède pour les 'quartiers sensibles': Histoire d'un engoument pour la démocratie locale." In *Démocratie et management local: 6e Rencontres internationales,* edited by Robert Le Duff and Jean-Jacques Rigal, 530–41. Paris: Dalloz-Sirey.

————. 2007. *L'État et les quartiers: Genèse d'une catégorie de l'action publique.* Paris: Seuil.

Topalov, Christian. 1994. *Naissance du chômeur: 1880–1910.* Paris: Albin Michel.

Touraine, Alain, Michel Wieviorka, and François Dubet. 1984. *Le mouvement ouvrier.* Paris: Fayard.

"Tous unis contre le CPE." 2006. *Le Populaire du Centre,* February 27.

Trincaz, Jacqueline, Bernadette Puijalon, and Cédric Humbert. 2011. "Dire la vieillesse et les vieux." *Gérontologie et Société* 138:113–26.

Troyansky, David G. 1996. "Limogé for a Year: An American Teaches French History in Provincial France." *The History Teacher* 29 (3): 379–89.

Trumbull, Gunnar. 2002. "Policy Activism in a Globalized Economy: France's 35-Hour Workweek." *French Politics, Culture and Society* 20 (3): 1–21.

Vail, Mark I. 2010. *Recasting Welfare Capitalism: Economic Adjustment in Contemporary France and Germany.* Philadelphia: Temple University Press.

Védrine, Hubert, and Dominique Moïsi. 2001. *France in an Age of Globalization.* Translated by Philip H. Gordon. Washington DC: Brookings Institution Press.

Villalard, Jean. 1985. "Les TUC: Dans quels organismes? Pour quels travaux?" *Travail et Emploi* 26:35–45.

"Voiture incendiée." 2005. *Le Populaire du Centre,* November 12.

"Une voiture partiellement incendiée." 2005. *Le Populaire du Centre,* November 9.

Voldman, Danièle. 1997. *La reconstruction des villes françaises de 1940 à 1954: Histoire d'une politique*. Paris: L'Harmattan.

Wacquant, Loïc. 2008. *Urban Outcasts: A Comparative Sociology of Advanced Marginality*. Cambridge: Polity Press.

———. 2010. "Crafting the Neoliberal State: Workfare, Prisonfare, and Social Insecurity." *Sociological Forum* 25 (2): 197–220.

Wakeman, Rosemary. 2004. "Nostalgic Modernism and the Invention of Paris in the Twentieth Century." *French Historical Studies* 27 (1): 115–44.

Weakliem, David L., and Anthony F. Heath. 1999. "The Secret Life of Class Voting: Britain, France, and the United States since the 1930s." In *The End of Class Politics? Class Voting in Comparative Context*, edited by Geoffrey Evans, 97–136. Oxford: Oxford University Press.

Weber, Florence. 1989. *Le travail à côté: Étude d'ethnographie ouvrière*. Paris: INRA-EHESS.

———. 1991. "Nouvelles lectures du monde ouvrier: De la classe aux personnes." *Genèses* 6:179–89.

Weber, Max. (1922) 1978. *Economy and Society: An Outline of Interpretive Sociology*. Edited by Guenther Roth and Claus Wittich. Berkeley: University of California Press.

Wieviorka, Michel. 2005. "Violence in France." November 18. http://riotsfrance.ssrc.org/Wieviorka.

Willis, Paul E. 1981. *Learning to Labor: How Working Class Kids Get Working Class Jobs*. New York: Columbia University Press.

Wright, David C. 1991. "Socialist Municipal Politics and Twentieth-Century Limoges, France." PhD diss., University of Wisconsin–Madison.

Wyllie, Irvin G. 1954. *The Self-Made Man in America*. New Brunswick NJ: Rutgers University Press.

Yardley, Jim. 2010. "India Asks, Should Food Be a Right for the Poor?" *New York Times*, August 8.

Zappi, Sylvia. 2012. "Banlieues: Mobilisation pour l'emploi des jeunes." *Le Monde*, October 4.

Index

Page numbers in italics indicate illustrations.

Clarke, T. J., 229n14

CNE (New jobs contract), 172–74, 238n5, 239n10, 242n34

Coca-Cola (company), 236n16

collectivism: as French value, 10; impact of housing projects on, 47; neoliberalism as opposite of, 13; and shifts to individualism, 17–18, 34–35; and *solidarité*, 14

color-blind policy, 28, 112

Confédération générale du travail (CGT), 41, 155, 156–57, 240n13

consolidation periods, 148–51, 162, 238nn7–9

Contrat à durée déterminée (CDD), 62–63, 166, 230n2

Contrat à durée indéterminée (CDI), 62, 148–51

Contrat d'accompagnement dans l'emploi (CAE), 91

Contrat d'adaptation (CA), 89, 233n11

Contrat d'autonomie (CA), 92

Contrat de qualification (CQ), 89, 233n11

Contrat de travail temporaire (CTT), 62–63, 166

Contrat d'insertion dans la vie sociale (CIVIS), 92, 234n20

Contrat emploi-solidarité (CES), 91, 92–93, 233n12

Contrat emploi ville (CEV), 91

Contrat initiative-emploi (CIE), 88, 90

Contrat jeune en entreprise (CJE), 90

Contrat nouvelles embauches (CNE), 172–74, 238n5, 239n10, 242n34

Contrat première embauche (CPE). *See* CPE (First job contract)

Coralie (interlocutor), 191

Corbin, Alain, 35, 40, 41

Cours Jourdan, 183

CPE (First job contract): compared to the CDI, 148–51; compared to the CNE, 172–74, 238n5, 239n10; consolidation period of, 148–51, 162, 239nn7–9; criticism of, 1–2, 151–52, 219; outer-city youth reactions to, 161–66; student opposition to, 163–66; targeting youth, 145–46, 147–48. *See also* protests (CPE)

CTT (temporary contract), 62–63, 166

culture, 123

Cupers, Kenny, 230n16

Dahlia (interlocutor), 135, 139

Dalil (interlocutor), 191–92

Dans ma bulle (album), 121–22

Davis, Fred, 55, 232n16

débrouillards, 104–5, 108

de Gaulle, Charles, 10

Diam's (French rapper), 121–22, 132, 236n14

dirigiste policy, 6–11

Divay, Sophie, 94

Dubet, François, 178, 186

Duflot, Cécile, 137

Dufoix, Stéphane, 197

Durkheim, Émile, 134, 235n26

L'Écho de la Haute Vienne (newspaper), 125–26, 127, 158–59, 172–73, 239n11

École polytechnique (Polytechnic school), 9

economic crisis (1930s), 43, 58–59

economic crisis (1970s), 10–11, 16, 60, 84

economic crisis (2008), 202, 204, 220

economy: and *dirigiste* policy, 6–11; growth during *Trente glorieuses*, 8–9, economy (*cont.*)

    225n6; impact on employment, 4, 84; under Nicolas Sarkozy, 202–3; in twentieth-century Limoges, 57–61

éducateur de rue (street educators), 97–98, 233n16

education: degree hierarchy, 165; government programs targeting, 84–85, 232n2; graduation statistics, 232n3; meritocracy promoted in, 56; outer-city youth experiences of, 74–78; popular education movement, 190, 243n11; vocational training, 85, 93, 165, 231n10, 232n6

electrical components industry, 229n11

Emergency plan for hiring youth policy, 87–88

Emplois-jeunes (Youth employment) initiative, 91, 93–94, 240n22

employment: adulthood linked to, 72–73; benefits of flexibility in, 15, 227n17; charges of racism in, 120; danger of flexibility in, 16–17; impact of global economy on, 4; impact of stereotypes on chances for, 71; job creation programs, 92–94; job insecurity, 98, 221–23; and national identity, 221–22; nostalgia over shifts in, 56–57, 72–78; purpose through, 195; and social inclusion, 111–12, 199–200; through social networking, 193; statistics on, 2, 225n1; in twentieth-century Limoges, 60; unequal access to, 2; work arrangements, 15–16, 62–64

employment agencies, 62–64, 202, 234n20

employment policies: creating jobs, 92–94; criticisms of, 88, 93, 162;

debated success of, 88; emphasis on *accompagnement*, 94–96; overview of programs, 89–92; stigmas associated with, 93–94; targeting youth unemployment, 84, 85–92, 101–2; under the Villepin administration, 147–48. *See also* CPE (First job contract)

ENA (National school for civil service), 9

Epstein, Beth, 47, 142–43

ESTER Technopole, 61

ethnicity: ban on statistics collecting, 28, 112; categorical relevance of, 18–19; changing views on, 112–13, 237n23; debates on, 5; labels based on, 168, 237n23

exclusion: *banlieues* as sites of, 52–53; based on social inequalities, 73; challenged by youth, 100, 170–71, 183–84, 218; contrasted with *solidarité*, 84, 99, 218; employment policy as response to, 87; in François Dubet's analysis, 186; Jacques Chirac's war against, 233n8; and the logic of indifference, 140; shopping centers as sites of, 67–68

Exo-jeunes policy, 90

Fabrice (interlocutor), 114–15

Fariba (interlocutor), 79–80, 163

faubourgs, 40–41, 229n8. See also *banlieues* (outer cities)

Ferenczi, Thomas, 185

Ferguson, James, 12

Fernando, Mayanthi, 133–34

Le Figaro (newspaper), 167–68

Fillon, François, 202

film project, 177–78, 194–97, 198–99

individualism (*cont.*)
    impacts of, 18; tensions between
    assistance and, 83–84. *See also*
    neoliberalism
industrialization, 7–8, 43–45
inequality. *See* social inequality
Ingram, Mark, 112
Initiation to the world of work intern-
    ship program, 88
insertion, 87
internship programs, 88, 233nn11–12
Interval (dry bar), 114–16, 157, 188–89;
    images of, *114*, *208*
Irvoas, Jean-Claude, 128–29
Isabelle (activity leader), 96–97
Islamic community, 65, 133–34, 191–92,
    243nn15–16
Islamic fundamentalism, 51, 230n19,
    231n4

Jablonka, Ivan, 168
Jancius, Angela, 21
Jaurès, Jean, 42, 228n2
Jeunes CGT (youth union), 155, 156–57
JOC (Young Christian workers), 83,
    190–92, 194–95
Jonathan (interlocutor), 70, 77–78, 131,
    164, 193, 199, 210–11, 231n12
Jospin, Lionel, 53, 244n1
Julliard, Bruno, 165–66

K., Benoît (murder suspect), 128–29
kaolin, 36, 228n6
Karim (interlocutor), 65–67, 181, 231n5
Khomeini, Ruhollah, 230n19

labor: and *dirigiste* policy, 7–8, 10–11;
    historic shortages, 15–16; impact of

neoliberalism on, 13–14; inequali-
    ties in, 20
Labor Day, 172, 241n32
labor law (French), 148, 201–3, 244nn1–
    2. *See also* legislation
labor movement, 41–42, 155–57
Lapeyronnie, Didier, 197
Larcher, Gérard, 113
Laurence, Jonathan, 243n16
Law for equal opportunities policy,
    147–48, 238n2, 238n4
Learning to Labor (Willis), 2–3, 222
Leblanc, Raymond, 95
legislation: anti-*casseur* law, 166–67,
    241n27; under Nicolas Sarkozy,
    201–4; under the Villepin admin-
    istration, 147–48. *See also*
    employment policies
Legrand (manufacturer), 60, 229n11
Le Pen, Marine, 204, 213, 236n14
Lepoutre, David, 187
Levy, Jonah, 11, 13
Limoges (France): author's fieldwork in,
    26–27, 28–30; CPE protests in, 152–57,
    239n11, 240n18, 240n20; economic
    development in, 35–38, 57–61; images
    of, *39*; immigration in, 27–28; impact
    of 2008 crisis on, 204–5; industry in,
    23–25, 229n11; leftist tradition in, 24,
    35, 228nn2–3; maps of, *22*, *52*; negative
    perceptions of, 130–31; population
    of, 21–23, 43, 45, 48; portrayed as a
    "haven," 127–30, 131–32; prostitution
    in, 229n9; unemployment rates in,
    61–62, 205, 245n6; urban planning in,
    40–41, 48–49; during World War II,
    229n10; youth homelessness in, 205,
    244n4. See also *banlieues* (outer cities)

Limousin cattle, 23
Limousin region (France), 21–23
Loïc (interlocutor), 177, 194
Loi pour l'égalité des chances (employment policy), 147–48, 238n2, 238n4
Louise (municipal official), 34

"Ma France à moi" (song), 121–22, 132
Malik (interlocutor), 68, 119
Manon (interlocutor), 215–17
maps, 22, 52
"Marine" (song), 236n14
market sector, 86, 87–90
Matthieu (interlocutor), 104, 177
Mauger, Gérard, 197
media. *See* news media
Mélenchon, Jean-Luc, 204
memories, 55–56. *See also* nostalgia
Mendras, Henri, 105–6
"Me revoilà" (song), 236n12
meritocracy, 56, 74–78, 80
Merkel, Angela, 203
Merriman, John, 35, 36–43, 130, 229n7, 229n9
Ministry of the Interior, 236n10
missions locales (youth unemployment offices), 94–96
Mitterrand, François, 10, 11
Le Monde (newspaper), 146, 157–58
Mouloud (interlocutor), 120, 169
Mucchielli, Laurent, 20–21
murals initiative, 136–37, 138
Muslim community, 65, 133–34, 191–92, 243nn15–16

National Front party, 51
national identity: linked to employment, 221–22; and the logic of indifference, 133–40; under Nicolas Sarkozy, 203–4; and *solidarité*, 218
Neilson, Brett, 226n13
neoliberalism: CPE seen as form of, 159; French lineage of, 226n10; French perspectives on, 6, 13–14; impact on adulthood, 79; impact on employment, 3; under Nicolas Sarkozy, 202–3; nostalgia as response to, 56; personal responsibility rhetoric of, 49–54, 56, 65, 71; scholarship on, 11–12; and social disintegration, 185–86. *See also* capitalism
Newman, Andrew, 230n18
news media: coverage of CNE protests, 172–73, 239n10; coverage of CPE protests, 145–46, 157–61, 167–69, 239n10; negative portrayals of *banlieues* by, 115–17; portraying Limoges as "haven," 124–30
Nicole-Drancourt, Chantal, 17
nobility, 9, 225n8, 232n15
noblesse oblige, 9, 80–81, 226n8
Noiriel, Gérard, 16, 227n19
non-market sector, 86, 87, 90–91, 92–94
nostalgia: and bonds with the *banlieues*, 189; combating negative stereotypes, 64, 71; defined, 74, 232n16; explanations for, 79–81; over shifts in employment, 72–78; social dimensions of, 55–57; structural limits of, 81–82
Noureddine (interlocutor), 64, 68, 71, 231n13

Observatoire des inégalités (Observatory of inequalities), 225n1
Ong, Aihwa, 11

OPEC (Organization of Petroleum Exporting Countries), 10
OPHBM (Public affordable housing office), 44
organic solidarity, 107, 235n26
Ousmane (interlocutor), 116, 162
outer cities. See *banlieues* (outer cities)
outer-city youth (*jeunes de quartier*): addressing differences, 135–40; bonds with neighborhoods, 187–89; commitment to *solidarité* ideal, 106–7; CPE targeting, 145–46, 147–48; disadvantages faced by, 80; follow-up interviews with, 205–17; and *galère*, 178–79; labels claimed by, 171–72; negative identities imposed on, 71, 200; negative stereotypes of, 54, 64–71, 168–70, 177–78; participating in the CPE protests, 154, 164–66; "perfect delinquent" role, 65–67, 231n5; portrayed as "at-risk," 96–99, 101; portrayed as "risky," 97, 99–102; pseudonyms used for, 228n28; reactions to CPE, 161–66; relationships with social service providers, 233nn15–16; struggles with naming, 81–82; unemployment rates among, 203, 205; use of cell phones, 179–82; views on social assistance, 102–5. *See also* nostalgia

Pactes nationaux pour l'emploi policy, 89
PAIO (reception, information, and guidance centers), 94–96
Patico, Jennifer, 244n17
personal responsibility: contrasted with *noblesse oblige*, 80–81; impact on outer-city youth, 71; nostalgia as response to, 56; shifts in understanding of, 65; shifts toward, 49–54, 143; and *solidarité*, 14; stressed by social services, 97–102; tensions between assistance and, 83–84

Pialoux, Michel, 17
Piketty, Thomas, 8
Pinkney, David H., 229n14
Plan d'urgence en faveur de l'embauche des jeunes policy, 90
Pôle emploi (Employment center), 202
police: charges of racism, 118–19; during the CPE protests, 167–68; increased presence of, 53–54; under the Ministry of the Interior, 236n10; and strikes, 240n16; during the 2005 riots, 118–19
populaire, 227n22
Le Populaire du Centre (newspaper), 127–29, 159, 168–69, 172–73
popular education movement, 190, 243n11
porcelain industry, 36–39, 57–58, 228–29nn6–7
positive discrimination, 133
poverty, 65, 205, 245n5
Prasad, Monica, 7
precariat (social class), 3, 147, 171, 174–75
A Precariat Charter (Standing), 220–21
précarité: contrasting results of, 198–99; and employment flexibility, 16–17; first use of term, 226n15; impact on *solidarité*, 98–99, 170–71; meanings of, 17; threat of CPE increasing, 146–47, 151–52, 160–61,

174, 239n10; worldwide prevalence of, 226n13

press. *See* news media

probationary period, 148–51, 162, 239n7–9

protests: against the CNE, 172–73, 239n10; in the nineteenth century, 39–40, 42; as "orderly disorder," 240n16

protests (CPE): *casseurs* during, 166–68; ending of, 240n21; estimated numbers at, 145, 241n29; images of, 153; in Limoges, 152–57, 239n11, 240n18, 240n20; media coverage of, 145–46, 157–61, 167–69, 239n10; outer-city youth participation in, 164–66, 241n33; student involvement in, 163–66, 241n25; unions in, 155–57, 240n13. *See also* CPE (First job contract)

public hygiene movement, 45–47, 230n15

public transportation, 83, 232n1

race: in America, 122–23, 142–43, 237n17, 238n24; ban on statistics collecting, 28, 112; categorical relevance of, 18–19; debates on, 5; French versus American conceptions of, 140–43; influence of American culture, 122–23, 237n17; labels based on, 168; and the logic of indifference, 133–40; shifting views on, 112–13, 123–24, 237n23

Rachid (interlocutor), 116, 131, 133, 164, 180, 185, 206–10

racism: in America, 122–23, 142–43, 237n17, 238n24; in employment,

120; in housing, 119–20; and immigration, 51, 121; outer-city youth claims of, 116–21; and *solidarité*, 132, 143

Reich, Robert B., 227n17

Renahy, Nicolas, 17–18

Renault Trucks Défense (manufacturer), 60

riots (2005): ending of, 237n19; frameworks for understanding, 197–98, 244n21; incident triggering, 118–19, 236n11; in Limoges, 124–29, 131; and Nicolas Sarkozy's inflammatory language, 117–18, 236n9; role of race in, 112–13, 117–19; scope of, 1–2; underlying causes of, 111–13, 185–86, 197–98

RMI (Minimum subsistence income), 14, 15, 86, 100–102, 202, 232n4, 239n5

Rogers, Susan Carol, 105, 124, 226n11

Rosanvallon, Pierre, 100

Rossiter, Ned, 226n13

Roy, Olivier, 197

Royal Limoges (porcelain factory), 58

RSA (Active solidarity income), 202, 232n4, 239n5, 245n9

Rue Charles-Michels, 183

rues de la soif (streets of thirst), 182–83

Rushdie, Salman, 230n19

Sabbagh, Daniel, 237n23

Saïda (interlocutor), 135, 138

Samira (interlocutor), 139

Sandra (interlocutor), 156–57

Sarkozy, Nicolas, 53–54, 117–18, 201–4, 220, 236n9, 244n3

Saviem (manufacturer), 60

Schmidt, Vivien, 203

Souad (interlocutor), 120, 131, 170

sports, 235n7

Stage d'initiation à la vie profession-nelle (SIVP), 89, 233n11

Standing, Guy, 3, 146–47, 220–21

Stewart, Kathleen, 55–56

Strauss-Kahn, Dominique, 204

street educators, 97–98, 233n16

strikes, 39–40, 42, 154–55, 240n16

students, 154–55, 163–66, 241n25

suicides, 131, 237n20

Tannock, Stuart, 81

temporary employment, 2, 62–64, 92–93, 203

termination, 148–51, 239nn8–9

Terrail, Jean-Pierre, 17

Thomas (interlocutor), 104–5, 163, 169, 193, 213–15, 241n31

Timothée (interlocutor), 71

Tissot, Sylvie, 50–53, 65

Todorov, Tzvetan, 113

"Tom Sawyer" (anime series), 231n13

Topalov, Christian, 15

Tours Gauguin (La Bastide project), 188, 189

Trajet d'accès à l'emploi (TRACE), 91

Travaux d'utilité collective (TUC), 90, 92–93, 233n12

Trente glorieuses (Thirty glorious years), 7–9, 15–16, 45, 106, 225nn5–6, 228n4

trial periods, 62, 148–51, 162, 238nn7–9

TUC (Works of collective utility) policy, 90, 92–93, 233n12

unemployment: anthropological literature on, 21; education programs targeting, 84–85; impact of neo-liberalism on, 3; impact of 1970s economy on, 84; under Nicolas Sarkozy, 201–2; among youth, 1–2, 61–62, 203, 205, 245n6

unemployment agencies, 94–96, 201–2, 234n20

unions: during the CPE protests, 155–57, 240n13; development of, 41–42; and the labor movement, 39–40; in Limoges, 24

universalism: impact on difference, 5; and race neutrality, 112, 140

University of Limoges, 60, 152–54

Urban Development Program (*Politique de la ville*), 50–51

Vaïsse, Justin, 243n16

Val de l'Aurence (housing project): images of, 114, 208; Interval dry bar, 114–16, 157, 188–89, 190, 208; JOC presence in, 190–92; map of, 52; mural initiative at, 136–37; shopping center in, 65–66; social mediators in, 207–8; during the 2005 riots, 125–26; as ZRU, 230n21

Védrine, Hubert, 13

Véronique (interlocutor), 102–4, 120, 172, 216–17, 241n33

Villepin, Dominique de, 14, 145–46, 152, 153, 160, 238n2, 238n4

vocational training, 85, 93, 165, 231n10, 232n6

Wacquant, Loïc, 25–26, 174

Weber, Max, 19–20

welfare system. *See* social services

Wieviorka, Michel, 197

Williams, Raymond, 123
Willis, Paul, 2–3, 222
working class: changing categorical relevance of, 3, 17–18, 227n19; emergence of, 35–40; housing shortages for, 43–45; in Limoges, 24; in the nineteenth century, 41–42; scholarship on, 200
World War I, 58–59
World War II, 43, 229n10

Yanis (interlocutor), 164–66, 170
Yasmine (interlocutor), 68, 133, 139, 180
youth: age bracket for research, 228n27; "at risk" category, 86; inequalities faced by, 15; prevalence of short-term jobs for, 63–64; unemployment rates, 1–2, 203; unemployment rates in Limoges, 61–62, 205. *See also* outer-city youth (*jeunes de quartier*)
Youth employment initiative, 91, 93–94, 240n22
youth hangouts, 190–92, 242n9
youth houses (*maisons des jeunes*), 96–97

ZEP (Priority education areas), 85
ZRU (Urban revitalization areas), 230n21
ZUS (Disadvantaged urban areas), 52, 53, 230n21

CPSIA information can be obtained
at www.ICGtesting.com
Printed in the USA
LVOW11*1516050317
526190LV00005B/324/P